BASIC TEXTS IN COUNSELLING AND PSYCHOTHERAPY

Series editor: Stephen Frosh

This series introduces readers to the theory and practice of counselling and psychotherapy across a wide range of topic areas. The books appeal to anyone wishing to use counselling and psychotherapeutic skills and are particularly relevant to workers in health, education, social work and related settings. The books are unusual in being rooted in psychodynamic and systemic ideas, yet being written at an accessible, readable and introductory level. Each text offers theoretical background and guidance for practice, with creative use of clinical

Published

Jenny ...
WOR...

Bill Barn...
AN INTR...

Stephen E...
WORKIN... TH... CENTS

Alex Coren
SHORT-TERM PSYCHOTHERAPY

Emilia Dowling and Gill Gorell Barnes
WORKING WITH CHILDREN AND PARENTS THROUGH SEPARATION AND DIVORCE

Loretta Franklin
AN INTRODUCTION TO WORKPLACE COUNSELLING

Gill Gorell Barnes
FAMILY THERAPY IN CHANGING TIMES 2nd Edition

Sally Modyes
COUNSELLING ADULTS WITH LEARNING DISABLITIES

Ravi Rana
COUNSELLING STUDENTS

Tricia Scott
INTEGRATIVE PSYCHOTHERAPY IN HEALTHCARE

Geraldine Shipton
WORKING WITH EATING DISORDERS

Laurence Spurling
AN INTRODUCTION TO PSYCHODYNAMIC COUNSELLING

Paul Terry
WORKING WITH THE ELDERLY AND THEIR CARERS

Jan Wiener and Mannie Sher
COUNSELLING AND PSYCHOTHERAPY IN PRIMARY HEALTH CARE

Shula Wilson
COUNSELLING ADULTS WITH LEARNING DISABILITIES

Invitation to authors

The Series Editor welcomes proposals for new books within the Basic Texts in Counselling and Psychotherapy series. These should be sent to Stephen Frosh at the School of Psychology, Birkbeck College, Malet Street, London, WC1E 7HX (e-mail s.frosh@bbk.ac.uk)

Basic Texts in Counselling and Psychotherapy
Series Standing Order ISBN 0–333–69330–2
(outside North America only)

You can receive future titles in this series as they are published by placing a standing order. Please contact your bookseller or, in the case of difficulty, write to us at the address below with your name and address, the title of the series and the ISBN quoted above.

Customer Services Department, Macmillan Distribution Ltd
Houndmills, Basingstoke, Hampshire RG21 6XS, England

AN INTRODUCTION TO WORKPLACE COUNSELLING

A Practitioner's Guide

LORETTA FRANKLIN

palgrave
macmillan

First published 2003 by
PALGRAVE MACMILLAN
Houndmills, Basingstoke, Hampshire RG21 6XS and
175 Fifth Avenue, New York, N.Y. 10010
Companies and representatives throughout the world

PALGRAVE MACMILLAN is the global academic imprint of the Palgrave
Macmillan division of St. Martin's Press, LLC and of Palgrave Macmillan Ltd.
Macmillan® is a registered trademark in the United States, United Kingdom
and other countries. Palgrave is a registered trademark in the European
Union and other countries.

ISBN 0–333–92255–7 paperback

This book is printed on paper suitable for recycling and made from fully
managed and sustained forest sources.

A catalogue record for this book is available from the British Library.

Printed and bound in Great Britain by
Biddles Ltd., King's Lynn, Norfolk

CONTENTS

Foreword by **Lisbeth E. Hearst**   ix

Acknowledgements   xi

Preface   xiii

PART I   COUNSELLING IN ORGANISATIONS   1

1   The Nature and Culture of Organisations   **3**
Introduction   3
Defining Organisations   3
Organisations, Systems and the Environment   6
Survival Culture   12
Thriving Culture   18
The Individual in the Organisation   18
Stress at Work   20
Summary   25

2   The Role of Counselling at Work   **27**
Introduction   27
Workplace Counselling   27
Managing the Workplace Counsellor's Role   33
Confidentiality   37
Developing the Counsellor's Role in the Organisation   42
Publicising Services   45
Summary   46

PART II   MANAGING THE PROCESS: FEATURES
          AND PRACTICE   49

3   Client and Practice Management   **51**
Introduction   51
Therapeutic Alliance   51
The Counsellor   52

The Client   55
Resistance to Counselling   59
The Interaction between Client and Counsellor   60
The Helping Process   62
Practice Management   65
Monitoring the Progress   69
Record Keeping   70
Summary   71

4   The Process in Practice   72
Introduction   72
Beginning the Relationship   72
Contracting   73
The First Session   77
The Initial Referral   80
Developing the Relationship   89
Ending the Relationship   97
Handling Endings   99
Summary   100

PART III   MANAGING THE PROCESS: ISSUES
           AND DILEMMAS   103

5   Therapeutic Issues and Techniques   105
Introduction   105
Subjectivity and Objectivity   105
Transference and Countertransference in Practice   110
Transference   110
Countertransference   118
Making Sense of Transference and Countertransference   126
Projective Identification   128
Self-disclosure   134
Power   138
Summary   140

6   Working with Diversity   142
Introduction   142
Race, Culture and Ethnicity   146
Working with Difference – the Counsellor's
  Role and Responsibility   150
Cross-cultural Perspectives   151

Sexual Orientation 153
Disability 155
Religion 156
How does Diversity Impact on the Counselling Process? 158
Learning the Language of Difference 160
Transference 163
Gender and Culture Matching 164
Summary 167

PART IV   INTERVENTION STRATEGIES 169

7   **Intervention** **171**
Introduction 171
Opportunities for Intervention 172
The Organisation as a Client 175
A Systemic Approach 178
Change Management 182
Stages of Individual and Organisational Change 186
Defence Mechanisms in Organisations 191
Summary 197

8   **Particular Approaches** **198**
Introduction 198
Short-term Therapy 198
Time-limited Counselling 199
Mediation 202
Telephone Counselling 203
Critical Incident Stress Debriefing 205
Co-working 206
Group Facilitation 206
Summary 218

9   **Practitioner Development** **219**
Introduction 219
The Initiate 219
The Relationship between Theory and Practice 224
The Counsellor and the Outside World 228
The Developing Counsellor 230
Personal Development 232
Counselling Supervision 234
Personal Therapy 236
Burn-out 236

CONTENTS

Caring for Yourself   239
Summary   240

Postscript   241

Appendix 1: Employment Law   242

Appendix 2: Useful Addresses   244

References   248

Index   255

FOREWORD

This introduction to counselling in the workplace is much more than the title promises. It offers in-house counsellors, organisational counsellors, and personnel officers, a comprehensive, detailed, eminently accessible guide to the maze in which they find themselves in the execution of their profession. For although the bookshelves are crowded with textbooks on counselling, this book manages to bring under one roof the various and manifold aspects of counselling not in the seclusion of the consulting room, but in the intricate network of the workplace. We are introduced to the conceptual foundation, the therapeutic issues, the institutional and legal implications, and the technique required to achieve the goals set. The comprehensive research is underwritten by numerous quotations; the case material brings to life the theory and practice of counselling in the workplace. The reader is taken by the hand and led through the landscape of their professional lives. It is, however, a light hand that guides: there is no imposition of a dogmatic baseline, not 'do this, don't do that'. The approach is facilitation rather than directive. As a group analyst, I feel at home with the underlying perception that all phenomena of a given situation have to be taken into account, and that includes the presence of the observer, in this case the counsellor. Only too often the conscious and unconscious assumptions and value judgements of the counsellor are left out of the equation. Not so in this book: here the place of the counsellor is explicitly treated as relevant to the process and outcome; this is convincingly modelled by the self-disclosure of the writer's emotional states and experiences in the execution of her profession where these pertain to the text.

In many textbooks on counselling the more complicated and controversial concepts, such as transference, countertransference, projection, projective identification, are left out or mentioned in passing, a backdrop of the text, as it were. This book presents these concepts in concise, comprehensible language and illustrates them with case material, which, as we know, is worth pages of theoretical exposition: it enables the reader to relate intellectually and emotionally to the states of real people in conflict or distress, the counsellor's response and their place in the complicated network of relationships in the workplace in which the dramas unfold. As in all drama, the participation of the onlooker is an intrinsic component of the experience. I hope the reader of this will allow him/herself to participate fully in the story here told.

LISBETH E. HEARST

ACKNOWLEDGEMENTS

My thanks to all who have read, made suggestions, or contributed in some way to the final form of this book. Space and memory won't permit me to express my individual gratitude to all those involved. If this book is a success it is largely due to the experience I have gained from working with what I describe as the first generation of workplace counsellors.

In all instances details of organisations, case work and practitioners have been changed to ensure that recognition would be prevented. I am particularly grateful therefore for the generosity of contributions from organisations, colleagues and counsellors who, for reasons of confidentiality, cannot be mentioned individually.

Several colleagues, friends and family members read parts of the manuscript and gave very helpful criticisms. I am particularly indebted to Irene Murdoch for her consistent encouragement and current knowledge of workplace issues; to Janet Cohen for her reflective and thorough suggestions; and to Jayne Franklin for her patience and honesty.

During the past 30 years I have had the great benefit of frequent communication with colleagues and students. In particular I would like to thank Relate for teaching me so much, the Civil Service College for the opportunities they afforded me during a challenging time in my life, the tutors of the Franklin Edgerton Partnership for the experience of working with a team dedicated to providing meaningful training, and the Civil Service Welfare Community, past and present, for their commitment to the development of workplace counselling. To all of them I owe a deep debt of gratitude, especially to those enthusiastic supervisees who sowed the seeds for this book's conception with their persistent requests to write what I conveyed verbally.

Lisbeth Hearst's professional guidance over the years and particularly her belief in my work has been invaluable. Knowing her continues to be a privilege. My dear colleagues on Links, whose wisdom and perception I value each time we meet, offer a forum where ideas can be exchanged freely regardless of age, culture, class or religion. I thank them for their love and friendship.

There are others who have played important roles. I am especially grateful to Richard Franklin for his loyalty and careful critique and to James Goldman and Lisa Jerrard for their calmness with computer calamities. I would also like to thank my editor Frances Arnold of Palgrave and Stephen Frosh for their belief in this book, Alison Caunt for her encouragement during its developmental phases, and Sandra Eriemo for easing the final labour pains with her objective contributions. I deeply appreciate the unswerving support of dear friends, family and the medical profession which has enabled me to complete this book. Collectively they ensure that I continue to 'break all the rules'.

I offer special gratitude to my immediate family for their tolerance over the years of my absences from home and their understanding when I returned utterly exhausted. In particular I wish to thank my husband Michael whose courage I admire beyond words. I thank him for his love and exceptional support.

Finally my thanks go to Covi, my four-year-old grandson, who succeeded where others failed, in wooing me away from the computer. He reminds me how simple and uncluttered life can be and how much one can learn from the young.

LORETTA FRANKLIN

PREFACE

According to Carl Jung, today's ideas, methods and thoughts come from the life experience of our ancestors and indeed from the entire human race. In that sense in this book I am merely offering back a collection of ideas gained from the work of famous theorists, past mentors, my current supervisor, enthusiastic students, courageous clients and my own life experience.

At the outset I believe it is important to declare that at heart I am a psychodynamic counsellor and although I am experienced in many other approaches I have never stopped valuing psychodynamic principles, including the self-discipline required to practice. I have experimented and at my better moments I have been involved in some extremely exciting and creative work, but when the going got tough, and it did, particularly in the organisational work in which I was involved, then the psychodynamic approach has stood me in very good stead.

'A scholarship girl who should have done better' might have been a fitting epitaph to mark my departure from a well-known south London public school. Then again maybe not. Whose decision was it that I should leave that respected place of learning in the summer of 1961? Perhaps I shall never fully know. However, the answers to 'how' and 'why' I ever came to be there in the first place have become clearer. As I look back on those days I realise that words such as 'projection', 'collusion' and 'the unconscious' did not exist for me, let alone have some meaning – I just lived them!

At some point in the 1960s I embarked on a journey of self-examination, discovery and enlightenment which led to my becoming a psychodynamic marital and family therapist and subsequently in the 1980s and 1990s to incorporating my clinical experience into my work with organisations and in particular within the Civil Service. It has been an enriching voyage.

When I first began my counselling career in the late 1960s the word 'counselling', if used at all, was spoken sparingly and in hushed tones. If asked at a party, 'What do you do?', I quickly found myself cut off when I answered, 'I am a counsellor.' Instead of being offered another glass of wine I found myself ignored or alternatively being the unwilling recipient of someone's secret distress. Perhaps some things never change. What certainly has changed is the public's perception of the word 'counselling'.

Then media attention was 'low key' and the average local bookshop devoted minimal shelf space to the subject. Times have changed and today the word 'counselling' is used anything but sparingly. Enter any bookshop today and there is sure to be a section headed 'Counselling' and a wide range of self-help books. Nowadays there is certainly no shortage of literature covering every therapeutic school, with new interpretations arriving each year. In short, counselling in general has become a growth industry and workplace counselling is now a part of that industry.

At that time welfare services in the workplace were well established in this country but staff counsellors were rare and EAPs (employee assistance programmes) did not exist in the United Kingdom. Employees subjected to discrimination of any kind, or sexual harassment, rarely had the opportunity of discussing the matter with a truly independent person. I do not recall assertiveness courses and communication skills training being seen as a priority; it was more a case of put up, shut up or get out. Well, times have changed: for example employment legislation now exists to protect individuals' rights at work and this combined with initiatives such as Investors in People (IIP) and Continuing Professional Development (CPD) challenge organisations to integrate best practice into how staff are managed.

With the changing nature of the employment contract, research in the 1990s began to demonstrate clear links between people management and development and business performance. There was a recognition that not only was there a need to recruit the right people and invest in them with proper training but that they then needed to be adequately supported. Organisations, both in the private and public sectors, were starting to take seriously the old mantra 'people are our greatest asset'. Offering a counselling service, whether it be internal or external, was not only perceived as a way of caring for staff, but was also seen as an innovative way of enhancing the productivity and profitability of the organisation.

Civil Service welfare officers were also on the move and with more professional training and supervision many of them saw themselves, as did their counterparts in the private sector, as agents for change within their organisations. A whole generation, perhaps the first generation, of workplace counsellors emerged, accompanied by titles such as 'staff counsellor' and 'employee counsellor'.

For the past 25 years of my professional life, as a provider of training – practitioner and supervisor – I have been privileged to play a part in the development of workplace counselling. It has been enormously challenging and I have learned a great deal. Often my own understanding of counselling has been far removed from those with whom I have been working. The word 'counselling' has been used in a variety of contexts, misunderstood in some and abused by others. As I began to integrate my systemic knowledge and clinical experience of groups and families I was better able to understand the dynamics of the organisations that asked me to train their staff, to act as a mediator or to advise them on best practice for counselling in the workplace. I very quickly discovered the influence of 'the organisational culture' (which until then I had thought rather naively to be a relatively simple term) and how it impacted on the activity of counselling. As like-minded individuals tackled this complex issue I began to realise that new ground was being broken and this appealed to my pioneering spirit.

Drawing on my work as a family therapist, I often felt the need to become part of the organisational system in order to truly understand what it was like to live in their world, whether it be in public service, multinational corporations, media or the law. Only then could I offer some useful interventions. Many of these 'cultures' reminded me of the families with whom I had worked where there was the 'presented patient', 'the child caught in the crossfire', 'the scapegoat', 'the aggressor' or 'the victim' and of course 'the helpless onlookers'. Familiar re-occurring themes were to emerge but now they appeared on a much larger scale. To use a musical metaphor, if the family was a quintet, then the organisation was like a full symphony orchestra. Whilst both could play quietly, they equally could play with great force, sometimes in unison and sometimes in discord. The work was fascinating.

Now some 30 years later this book represents an opportunity to share some of the knowledge I have gained along the way about how counselling, and in particular workplace counselling, works in practice. It is my hope that this book will serve as a practical and easily accessible guide to those who follow me and who are interested in developing 'workplace counselling'.

Whilst I believe that it is important for counsellors to study and to compare the different therapeutic schools that exist it is not my intention in this book to debate the merits of any one particular theory. Nor is it my intention to record the history of workplace counselling. I am making the assumption that you will have read a little, recognise some of the counselling terms mentioned and realise you are already involved in using some approaches. I am also taking the view that readers will have varied work experiences, come from a range of organisations with different types of counselling training. This book therefore is not about research, it is not about defining theory, it is about what happens in practice. I seek to discuss a variety of approaches and theoretical views, to help make sense of concepts and to integrate them in a practical way.

What I hope will be new to those of you involved in workplace counselling is the focus on *how* the wealth of theoretical information and the experience of a generation of workplace counsellors relates to current counselling practice in organisational settings.

Although this book is intended primarily as a practitioner's guide for workplace counsellors and for those for whom counselling forms a significant part of their role at work, I would also like to acknowledge that there may be other professionals – personnel officers, nurses, head teachers – operating in the workplace for whom counselling is an unrecognised part of their day-to-day work and who may wish to integrate counselling skills into their work environment. I hope they too may benefit from a greater understanding of the dynamics of counselling at work.

When deciding how to structure this book I agonised over its order. Should the section on 'Managing the Process' come first, followed by 'Counselling in Organisations' or should it be the other way around? My dilemma illustrates beautifully what actually happens in practice. So often the new workplace counsellor, in a desire to get on with the job, just wants to know about 'the nuts and bolts' of counselling, only considering the organisational system when they encounter its difficulties. By that time they are already in the system and then the impact of the setting on the counselling process becomes all too clear. It is naive to think that one can just enter the counselling room pretending you are in a 'bubble' and ignoring all other systems. So after much deliberation I am taking a phenomenological approach, which believes that no therapeutic theory or practice is adequate if it does not place people in their social context, and for the purposes of this book that is the workplace.

Initially I will consider the setting in which counselling takes place, exploring specific workplace issues, including organisation culture and the role of counselling. Then in the next two sections I shall focus specifically on the counselling process: examining how it works in practice, including some of the ethical and professional issues that occur for practitioners in organisations.

Having considered in some depth the intricacies of managing the counselling process I hope the reader will feel more informed and confident in their abilities. The fourth part of the book returns to the opening theme, that of the organisation and how workplace counsellors might wish to intervene and practice. In the concluding chapter I will discuss professional development issues central to all therapeutic work and in particular the counsellor's approach to learning and development. Ultimately this book is for you and so, ever mindful of the differing needs of individuals, it is designed in such a way that you can select the sections which are most crucial and read them in the order of your choice. I feel sure that you will know where to begin and where to end.

Given the ongoing challenges facing any organisation, for example new legislation, I believe there is a need for greater interdependency between staff counsellors, other functions and professional disciplines. However, whilst interdependency offers creative opportunities for influencing the way organisations work, change can also impose additional constraints on workplace counsellors' roles, and pose the individual practitioner with further counselling dilemmas.

Working with these dilemmas and the inherent conflicts of different professional and organisational cultures can affect counsellor autonomy and that of the counselling function. Therefore two re-occurring themes throughout this book will be the role of the workplace counsellor and the impact of the organisation on the counselling process.

Those involved in the field of counselling in organisations use different titles to describe the services they offer. I shall therefore for the purpose of this book use 'staff counsellor', 'welfare officer' and 'counsellor' inter-changeably. The examples offered are fictionalised to preserve client identity but are based on real casework to help, you the reader, relate ideas to your own practice, and where the term 'we' is used it refers to collective therapeutic issues.

Finally, I firmly believe that because of the complexities facing counsellors working in organisational settings it is essential to set aside time, perhaps more frequently than independent practitioners, to assess the context in which we practice, to reflect upon the consequences of our actions, our interventions and their impact on the organisation. Perhaps making time to read this book will go some way to satisfying that need.

Counselling can be an isolating experience and nowhere more so than in an organisation. In the film *Shadowlands* Anthony Hopkins, in his portrayal of C.S. Lewis, said 'We read so as to know we are not alone.' It is my hope that this book will not only be of practical help to counsellors but that it will also give support to those of you working in organisations so that you too may realise that you are not alone.

Part I

Counselling in Organisations

INTRODUCTION TO PART I

In the numerous books on organisational psychology, counselling is rarely mentioned. Likewise, books on counselling seldom refer to organisations. In this section I seek to narrow that gulf and embark on the process of integrating the importance of both, thus minimising the potential for division.

As mentioned in the preface, the book is written for three groups of people: counsellors working for an in-house counselling service; employees who have a counselling role as part of their function; and those who provide counselling through EAPs (employee assistance programmes). Whatever differences exist between counselling in general and workplace counselling, all three groups need to know about:

- the context in which the counselling activity takes place;
- issues that arise in organisations;
- where a counsellor can help;
- how they can develop their role.

Counselling in organisations dates back to work done in the United States in the 1930s. Over the past two decades there has been a movement towards acknowledging the need to provide counselling in organisations in the United Kingdom. Whether it is merely the concept of counselling itself that is increasing or whether it is the actual provision of counselling services involving identifiable counselling functions that is increasing, is debatable. Certainly an increased awareness of the impact of legislation and employers' legal obligation to their employees may be a contributory factor.

Therefore in this section I will offer an overview of the setting in which workplace counselling takes place; the opportunities and limitations which exist for counselling and the interaction between the workplace counsellor, the organisation and the client.

THE NATURE AND CULTURE OF ORGANISATIONS

Introduction

When counselling takes place in organisations we need to consider the effects of such a setting and what the word 'organisation' actually means. By standing back and thinking about organisations, their structure and the way they work we are better placed to consider potential interventions. Initially I wish to consider the organisation as a system, the individual within that system and then the effects of internal and external changes, including social, political and technological change, on the individual.

Defining Organisations

Organisations conjure up many different images with associated words such as 'impersonal', 'dynamic', or 'entrepreneurial' often being used to describe them. Frequently the simple fact that they are merely a collection of people doing some form of work gets lost.

Bell (1967) suggests contrasting social groups and work groups, as a way of discovering the distinguishing features of an organisation. What is it that people do at a social gathering – say at a party – which is different from a department in a work situation? After all, they both gather for a purpose requiring organisation and allocation of roles. Schein offers this definition:

> An organisation is the rational co-ordination of the activities of a number of people for the achievement of some common explicit purpose or goal, through division of labour and function, and through a hierarchy of authority and responsibility.   (Schein, 1980)

Much of the literature on organisations supports this definition and sees organisations in terms of rational, planned activities with specific objectives. However, this does not offer a complete picture.

3

Schein's definition is a rather traditional view of organisations, which does not adequately refer to social relations and interactions such as friendships and communities, which evolve as a result of people undertaking specific tasks to achieve their goal. These occur over and above those required by the formally prescribed roles.

So where do people fit into this rational definition? How do individual characteristics, behaviour of people and small groups interact with the nature and the structure of organisations? What about the individual's emotional experience of work and how does this affect the structure and performance of the organisation?

Emotions in organisations

My experience of organisations is that there is too much emphasis on management and insufficient attention paid to the heart and feelings of the organisation. Although control is necessary for an organisation to function effectively it is possible that creativity is stifled by a repressed organisational 'super ego', a term used by Freud (1923), that restricts the range of feasible ways in which it can operate. There is much emphasis on the cognitive and purposeful deliberations of individuals, which gives an impression of organisations as places where there is much headwork, but little of the heart. A more balanced approach is not only desirable but would enhance productivity.

Fineman (1993) talks about organisations as emotional arenas and notes that feelings contribute to and reflect the structure and culture of organisations. It has been suggested that emotions in organisations are controlled by those in power who define what is an acceptable expression of emotion. By defining what is acceptable emotionally, employees who do not fit the 'identified' criteria of organisational strength are vulnerable to being stigmatised or ostracised.

Case example: the ostrich syndrome

A Managing Director would not address a personal issue in which he had behaved inconsiderately towards his assistant who had a serious illness. This caused communication problems between them and amongst the staff, to whom it was made quite clear that the assistant's illness 'was not to be discussed'. All emotions were therefore expressed in subgroups 'behind closed doors'. Even though these issues needed addressing the Managing Director had the ultimate power to prevent them being talked about openly.

4

Clearly what was happening was having an effect, but it was a taboo sub-ject and not for discussion. In such situations individuals may talk to the staff counsellor and while this may be very therapeutic for them, it raises the question of whether or not the counsellor is colluding in reinforcing a dysfunctional organisational culture.

Organisations can use counselling services as an excuse to avoid legiti-mate managerial responses to emotional messages from their staff. Parkin (1993) suggests that the growth of workplace counselling could be a way in which emotions are dealt with, restricted and controlled. If the expres-sion of emotions is only acceptable within the counselling arena then this reinforces the stigmatisation of strong emotions at work and they become pathologised.

The influence of organisations

Organisations play a significant part in most people's lives without them even realising it. Some people identify strongly with the organisation for which they work and they can become very attached to its ethos. Understanding the factors that have an influence on individuals' attitudes towards – and choice of – work can assist the development of empathy with clients who will present with a variety of workplace issues.

People's early experience of organisations is quite extensive, starting with childhood experience in schools. Blackler and Shimmin (1984) sug-gest three main influences.

- **Context of social learning** – it is in organisations that we develop con-cepts of ourselves and the world about us. We experience competition and power, authority, co-operation and the ways people seek to influ-ence others.
- **Life sequence** – as we go through life we define ourselves and are defined by the stages of life through which we pass – school, work, leisure, retirement home. General and particular titles such as pupil, youth worker, teacher, volunteer, nurse, doctor, director, resident will be given, adopted or sought.
- **Providers of education** – employment, career opportunities, health care or therapy, the means through which organisations can satisfy people's hopes and aspirations.

As we can see from the above there are many opportunities for organisa-tions to have a significant impact on people's development which can help us to understand how and why they behave as they do in the workplace.

Work, society and identity

It is important for workplace counsellors to understand what work actually means to people and the importance individuals attach to their work. People often define themselves by their jobs, introducing themselves by saying, 'I am a doctor' or 'I'm an engineer'. Any counsellor working with someone who has lost their job will not underestimate the meaning of a social framework, colleagues, a daily task, a place to go, time-markers to pace the day, sense of identity and in some cases a purpose to living (Fineman, 1993). Individuals' attachments to organisations and the many functions that the organisation provides need to be borne in mind. These can include a source of creativity and mastery, self-value, status, income and an opportunity for social interaction.

This is true not only at the point of entry but also at the point of withdrawing from the organisation. If work represents all of the above it is not surprising that although some people cannot wait to retire, others cannot believe it will actually happen and some people do not wish to think about it at all.

For some years I contributed to a seminar called 'Life After *Yes Minister*' which addressed retirement issues for senior civil servants. It would be easy to assume that those who had 'made it to the top' of their organisations would have their future retirement all sorted out. This was not the case. Whilst many had indeed made plans for the future they were still 'psychologically' adjusting to what it would mean for them to no longer have their job or their position. Some had not even given it a thought. As one man who had retired put it: 'I only realised I had retired when I put out the lights, went out of the office and walked down Whitehall – then it hit me.' In this illustration he just worked up until the last minute but others, realising the significance of the adjustment they would need to make, withdrew more gently.

This underlines just how large a part work plays in people's lives not only in terms of identity but also of affiliation and meaning. Although many of us dream of the day we no longer have to work, we tend to deny the importance of the relationship we have with our work.

Organisations, Systems and the Environment

Counselling takes place within a system and the counsellor needs to know about that system. By understanding organisational cultures, systems and pressures, they are better placed to help the client who says 'but you don't realise what it is like to work here' how to consider realistic options or change. In order to fully help the individual make realistic changes within the world in which they live and work the counsellor needs to appreciate the impact and constraints of their workplace.

One theory about organisations and businesses which has been particularly influential is the concept of organisations as systems. Four perspectives for considering how organisations operate are outlined below.

The socio-technical system

This system describes the interaction between technical activities and what is happening at a social level. It implies that if you try to optimise one it will be at the expense of the other and ultimately it will cost the system as a whole. Trist and Bamforth (1951), together with Rice (1958) and Miller and Rice (1967), were interested in developing a framework to understand the interaction between a system of *technical activities* necessary for task performance and a social system of *relationships*, which met the psychological and social needs of the workforce.

Most of us don't even think of the workplace as a community even though we spend the majority of our waking hours there. The degree to which a work community operates cohesively will directly affect the task. Good communication, when individuals' needs are considered, facilitates the technical task. Where this does not exist, time delays and even sabotage occur, generally accompanied by low morale. It is often at this point that the workplace counsellor is approached.

Example: the ideal office

I was involved in a relocation project, which required families to make decisions about whether to stay in London or to move to the north of England. Naturally there were many personal considerations to be taken into account but any doubts seemed to be offset against the promise of improved working conditions in a new high-tech, state-of-the-art office building. A completely new structure was to be erected. The possibilities were endlessly exciting.

However, follow-up work with the organisation showed a high level of dissatisfaction about how the relocation had been managed and, in particular, about the lack of consultation about the design of the new building and its impact on practical working arrangements.

Sadly innovation is all too often obsessed with logistics and technology while the human aspects are considered only as an afterthought or when changes have been resisted. Clearly both sub-systems as described above were important. There was a real opportunity for these principles to be applied but they needed to be introduced at the strategic planning stage of change with a plan for effective consultation throughout the process.

The open system

The comparison is often made between living organisms that have to adapt to environmental conditions in order to exist and organisations as systems that face similar challenges. This biological approach is simply saying that human organisations are living systems that need to interact with the world around them in order to survive. Like nature, organisations need to be interdependent and cross boundaries where necessary. The concept of open systems is about the interconnectedness of the parts of an organisation – meaning that when you change one bit of the organisation it will have repercussions in the other parts.

In the commercial world businesses have customers, they have suppliers and there are wider social and economic forces that affect them such as government legislation, labour markets and economic forces. With transactions taking place daily across their organisational boundaries one could say that they are 'open systems', competing for survival and needing to adapt to current environmental conditions. For example, the wider forces of worldwide events and fluctuating financial markets have an effect on the European economy. Acts of Parliament affect local authorities, taxation affects small companies and the financial pressures on central government have an effect on public sector organisations.

The internal environment of an organisation is affected and potentially changed by events in the external environment as described above. As a result, the external environment is then affected by the level and quality of the organisation's outputs and so the circular process continues. Internal changes, such as relocation, reviews, restructuring, changes in working practices and accountability will also have their effect. They are all interconnected.

Open systems provide for change, offer choices and successfully meet reality. Rules are overt, up to date, humane, and can be changed when needs arise. In contrast, closed systems provide for very little or no change at all and depend on edict and law and order operating through force. Rules are covert, out of date and fixed. If the boundary of an organisation is too impenetrable or rigid then there is no opportunity for exchange. If the system doesn't interact then it cannot be sustained, grow and develop, and if it fails to restrict exchange across the boundary, then it would cease to exist, as it would be undifferentiated from its surroundings. I expect you can think of an individual who is seen as closed – not interacting with people around them, often isolated and not benefiting from mutual exchange – and the opposite type whose boundaries are so blurred that they appear not to have an identity of their own.

This way of considering open and closed systems can be applied to individuals, groups, families and organisations alike. A balance needs to be struck in the degree of openness, for if an individual, a group or an organisation operates by being completely open, it could become submerged and then there would be no individual or corporate identity.

There are comparisons to be drawn here with boundary maintenance in the counselling process. In the chapter 'Therapeutic Issues and Techniques' I will consider subjectivity and objectivity and the potential for the counsellor to become enmeshed and undifferentiated from the client's world.

The political system

To the extent that an organisation is engaged in negotiating and allocating power between groups and individuals the organisation is a political system. Aristotle supposed that 'Man by nature is a political animal.' Shared assumptions about the distribution of power are significant in maintaining any system. In other words, it is the belief of the employee that the manager might fire people or make them redundant, and the belief that the union members could go on strike or the belief that the counsellor has the power to support early retirement that support the system.

Political activity is universal and inevitable. I recall my own resistance to acknowledging that politics existed in the therapeutic world (let alone the world of organisations) and rather arrogantly decided that the game of organisational politics was not something I wished to play. I learned the hard way and so feel it would be remiss of me not to draw your attention to the fact that it does exist and that you will not be working in a vacuum.

The workplace counsellor works within a political system and, by relating to particular departments, e.g. personnel, they will be perceived as part of the power structure. It is important for workplace counsellors to recognise this and be aware of the consequences of any unrealistic perceptions. They will need to know about the shared assumptions of the organisations in which they work and to recognise their potential for empowering their clients.

It often comes as a surprise to new workplace counsellors that employees perceive them as having more power than they feel they have. For example, employees may believe that the counsellor has the power to arrange a transfer on their client's behalf, that they will stop the bully or that they will take the grievance procedure forward for them. The point here is that counselling is about enabling clients to realise that they are not powerless and that they have choices. It is for them to decide which way they prefer to live.

Organisations and culture

How often have you heard someone say of another, 'They don't mean any harm, it's just their nature'? We refer to a person's nature as being 'kind hearted' and in a similar way one can consider an organisation's nature. Yes, organisations have personalities too!

Fineman (1993) argues that people rely heavily on cognitive indicators to describe how the organisation works: for example, how people think about their organisational life, the language they use and the myths and stories that are circulated and cultivated. The word 'culture' as used by Fineman (1993) describes the feelings as well as the thoughts which characterise a particular organisation. Culture can be a pervasive way of life and a guest or visitor to an organisation can quite quickly pick up the 'vibes' that exist to describe the 'mood' of the company.

> **Example: 'Good morning'**
>
> The greeting I receive at reception and the exchanges between staff entering and leaving the building have often given me a snapshot of the issues I might be discussing when I meet with senior management. On one occasion a simple question en route to the lift – 'How is it going now that you have moved to these lovely new offices?' – elicited an outpouring about what it was like at lunch-time with nowhere decent to shop and the extra travelling time involved: a clearly disgruntled employee. The company had relocated a mere mile up the road.

The actual task of an organisation can be reflected in the way that people behave; for example, it is not unusual in accountancy firms for there to be a culture of logic, fact and 'bottom line' thinking. In legal firms argument and debate exist to service clients but can also become the norm for dealing with colleagues. In government departments rules and procedures can dominate the way people behave. Sometimes the culture is clearly visible in the type of logo, the mission statement or the way the building is designed, or it is reflected in its product and the way it operates – for example, The Bodyshop uses only environmentally friendly materials in its shops. Naturally cultures will vary according to the organisation's function.

Within an organisation each department might have its own subculture; for example, the research department may vary from the culture of the personnel department. One way of exploring cultures is to classify them into types, as proposed by Harrison (1972):

- **The power culture** is where key individuals exercise control, and policy and strategic decisions are centralised.
- **The role culture** is highly formalised, resources are controlled and it is assumed everybody is doing their job according to the rules co-ordinated at the top by a narrow band of senior management.
- **The task culture** is job- and project-orientated with the main emphasis on getting the job done. It has a strong sense of the basic mission of the organisation.
- **The person culture** is one where the individual is the central point and the power base is usually expert e.g. collectives, barristers' chambers. There is minimal structure and influence is shared.

It is not enough for a culture to be precisely defined, it also has to be perceived. Peters and Waterman (1982) suggest that where a pattern of beliefs is known, understood and shared by most people in the organisation then that organisation is most likely to be successful. This supports the use of 'mission statements', when they are understood, accepted by all employees and above all acted upon. It seems like the ideal scenario. Not everybody agrees that there is a clear perception of culture, perhaps it is an illusion. It is more likely that there are clashing subcultures or even no fixed consensus at all. Whilst there can be subcultures within cultures which enhance the overall success of the organisation, sometimes there are covert disruptive subcultures which, if they go unrecognised, can become destructive forces. Closing the gap between rhetoric and reality requires commitment of time, attention and resources.

De Vries (1991) argues a need to understand the psychological rationale behind common patterns of irrational organisational and individual behaviour. The counsellor is better placed to identify the culture in which they operate by standing back, observing and understanding where people focus their attention and also which areas get overlooked. This perceptiveness assists effective and objective intervention. The workplace counsellor

11

may observe and enquire about the written and unwritten rules of behaviour, how clients think about and describe themselves, the emotions or collection of feelings that underlie their activities, and the externalised symbols of an organisation such as the logo or mission statement.

The following exercise invites you to think about the culture of organisations you know.

Exercise

Honest questions such as the following may help clarify the nature of an organisational culture:

- Is there a mission statement?
- If so, how does it relate to what happens in practice?
- Is control with individuals or committees?
- How long do people stay?
- Are working hours flexible or inflexible?
- How formal or informal is the organisation?
- How open or closed is the organisation?
- Is there a general level of education?
- What is the mood?
- Do people take risks?
- What is the dress code?
- What language do people use to describe the organisation?
- What are the incentives, bonuses and stock options?
- What are the symbols?

Two extremes of organisational culture, the 'survival culture' and a 'thriving culture', will now be discussed. A survival culture may be characterised by corporate abuse or workplace bullying. Features of both are described along with case examples. This is then contrasted with what a counsellor may recognise as a thriving organisational culture.

Survival Culture

The last decade has produced a culture of survive rather than thrive. The survival culture, described as a 'culture of fear', can often lead to bullying and other problems. For example, it is quite common for people to be working very long hours and not taking holidays. Levels of sickness and absenteeism, traditionally used as indicators of stress in organisations, can no longer be relied upon. Staff may be working hard but this does not necessarily mean they are working productively.

It would appear that the trend towards 'downsizing' and the effects of job uncertainty have meant that staff are reluctant to take time off even when they would benefit from so doing. Although people might not 'absent' themselves from work, one might enquire to what extent they are really there and how effective they are when at work. Because of the fear of uncertainty it is likely that individuals will continue to operate using compromise and trade-offs. A new member of staff, unsure how secure her position was, described this process very clearly when she told me: 'To help you keep your job, you take on this, take on that, more and more – then they won't be able to get rid of you!'

That member of staff was a staff counsellor. Demotivation, unexpressed dissatisfaction and indirect communication are just symptoms of more fundamental causes leading to the 'go with it', 'get out of it' or literally 'become sick of it', phenomena. If this is the case then there is a danger that in a culture where there is significant level of anxiety about job uncertainty a counsellor could compromise to the point that they lose their identity, independence and autonomy.

If the climate of the organisation is 'achieve an end result in a cost-effective way' – how does the organisation achieve this with people? Aldrich's (1979) idea about organisational culture as a jungle is thought-provoking. If indeed the culture is one of a 'jungle', how should the counsellor operate in such an environment and how will it affect their role?

I do not underestimate the task which workplace counsellors face in survival cultures. In my view there has never been a time when they were more needed in organisations, yet when resources are reduced and standards compromised counsellors may feel their contributions are devalued. Sometimes ethical and effective practices are challenged without a sound basis or professional knowledge. All these forces, I would suggest, are familiar to our clients in their own pressurised work settings, a reflection of what is happening in many organisations as they face an economic downturn.

Workplace bullying

The survival culture often arises where changes at work are brought about by deregulation, privatisation, restructuring, downsizing and new technology. These changes can contribute to an erosion of working conditions for many. Casualisation and job insecurity can create a climate where people are increasingly powerless and at risk from being bullied. Research suggests that millions of adult working days are lost each year as a direct result of workplace bullying (see Hoel and Cooper, 2000).

The perception of bullying is often one of persecuting and ganging up on an individual, but it can be subtler than that. Bullying is an abuse of power and it can occur in conjunction with discrimination. The psychological well-being of staff is important at work, but sadly there are many devastating personal stories which tell of the demoralising and isolating experiences of people who are bullied at work. Those who seem to be most vulnerable include young workers, apprentices and trainees, women, older workers, and people from non-English-speaking backgrounds who may experience sexual and/or racist harassment. However, bullying can happen to anyone. It occurs across all industries and in all professions.

Under occupational health and safety legislation employers have a legal duty to control all health and safety hazards in the workplace. This includes organisational structures and behaviours that may lead to bullying. At worst bullying can result in serious health problems such as stress-related illness, anxiety and depression, suicidal thoughts and heart disease.

Example: 'You cannot be serious'

Dennis was an efficient public servant who was known 'to get the job done', but who also had a reputation of being difficult to work for. Consistently good job appraisals led to regular promotion.

When a new manager arrived and heard from a robust character that he had been 'broken' by Dennis, he decided to take action. Dennis was admonished in a meeting with a third party present. This was very distressing for him as it was tantamount to a disciplinary meeting for a senior person. 'You cannot be serious', he said, but they were and he was given 'gardening leave' and offered counselling.

Dennis at first appeared brusque, non-smiling, took control and was business-like. He had lots to say at a factual level and was deeply shocked and hurt. When this was acknowledged he burst into tears. He spoke of having been under considerable pressure for some time, always introducing unpopular changes on behalf of the organisation. Now he felt aggrieved, angry, generally betrayed and was struggling to make sense of the allegations. From always having been valued for his ability, under new management he now found himself accused of being a bully. His view of himself was shattered.

He accepted there were problems with his 'people skills' but thought they were well under control. He knew there was more to do but thought he was making progress. He was horrified at hearing that people dreaded his footsteps and that he was terrorising people. Aware he was intolerant of slowness or lack of commitment in others and was

---

quick-tempered, he also thought he had been improving in his inter-personal style. That this was not evident to others was a double blow and he was filled with self-doubt.

The focus of the work in the short term was to help him work through the shock and pain. In the medium term the underlying causes for his behaviour towards others were addressed. He found it difficult to toler-ate the vulnerable softer side of himself and there were unresolved issues in his personal life, with suppressed emotions, including anger, which when he was under stress was discharged inappropriately onto others. In the long term he committed himself to a development programme to change his interpersonal skills.

But what about the organisation's responsibility for allowing such a situation to arise? Should one just work with Dennis or does the workplace counsellor have a responsibility to address a system which allows such a situation to occur?

Unfortunately scenarios like this are all too common. In cultures that reward results without regard to the process, managers are promoted with-out the necessary training to manage staff effectively. The system puts strain on managers and staff alike. Some become addicted to pressure to the extent that they behave like express trains, not alert to the danger they may cause to others that get in their way. This was the case with Dennis. In a sense he too was a 'victim' of the system, which did not care enough to confront his behaviour at an early stage, nor give him the necessary training for his position.

Bullying is characterised mostly by a combination of the following conditions:

- unreasonable demands and impossible targets;
- restrictive and petty work rules;
- being required to perform tasks without adequate training;
- being forced to stay back to finish work or additional tasks;
- compulsory overtime, unfair rostering or allocation of work;
- constant intrusive surveillance or monitoring;
- no say in how your job is done;
- interference with personal belongings or sabotage of work;
- shouting or abusive language;
- open or implied threat of the sack or demotion;
- oppressive, unhappy work environment;
- people afraid to speak up about conditions, behaviours or health; and
- compromise of safety.

Corporate abuse

Many people dread each day because they have to work in places where they feel abused and powerless. Some organisations have gone beyond being tough and competitive and their desperation to be successful has obscured common decent behaviour. Autocratic, inconsistent management, illogical rules, red tape and ruthless downsizing have led to a climate of hostility and fear. In such workplaces, the modus operandi of the organisation could be described as corporate abuse.

Employees expend so much energy just surviving the day that often there is nothing left to give when they return to their families. This has a significant impact on personal lives, for example exhaustion, preoccupation and frayed tempers. Abuse makes people doubt themselves; they begin to think it is only they who are undervalued and that they are going 'mad', even though that is not the case. Everyone else is just busy surviving and conforming to the system.

Example: Big Brother

A telecommunications organisation was struggling to survive and in order to improve cost effectiveness it introduced changes. It employed a team of supervisors whose job it was to observe and report back on the customer advisers' working patterns, including time taken for coffee, lunch and toilet breaks. In addition employees were asked to present evidence to justify their positions and remuneration – a form of performance-related pay. The level of accountability became excessive. Not only did the employees at the call centre feel that they had no autonomy but that there was a divisive atmosphere because some of the 'observers' were personal friends of the operators and it was considered that favouritism existed. The staff described it as 'a big brother culture' where the degree of personal scrutiny regarding their personal habits was experienced as an infringement of personal liberty. The employees felt dehumanised. The effects of continually having to prove themselves and not being valued meant that staff morale was low. Whilst some felt trapped as a result of fear, others had no loyalty to the firm and left. This left the company with staff shortages and difficulty in retention.

Why do people stay? Corporate abuse is similar to domestic abuse in that it goes through a cycle of hope, expectation and disappointment. I am reminded of spouses of violent or alcoholic partners who would genuinely believe that 'it won't happen again', only to have their hopes dashed.

Characteristics of an abusive environment are when staff are furtively looking over their shoulders and feeling increasingly vulnerable. They may be aware of their every move and sentence and can appear depressed, withdrawn and have low self-esteem. Although working hard they may never feel fulfilled and stop trying to excel or take initiative. Such staff may feel overwhelmed by fear and suspicion.

Recession and survivors

It was argued that there was a slow-down in the economy prior to the attack on the World Trade Center, 11 September 2001, but the impact of that day will be very significant and may well bring about recession. We have already seen the restructuring in the airline and travel industries with job losses being announced weekly. There is likely to be a squeeze in public spending, probably the most severe for years, to cover the cost of disaster recovery and war.

Living with uncertainty or change for short periods of time is manageable but what are the effects on individuals on a long-term basis and how do they affect corporate performance? In recession some companies, in the interests of 'the bottom line', become so preoccupied with surviving that they do not have time to deal with management problems until a crisis point is reached. In the face of lack of external control one way organisations react is to increase rules and regulations and have more security measures to 'cope with the chaos'. This can lead to the 'watch your back syndrome' illustrated earlier in the Big Brother example.

As the economy emerges from recession organisations will need to respond to an increase in customer demand. Expansion caused by a buoyant market, although most welcome, still requires skilful handling but is often overlooked. Investment in the 'people' side of growth does not always keep pace with systems and productivity.

Companies who survive recessions are much tougher. They believe they have seen off any threat and start to feel positive, wanting to move on. Perhaps what is forgotten at the point of upturn in the market is that it is not just a question of luck. Companies in such positions could, if they invest time and expertise, reflect on and assess what they have learned, enabling them to go forward with renewed vigour. In an effort to restimulate the economy they could share not only what they have learned about how to survive but also how to thrive. Sadly the workplace now provides little time for development, individual reflection or coaching. In today's environment of continuous change, it is vital for companies to motivate and develop management so that they are able to handle the challenges they face every day. Such issues need to be addressed otherwise mistakes will occur which could adversely affect organisations' reputations and company profits.

Thriving Culture

Of course, not all organisations are abusive. Many offer wonderful opportunities for development and fulfilment. An organisation that does so is seen to have a 'thriving culture'. Thriving organisations manage rather than are managed and problems are perceived as opportunities not as crises. Thriving cultures are ones where individuals and companies are in partnership together through the vagaries, uncertainties and brutalities of modern-day commercial life. They seek success for themselves and for their organisations.

Counsellors working remedially should consider the features of thriving organisational cultures and what it is that makes people happy and productive at work. Some examples of a thriving culture are when staff have a sense of purpose and there is a high level of initiative. They are supported, encouraged and feel secure about sharing their thoughts and feelings. Their views are valued and there is a respect for difference. Communication is direct, clear, specific and honest and there is a willingness to negotiate. Staff stress levels are productive and there is respect for the organisation's objectives. Leadership coalitions are complementary and there is an appropriate sharing of roles. The world of work is changing and Handy (1993) urges organisations to give more freedom to individual employees, to maintain a balance of commitment and creativity.

The Individual in the Organisation

Clients might present with a range of issues regarding their role at work and their relationship with the organisation. To understand what lies beneath presenting problems such as bullying, anxiety and stress, you might consider the psychological contract that an individual has with their organisation. A psychological contract is a term used to describe the less formal expectations and the nature of the relationship between the individual and the organisation. Some of those expectations are explicit and others are implicit. The psychological contract can have a powerful effect on people's behaviour, including their degree of motivation, commitment, affiliation and how they expect to be treated.

Jaques (1961) suggests that there are three factors that need to be in balance if a person is to be in a state of 'psychological equilibrium'.

These are equitable payment, the content of the work itself and the capacity of the individual. In addition Handy (1976) suggests that where a fit exists between the prevailing culture and the individual's personal, cultural preference, this should lead to a fulfilled psychological contract with the organisation and to satisfaction at work. If this contract is broken, for example where individuals perceive their value system is being violated, people can react strongly, behaving quite fiercely.

The nature of changing work contracts is another aspect to consider regarding clients' presenting problems. Organisations are increasingly offering jobs rather than careers. The experiences of recession, downsizing and restructuring in the 1980s and 1990s led to a new reality for employees. A job is no longer a job for life. The emphasis is placed on being employable rather than being employed. Short- or fixed-term contracts, career breaks, being multi-skilled or acquiring transferable skills are phrases which highlight this shift. People are retiring earlier and there is a move towards job portfolios, where people are self-employed with more than one job. We are witnessing a major change in the way in which work is interpreted, signifying a shift from dependency to being independent, taking charge and control of one's own career path within a changing world.

Changing work practices present other challenges. For example, accompanying the attraction of working from home is the potential for isolation and lack of opportunity to learn from others through regular human interaction. Some of the more structural work changes are, for example, open-plan offices, job sharing, flexitime, hot-desking, information technology, call centres, E-talk or detached duty where people are away from home for long periods. All these changes have implications for client work and wider counselling interventions. Whilst some individuals seek change and thrive on it, others find it stressful. People who find transition to a new working culture difficult may need counselling to help them adapt or move to a function in which they can continue to contribute and to feel valued.

Role ambiguity and role conflict can feature highly as a source of workplace stress. When a person's role in an organisation is clearly defined, understood and where the expectations placed upon the individual are also clear and non-conflicting, then stress can be minimised. This is particularly relevant for counsellors in organisations.

Role stress

Handy (1976) differentiates between beneficial stress, calling it 'role pressure', and harmful stress, which he calls 'role strain'. Potential areas for role stress leading to strain are:

Expectations	Lack of clarity about scope and responsibilities of job Lack of clarity of objectives for a role
Role conflict	Between different departments Between the organisation and the outside world Contradictory instructions from superiors Inter-role conflict – two sets of competing pressures Personal values versus organisational values Professional values versus organisational values
Role ambiguity/ inadequate information	Uncertainty about evaluation Promotion prospects Extent of power Others' expectations Poor communication
Role load	Overload or underload

The effects of the above are numerous. Some of these include low job satisfaction and motivation, aggression, depression or a decline in self-confidence and self-esteem. Clients present with 'general dissatisfaction', 'a sense of futility', 'mental and physical health problems' or 'an intention to leave the job'.

Role underload results from people occupying jobs that do not allow them to make full use of their skills and abilities. Promotion is an interesting example. Where employees with specialist technical abilities, e.g. a nurse or scientist, are removed from a job with which they particularly identify they can be vulnerable to role stress, despite the increase in status. Too often it is assumed that because they are effective in their areas of expertise they will make good managers.

Increases in workload, arising from the desire for cost-effectiveness and increased throughput in organisations, can in turn lead to stress. In this context emotional and physical strength are taken for granted. Often stress and uncertain emotions are regarded as personal weakness and are not recognised as being a result of organisational structures and pressures.

Stress at Work

Stress? You don't believe in all that fashionable mumbo jumbo – much too much is made of it.

The above comment was made to me by a chief executive of a large company. I partly agree with him. Stress is a popular word much overused. When trying to understand a colleague's forgetfulness we might lightly use the phrase 'she [or he] is under a lot of stress at the moment' or we might attribute our own varied reactions to 'work is stressing me out of my mind right now'. In the current economic climate it can be considered fashionable to be in a 'high-stress job' and even to suffer from it, proving that you are conscientious and in high demand! Stress can easily become as addictive as alcohol or other drugs.

What is lacking is a clear understanding of the distinction between 'healthy stress' and 'distress', which can lead to illness if not addressed. Stress means arousal or stimulus, which we need as part of everyday life – to get up, to catch trains, to complete deadlines, to play sport and to perform. We need healthy stress to achieve, feel motivated and satisfied. What we do not need is strain. Too much stress is as bad as too little. I think it would be helpful if organisations were more informed about stress, and encouraged to look at the way their systems operate, to see if they are robust enough for staff to work creatively and productively.

From my work with teams of staff and management, I have come to believe that stress usually begins at the top. Often it is kindled by a straight denial that stress could possibly exist in the organisation. This is expressed in a variety of ways, from a completely blank stare to a trivialising of the whole subject. Senior managers are not superwomen and supermen, but by the time they get to the top they do have secretaries and assistants to help them and perhaps they have learned the art of delegation. This may be one of the reasons they achieve their high status. Perhaps the fact that it appears that they are less vulnerable to stress could be a form of defence, which manifests itself as lacking a degree of sympathy with those who are. Stress does exist at senior levels, even if it is not talked about. For the most part, people in senior positions have autonomy, which helps them to cope with stress more effectively.

Case example: pressures and possibilities

Simon was a trial lawyer in his mid-forties working in a city legal firm. He had progressed well and was known for his meticulous methods. Low in self-confidence and sensitive to criticism, he was involved in a high-profile trial and the media coverage with which it was accompanied. Were he to make a mistake and 'get it wrong' he would not only be vulnerable to criticism from his management, but also exposed to the press and the general public's criticism. Working in a culture, which was 'rife with criticism' and where, because of the nature of the task, the emphasis was understandably on facts and evidence, he felt he must keep his worries to himself. Simon as a trial lawyer was struggling with whether or not he had disclosed information inappropriately. A tough management style was perceived as 'lacking in support' (of individuals' professional judgements) where little concern or praise was demonstrated. This, combined with a macho culture where emotions were trivialised, reinforced his prior life experience.

He feared that if he were to talk about his professional concerns he would be criticised harshly and therefore he found it difficult to talk about his anxieties at work. His manager was newly appointed and was himself feeling under pressure having just been promoted; therefore he in turn did not realise that there was a problem. The lawyer continued to worry about whether or not he had made a mistake and spent sleepless nights, compulsively checking every detail until his anxiety level rose to the point where he had panic attacks. At this stage the situation had deteriorated to the point where it became clear to his colleagues that he needed help. Simon went off sick with stress and the organisation referred him for counselling.

The relief he experienced was striking, as was his scepticism, when he first entered the counsellor's room. The counsellor, after initially helping him on a practical level to reduce his immediate stress levels, began to help him talk about his low self-esteem and his response to criticism. Part of the work involved exploring Simon's work environment, his background and how it affected him in his current life. He was able to see that he had always found it difficult to turn towards authority figures and, as an experienced lawyer, himself responsible for managing a staff team, he felt he 'should be able to cope'. Having found his senior management supportive, his perception of both how he and others could be managed changed. From the knowledge he personally gained he changed his approach to the way he managed his own staff, thereby improving his own team's ability to communicate more openly. This in turn created a mini culture where individuals could raise professional concerns and obtain constructive support. Simon's own resentment towards the organisation turned to appreciation of the help they gave him and he returned to work both motivated and committed to trying to change his immediate work environment.

This case illustrates both the opportunities and the limitations of the counsellor's role. The initial contract with the organisation was quite clear: to help Simon with his anxiety attacks. However, through the counselling process, Simon was able to influence a small part of the organisation, although there were clearly other issues that could have been (and, some would argue, should have been) addressed if similar situations were not to re-occur. For example, what happened to the new manager, left feeling quite guilty about his management style and who was under pressure for quite different reasons? What about other members of staff in the organisation who felt similarly to Simon? What would happen to them in the future? Although there were further opportunities to become involved, the staff counsellor himself was influenced by the enormity of the task of addressing the overall climate within the organisation, and he too feared that a larger organisational intervention would not be heard and might be perceived as being critical.

Causes of workplace stress

The assumption that death, divorce and moving house are the three biggest causes of stress was challenged by a 'Mind' survey conducted in 1992, which shows that the office has replaced the home as the principal focus for stress. The biggest contributing factors to stress were:

Pressure to perform	31%
Fear of redundancy/job uncertainty	29%
Recession	28%
Change/pace of change	15%
Personal/home life	12%
Increased job load	6%
Excessive hours	3%
Maintaining quality	2%
Other	7%
Don't know	6%
(Sample group of 109 UK companies)	

Over half of the respondents (52 per cent) were at director level or above. One-third were managing directors, partners or chairmen, while 19 per cent were human resources personnel or medical directors.

Organisations are currently under pressure to implement strategies that will ensure that they are doing all they can to fulfil their obligations as employers. Counsellors may well be involved in preventative work as well as remedial work, for they frequently pick up cases of stress-related illness.

Various provisions in legislation are in place to ensure the health and safety of all the organisation's employees. In addition, the employer owes a duty of care under common law to ensure the health and safety of its employees. Stress in the workplace is gaining a higher profile, perhaps as a result of recent legal test cases, but is legislation enough? There is a view that, in reality, organisations pay stress awareness 'lip service' and the counsellor may, under the therapeutic/psychological contract with the organisation, wittingly or unwittingly become the 'lip service' in the organisation's attempts to deal with stress. One employee in a city firm suggested a 'name and shame' policy:

> Perhaps commercial organisations would only start to take it seriously if, say, *Company Magazine* or the *Financial Times* published a 'league table of nervous breakdowns' identifying the number of employees/directors in various industry sectors ... or better still naming national companies who had suffered over a specific time period.   (Anon.)

When problems are presented as occupational stress overload it is often difficult to assess how much of the emotional distress is to do with the individual's own personality and how much is to do with the conditions at work, demands of the job and taking little or no time off. Some organisations do take work stress seriously and in recent years we have seen the growth of various techniques in industry which have at their heart the control of stress. These include job-enrichment programmes and more generally improvements in job design. In some Swedish companies a great deal of job design is left to the individual worker. They claim it produces more effective working patterns and allows for the optimum fit between an individual and their job.

Organisational structures and culture

Causes of stress in the organisational culture include lack of communication, consultation and participation in decision making, and unjustified restrictive behaviour as described earlier in the section on bullying culture. Without policies there will be no clear standards for the behaviour that is expected and no system for individuals to challenge discrimination or harassment. This cultivates a message that people should just cope alone. Organisations that operate on fear, or interpret stress as individuals not coping, will just generate more stress.

It is tempting for me to go further into the whole area but there are many excellent books written on the subject, for example, Sutherland and Cooper (2000). So far as workplace counselling is concerned, providers are reporting an increase in casework with stress-related illnesses, which then go to industrial tribunals. The reason for this trend remains open to interpretation. Some interpret this as employees 'jumping on the bandwagon' following recent test cases, and seeing legislation as a remunerative way out of work. A cynical or realistic view, I wonder?

Stress management

The old maxim 'prevention is better than cure' is simple but true: finding the right person for the right job is the first step in reducing the potential for stress in an organisation.

Warr (1987) identified job features that are considered as being responsible for reducing employee stress:

- utilisation of skills and ability to make decisions about work;
- balanced work demands;
- work variability, challenge and adequate training;
- environmental clarity – organisational information and feedback;
- fair and adequate pay;
- working conditions that are pleasant, safe and secure;
- interpersonal support;
- sense of making a contribution to society.

Sick absence, together with other indicators, has for a long time been seen as a symptom of organisational illness. Identification and recognition of stress within the workplace helps to address effective interventions. Implementing stress audits using a range of techniques – questionnaires, psychometric measures and focus groups – it is possible to assess the levels of stress experienced in a particular organisation. This information can be used to influence and change work practices.

Whatever the causes of workplace stress, whether it is the organisational culture, changing psychological contracts, role ambiguity or the way the job is organised, for many there still remains a stigma attached to this area of work. Many struggle on without seeking help until what started out as healthy stress – the desire to get up in the morning and achieve satisfaction in work life – begins to manifest itself in serious mental and physical problems. It is at this point that the workplace counsellor is likely to be involved.

Summary

An organisation has a will and life of its own; it is an organic being with a unique personality. Often people view the organisation as a single entity – 'the company' or 'the department' – as though it were separate from them, disconnected from them as human beings. It is essential for counsellors to recognise the culture and dynamics of the organisation with which they work in order to be aware of its potential impact on their ability to perform their role.

Opportunities for intervention in organisations are abundant but counsellors are not immune to changing work practices, particularly when counsellors, like many of their clients, face increasing uncertainty. This could undermine their sense of autonomy and leave them feeling less convinced about the impact of their interventions. It is important therefore for workplace counsellors to be aware of the potential for parallel processes to occur.

In this opening chapter I have attempted to acknowledge the internal, often hidden, demands of organisations, which place constraints on how staff counsellors operate and can add extra pressure onto their role. I have also sought to acknowledge the external forces, such as technological, social and political change, which affect the way organisations behave. The next chapter will look at some of the issues to consider in organisations and their implications for a counselling role.

2

THE ROLE OF COUNSELLING AT WORK

Introduction

As you embark on your career as a workplace counsellor I would dearly love to begin by telling you all about the pleasures and creativity of counselling. However, in order that you 'travel safely' I would like to alert you to some of the pitfalls and the 'road conditions' you will encounter on that journey.

The activity of counselling is taking place in a changing world – the world of professional and organisational accountability. When counselling in an organisational system it is important to bear in mind that there are always three dimensions involved: the client, yourself and the organisation. All three are operating in a world of increasing legislation and professional regulation, which has a direct impact on the counselling process. Metaphorically speaking, you need to read your 'highway code' as you take to the 'road' or you could be on a collision course with others in the organisation or innocently end up being subpoenaed by a court, not knowing how you got there or what to do. This chapter will therefore focus more specifically on how workplace counsellors should manage their role, looking at its potential and also its limitations.

Workplace Counselling

It is often said that 'people are our most important asset' but how do organisations demonstrate this? Providing counselling services is just one of the ways organisations can value their staff as human beings – so long as they are not used as a way of avoiding dealing with fundamental structural problems.

Effective management recognises that the well-being of staff is of importance for the growth and development of organisations. Apart from any legal requirement or humanitarian obligation of employers to their staff, it is recognised that people give of their best and work productively and co-operatively only if they are free from unnecessary worries and strain. Counselling is one way of ensuring that both individual and organisational concerns are addressed and resolved. Provision of face-to-face confidential counselling for employees has emerged as a significant way in which both public- and private-sector organisations are providing support for their staff.

According to the British Association for Counselling and Psychotherapy,

> people become engaged in counselling when a person, occupying regularly or temporarily the role of counsellor, offers or agrees explicitly to offer time, attention and respect to another person or persons temporarily in the role of client.
>
> The task of counselling is to give the client an opportunity to explore, discover and clarify ways of living more resourcefully and towards greater well-being.   (BAC, 1995)

Counselling begins when the client understands and wishes to make use of the offer of counselling. Counselling in organisations aims at providing opportunities for the individual and groups of individuals to work towards living and working in a more satisfying and resourceful way. At a macro level workplace counselling is about helping the organisation to help itself.

Recent research by McLeod (2001) found that there is strong evidence that counselling is effective. He found that the majority of clients in several studies improved significantly within six to eight sessions of counselling and virtually all clients were highly satisfied with the help they had received. Counselling was considered cost effective, in terms of covering costs, increased efficiency, reduced recruitment costs, and savings in employee absence etc.

It is encouraging to have detailed evidence to support what many workplace practitioners currently witness in their daily practice. Today counselling services in organisations are usually provided in some form of generalised counselling or welfare service provided either internally or externally. Both methods have advantages and disadvantages in the way they operate and we are seeing a trend towards 'partnerships' where in-house and external counsellors work together to provide an overall service to the organisation.

Internal and external provision

In-house counselling services, where staff employed by the organisation provide the service, are a valuable asset in that they have knowledge of the organisational rules and methods of operation. In addition they often provide other internal advisory and consultancy services to the organisation. However, knowledge of the organisation can be a mixed blessing. On the one hand, it is helpful to know the ground rules, and it also offers access to key people who can assist but, on the other hand, one can become 'part of the system' and affected by the environment to such an extent that it would be easy to collude with it. This would then affect the counselling process.

Where counselling is available to staff members through the provision of an externally contracted provider this is called an Employee Assistance Programme (EAP). There are currently about 14 major EAP providers in the UK and they provide counselling through an affiliate network of qualified counsellors. Staff members are made aware of the service and are able to contact a confidential telephone number or help line. EAP providers emphasise the independence of their services and promote the fact that in terms of human resource management they are an organisational intervention.

External counsellors can offer fresh perspectives to an organisation but EAPs can encounter other difficulties, such as gaining acceptance by the organisation and understanding its culture, rules and hidden agendas. The individual counsellor provided by an EAP, known as an affiliate, is usually a private practitioner with no knowledge of the particular organisation. They will be responsible to the EAP caseworker manager who allocates the case. Whilst the external counsellor may take longer to understand the culture, it could be argued that this is an advantage as with less involvement they are freer to ask questions. For example, 'Can you help me to understand how things work in your organisation?' can elicit a very direct response. By asking the client to explain what they mean, the client may gain some insight that perhaps leads them to challenge their own system.

The range of problems

As far back as the early 1920s research into the effects of work on human performance were being carried out. The Hawthorne Experiment, conducted in Chicago between 1927 and 1932, subsequently led to a long-term counselling programme which lasted until 1958. The findings showed that the five major concerns of employees were keeping and losing their job, unsatisfactory work relations, felt injustices, unsatisfactory relationships with authority and job development. Despite a changed world the concerns identified in the experiment are familiar to those expressed by the people I meet in organisations today. De Board (1983) suggests three categories of people-problems that present at work. These are personality problems, organisational problems and external problems. I would add a fourth category, the life stage of the individual.

Personality problems, says de Board, stem from the individual and would manifest themselves to a lesser or greater extent in the way that the person behaves – exhibiting, for example, lack of confidence or a dislike of authority figures. Case studies by Firth (1985) support this view, saying that with many of the managers who presented with job-related issues, their difficulties were related to their personality – they stemmed from childhood relationships and conditions, which operated at an unconscious level and impaired the subjects' attitude to work and their relationships with colleagues.

Organisational problems are those which occur as a direct result of people working together within the same organisation: for example, work relationships, career opportunities, overwork, underwork, technical abilities or job design.

External problems arising outside the organisation, for example, poor living accommodation, bereavement, ill health or financial difficulties, affect work performance just as organisational problems affect peoples' lives outside of work. An interesting way of distinguishing whether or not the problem is organisational or personal is by asking whether the problem would still exist if the client left the organisation.

At each stage of our lives we have differing needs and priorities, which alter our relationship with and perception of work. For instance, a job change is bound to affect other areas of our lives. When redundancy threatens it is a very different situation for a person in their mid-thirties with dependants than for someone in their early fifties with grown-up children and the mortgage almost paid. Relocations take on a different meaning for a young adult than for an employee in middle or late adulthood, where children's education and the care of elderly relatives could be major considerations.

Types of counselling interviews

I think it is important to bear in mind that counselling is only one way of helping people. Education, advice giving and practical assistance all have their value, and counselling skills can be useful in a number of workplace situations where employees will not necessarily present for 'formal' counselling interviews.

Nelson-Jones (1993) suggests several main types of interviews, which could be seen as having a counselling component in the workplace:

Developmental:	career counselling
Problem-focused:	bereavement, stress etc.
Mediation:	equal opportunities, harassment
Decision making:	redundancy or early retirement
Crisis interview:	after armed robbery, abusive attacks, trauma
Supportive:	mobilising the individual's ability to move forwards

Whether problems arise from something that has happened at work or from personal, family, domestic or social situations, a good manager will recognise the early symptoms, and take action. For example, they may decide to offer some help themselves by affording a staff member an initial opportunity to talk. This may involve the use of counselling skills but cannot be described as counselling (see BACP, 2000). These skills can be extremely useful for people in management and personnel functions, particularly with regard to referral. The power of being listened to at the right moment in time should not be underestimated.

Perhaps acknowledging the employee's situation is all that is necessary to mobilise their internal resources and nothing more will be required. However, there are times when it is necessary to call upon others who are specially trained in this aspect of staff management. Where specialist knowledge and more depth of expertise are required an identified specialist function such as a staff counsellor, welfare officer or external counsellor is preferable. They will have counselling experience and specialist training to cope in greater depth with people in crisis or experiencing problems.

Who is the client?

The use of the word 'client' assumes a singular perspective but what about the multiple and collective perspectives of an organisation?

When a client arrives to see a counsellor in private practice the focus of attention is clearly on the individual and their concerns. It is usually quite clear who that client or potential client might be, and although their problems may well be related to other people, perhaps members of their family or colleagues, there is no requirement to intervene at their place of work or with their families. When counselling in organisations, however, it is less clear where the primary focus of attention might be. Take the line manager who seeks to refer a member of staff who is 'experiencing difficulties'. Who is the client? It could be the line manager who has the 'problem' managing that particular member of staff.

Whether they seek personal counselling or some form of advice or support the primary client is usually seen as the individual who makes the telephone call or who walks through the counsellor's door. It is very easy to slip into talking about 'solving' the difficulties of an absent member of staff and reminds me of family work where parents present the child as 'the patient' when often the difficulty lies within the couple's relationship. Taking that comparison a step further, whilst there could be value in involving the child and treating the family system as a whole, in practice one begins the process with whomever is in the room with you, whilst keeping their relationship to the whole system in mind. This is an equally valid approach with organisations. The client is the person talking to you but I think it is extremely important to remember that they have arrived from a system and will have return to that system.

Example: the client manager

A counsellor described to me her experiences of what she described as 'client manager type situations':

> It's a bit like couple counselling with one of the couple missing! I feel as if I'm talking behind the other one's back! The other person is very present and again impacts on the dynamics of the counsellor/client relationship. Most of the time I am privy to some information that the client isn't aware of and it can get very confusing! I assume this only occurs in workplace counselling as I am sure this situation would not arise in any other sort of counselling as a counsellor would not build a separate relationship with both parties involved, would they?

A good question. In practice they do. Workplace counsellors might see several members of staff from the same office and then the experience is not one of 'couple counselling' but more like 'family therapy'. Ideally one needs to gain all parties' consent and make clear what would and would not be shared. The dilemma described in the above example is common and I think it is useful to remind oneself of the pitfalls of becoming 'a post-box' and colluding in a system of lack of direct communication.

The counselling room is often a rehearsal room for clients to face difficult interpersonal relationships and this is where the counsellor can be of use in helping the client to address particular concerns, gain insights, and explore their options and consequences.

When working with organisations a balance needs to be struck between the following three factors:

- the work task of the client and/or organisation;
- the process of the counselling;
- the environment.

In answer to the question 'Who is the client?' most workplace counsellors believe that by addressing the needs of individuals or small groups they benefit the organisation as a whole.

Managing the Workplace Counsellor's Role

Counsellors in organisations find themselves working in increasingly complex environments against a backdrop of continual change. Whether or not you as the reader are an in-house or an external provider of counselling, you face the issues of understanding the organisation with which you are working, and understanding your role and your ethical responsibilities. The way in which you manage your role is central to the effectiveness of workplace counselling.

Counselling and role conflict

Counsellors are likely to come across mixed expectations of their role. Counsellors in organisations could become all things to all people and take on tasks – such as breaking bad news, sick visiting or charity collections – which should be carried out by others, for example the line manager, personnel officer, disablement officer or occupational health officer. The workplace counsellor needs the confidence to put a boundary around their role, otherwise internal and external conflicts may arise. They may be asked to provide a confidential staff service whilst reporting to management, which can place limits on confidentiality.

Counsellors in organisations need not only to manage the external perceptions of the role but also to deal with potential internal conflicts, as described below by a supervisee.

33

Example: a counsellor's dilemma

'Working from a humanistic approach, my belief is that a crucial element in a good working relationship is that it is an equal relationship. As a workplace counsellor I initially had problems with setting up the working alliance with my clients. I had a responsibility to my employer, who had very different boundaries and expectations to those which I would have liked to offer to my clients. They also had a set of rules, which they wanted explained to every client at the beginning of the therapy. This caused me great concern. I felt it was impinging on the openness and genuineness of our relationship and placed me in an authoritative role from the outset. I believed this therefore led to an imbalance of power and affected our relationship. I felt I needed to establish a genuine and real relationship with the client before I discussed the rules and workplace boundaries (other than the confidentiality issues). I wonder therefore if this is a problem other counsellors have experienced in their role as a workplace counsellor.'

At a personal level staff counsellors might prefer to work in a person-centred way, but organisational constraints could mean that only a limited number of sessions can be offered to the client. This is invariably so with EAPs and increasingly common with internal counselling services. Remembering the balance that needs to be struck between the client, the organisation and the environment in which they are working, the counsellor then has to decide which approach is appropriate (see the section in Chapter 8, 'Short-term therapy'). The counsellor will not find it practicable to use one particular theory consistently in their work and needs to be flexible to a point, but not to the point where their integrity is compromised. That will not only do an injustice to them but it will not be of benefit to the organisation.

So in terms of their own 'psychological contracting' a workplace counsellor needs to bear in mind three levels of contracting: their contract with the organisation, with the client(s) and with themselves. Pressure to conform to a role and not to deviate can be very strong and, therefore, to avoid role conflict, all three contracts need to be clear and as congruent as possible. It might help you to consider these questions. What do individual members of staff in your organisation expect of you in your role? What are management's expectations of you? What expectations do you have of yourself? And finally, are there any conflicts between the above? If there are, now is the time address them.

The challenge in managing the role is to maintain credibility and independence within the limits of organisational rules and within the professional codes of counselling practice. In workplace counselling there are potentially more conflicts of interest and pressures 'to come out of an independent role' and to act on behalf of the client or management. It requires careful contracting, boundary management and the use of recontracting where necessary. It is important, therefore, to have a clear understanding of the counsellor's relationship with members of staff and the organisation. For instance, pressure can be exerted on a counsellor 'to get people back to work', or it might be suggested that it would be 'helpful if they were to go on medical grounds'. Similarly, individuals can attempt to manipulate the counsellor into 'taking sides' against unpopular management decisions. Frequently, in cases involving sexual harassment or racial discrimination, the staff counsellor is the first port of call and in time they may even be called upon to be a witness at an industrial tribunal.

A counselling service is often perceived as, and describes itself as, 'an independent source of counselling and advice available to all members of the organisation'. However, tensions do exist between the needs of the individual and those of the organisation as a whole. Much is talked about the 'independent role' of a staff counsellor but this requires individual reflection, definition and negotiation. It may also be useful to ask and answer the question of where the counselling service stands in the organisational structure. Discussing these issues in supervision is a useful way of monitoring one's own neutrality. The counsellor can seek clarification at each stage by asking questions such as: 'Who is the presenting client on this occasion?' and 'What is my role in this situation?'

Using some of your own casework examples, where on the following continuum would you see yourself in terms of allegiance or identification? Can we include a symbol for either end?

Organisation--Individual

Multiple relationships

Counselling in an organisational setting is challenging work and it has the potential for role conflicts when managing more than one relationship at a time. Perhaps a line manager might present for help regarding a member of staff who, unbeknown to the line manager, is already a client of the very same counsellor. Therefore counsellors need to be approachable and also trustworthy so that people can come to see the counsellor and know that they will be able to hold information. The challenge is in enabling people to feel safe where there are multiple relationships.

Independence is particularly difficult for in-house counsellors where counselling is not seen as a discrete activity and a 'stand alone' unit within the organisation. If the counsellor's own line manager is, for instance, a personnel manager it is not surprising if the client group has difficulty in understanding and accepting that the counsellor is truly autonomous. This can apply equally to EAPs, where it is usual practice for counsellors to make a report to the organisation at the end of their counselling contract.

In-house counsellors often do their work in settings where they cannot help but know the people who seek their help. They might have been a colleague or in a former post they may have been their subordinate or line manager. In such situations potential conflicts of loyalty and confidentiality issues arise, which will be addressed later in this chapter.

Mixed roles

When counselling is only a part of the function it could be said that the practitioner has a 'mixed' role. The practitioner needs to be quite clear about which role they are occupying at the particular moment and make that quite clear to the other person so that they too are aware of the task and roles each of them are occupying at that point in time.

Case example: 'Which hat?'

A personnel officer had a counselling role, albeit a limited one, with a member of staff whose wife had died in tragic circumstances. The personnel officer was then faced with issuing compulsory redundancy notices to the division in which this particular man currently worked.

Obviously this was not an easy situation and it was one where there was potential conflict in perception of role. The personnel officer clearly had two roles.

Managing those two roles takes skill. When the personnel officer responded to a specific situation (death of staff member's wife) he assumed the role of 'counsellor' in a tangible way (setting aside time, privacy, being clear about confidentiality etc.) at and for a specific time. In addition the staff member knew that this was the purpose of their time together. Thus for the role to be clear the workplace counsellor needs to assume the role that is congruent with the specific situation, and be clear about the role they are in at that particular time.

Confidentiality

Confidentiality is one of the cornerstones of counselling practice. But how confidential is confidentiality? What are its limits? When working with a client in the relative privacy and seclusion of the counselling room it is easy for a workplace counsellor to lose sight of some of the external forces which might encroach on the counselling relationship.

There has been a definite shift in practice. Not so many years ago confidentiality was understood as being between client and counsellor. Keeping case notes was considered to be good practice, for the benefit of the client, and it was understood that they were the private property of the counsellor. This relatively simple way of working allowed for a degree of openness with other professionals based on mutual trust and integrity. In general counsellors, unlike doctors and other health professionals, were much less bound by rules and regulations, which in turn encouraged flexibility and a sense of autonomy. Were they less professional? I think not. Were they less accountable? In terms of being answerable to outside bodies, yes, but that did not make them less responsible. They believed they were accountable to their clients, themselves and (where applicable) the agencies for whom they worked.

Now, however, counsellors are more constrained – and guided – by the law.

Confidentiality and the law

The law regarding confidentiality and professional responsibility is complex and evolving rapidly. Government legislation regarding discrimination, employment law and data protection have become a reality and this impacts not only on the counsellor's role but also on confidentiality and the counselling process. Counsellors are advised to work within the law and have appropriate knowledge of the law as it applies to their work. If in any doubt it is important to seek legal advice as early on in the process as possible.

Some counsellors are still at the stage of 'denial' and continue to promise absolute confidentiality, only to be rudely awoken when subpoenaed for their case notes or required to attend an industrial tribunal. It is ethically and legally unwise to promise total confidentiality because there are statutory laws which require disclosure, such as the Children's Act 1989, the Prevention of Terrorism Act 1989 and the Disability Discrimination Act 1995. Being clear and realistic about what you can and cannot disclose is fundamental to your credibility.

Conflicts of interest in legal matters can arise. For example, the staff counsellor may offer a confidential service, the client may expect it and yet because of employment contracts, employer's duty of care or government legislation they may be required to break confidentiality. For example, British Rail has an alcohol policy for the safety of their passengers, banks and the Inland Revenue have financial regulations, and the Ministry of Defence and GCHQ (Government Communications Headquarters) have security as part of their contracts with employees. The counsellor needs to make quite clear at the outset the limits of confidentiality. So at the beginning of the interview (or if that is inappropriate because the client is in great distress, then at the contracting stage of the first interview) they might say something like: 'As you know we are both employees of ... and other than the organisation's special rules regarding ... anything you say will be treated in confidence', or 'This is a confidential service and everything you say here will be treated in confidence unless working for this organisation we are both under a duty to disclose.' Most clients are perfectly aware of this and will be understanding. In my experience it seems to perturb the workplace counsellor much more than the client. Some counselling services have an information sheet, which includes codes of ethics and explains how the service works, including the organisation's policy on record keeping, disclosure and the limits of confidentiality. Some include a written contract to be signed by both parties.

When the counsellor is external to the organisation the boundaries of confidentiality can be limited to anonymous statistics, numbers of sessions and general trends, but when an in-house counsellor is also an employee of the organisation there are potential conflicts regarding absolute confidentiality. Often line managers and personnel officers, in addition to statistics, seek follow-up support. Perhaps they wish to know when the client will return to work, how to handle their return to work or how to deal with delicate situations involving the client and their colleagues. They may wish feedback to highlight sickness trends, the effects of changes in working practices or discriminatory behaviour.

It takes time to educate others in the organisation and to adjust their expectations of the counsellor. For a new workplace counsellor this comes just at the point of trying to get to grips with their own role. At the risk of being considered prescriptive let me suggest that when in any doubt regarding confidentiality, particularly where a third party is concerned, listen, acknowledge the importance of what they are saying to you and then give yourself time to think, offering to get back to them. Above all, keep your promise.

Confidentiality can reinforce myth, mystique and misinformation about the service. This was described by one manager as 'hiding behind a mysterious cloak'. Striking a balance between maintaining client confidentiality whilst keeping management appropriately informed is delicate work. It is easy to assume that the individual client is unhappy for anything to be disclosed and yet, if asked, they might not take this view. Wherever possible, encouraging the client to have direct contact with others involved, say their line manager, prevents distortion and manipulation occurring.

Disclosure

There are situations which pose dilemmas for counsellors, where conflicting responsibilities exist between the client and others who may be significantly affected, or society in general. Wherever possible the counsellor should encourage the client to disclose significant information to the appropriate third-party authority whilst offering support during the process. Two personal examples spring to mind.

Example: who needs to know?

The first client was a battered wife who told me that her child was being severely abused and the second was an angry grieving father (confidentiality prevents me going into further details) who was bent on revenge and was in possession of a firearm. In both cases, apart from any personal moral duty, I realised there were ethical and legal implications. Although I knew that disclosing confidential client information in the public interest was possible, I was also keen to try and maintain the trust of the clients with whom I was working – after all, our relationship was based on the client being able to disclose all manner of information. Each case required some form of risk assessment.

In the first example I made it clear to the client that if she would not take action I would feel bound to do so and did. In the second example I had no hesitation in contacting the client's general practitioner, as a first step, to discuss his perception of the client's state of mind so that we could make a joint decision.

Any disclosures should be undertaken in ways that best protect the client's trust. BACP (2001) states that respecting client confidentiality is a fundamental requirement for keeping trust. The professional management of confidentiality concerns the protection of personally identifiable and sensitive information from unauthorised disclosure. Disclosure may be authorised by client consent or the law.

How to respond to a suicidal client is one of the most challenging situations counsellors encounter. When does one act in order to attempt to preserve life and when does one remain silent out of respect for a client's autonomy? Counsellors vary in their philosophies and where they feel strongly either way then it is best to make this clear as part of the contract or in pre-counselling information.

Although clients often fear discrimination if they disclose certain information, managers, who are usually considered the first line of staff welfare, have concerns regarding their duty of care to all their staff. In the case of bullying or alcohol abuse in a machine-based environment they might argue that they need to be informed in order to assess the level of risk to the rest of their teams or sections. Both managers and counsellors need to think carefully about their role and responsibility. Requests 'not to tell anyone else' place a burden of responsibility on the recipient. Keeping secrets is fraught with dilemmas and can be distressing for staff and managers alike, particularly where others may be affected. The staff counsellor can help those involved clarify the implications of such issues.

Vicarious liability

Here is an example where there is potential conflict regarding disclosure. This time it is an organisational issue.

> ### Example: 'I have just found out that ... '
> A client presents saying that they have just been diagnosed with multiple sclerosis. It is in its early stages and they do not wish their line manager to know. The client asks the counsellor for this information to be treated in confidence.

At this early stage of diagnosis the client is clearly in shock, worried and concerned about their job security. What should the counsellor do? How does the counsellor, having regard to the Disability Discrimination Act (1995), deal with the issue of disclosure? This Act has implications for employees regarding disclosure about employees' disabilities as it not only requires organisations 'to make reasonable adjustments' for staff with disabilities but also says that should any representative of an organisation know of a situation, as described above, then this could involve 'vicarious liability'. This means that if one person knows then the organisation is deemed to know and is considered liable. Non-disclosure may jeopardise the employer's position should legal proceedings occur at a later stage. Clearly this is a dilemma for the counsellor. What is their professional position? It will not necessarily be a defence for an organisation to claim they did not know about the disability and so could offer a reasonable adjustment. They would be vicariously liable.

Workplace counsellors need to be aware of how their own organisations are managing the effects of this legislation. Some organisations may accept liability in order to preserve the confidentiality of their counselling service.

Example: non-disclosure

A client on a period of probation seeks help from the staff counsellor and tells them that when they applied for the job they didn't disclose information about their disability for fear that they would not get the job.

Some employers will be prepared to take the risk and advise counsellors to maintain confidentiality, subject to the client signing a disclaimer, others will not. Clearly, seeking clarification from the organisation's legal department in conjunction with the counsellor's professional body will be helpful in the early stage of employment.

Confidentiality contracts

Here are two examples of how counselling services make clear their policy regarding confidentiality and disclosure.

> Your sessions with a counsellor are in strict confidence. On occasion it may be necessary, with your permission, to obtain support from your line manager personnel or an external agency with reference to your concerns. The only exception is if you disclose a breach of company policy/staff rules or if there is a serious breach of the law or when it is considered that you are at risk of causing serious harm to yourself or other people.
>
> (BootsHelp, 1997)

> The only exceptions we make are when there is considered to be a serious risk to self or others. This includes disclosure of risk to children by people other than the client and acts of terrorism. In the rare event that we break confidentiality this is done where possible with your consent and only to parties (e.g. GPs) who absolutely need to know.
>
> ('Counselling Contact Service' – from a private practice)

Usually such contracts are signed and dated by both counsellor and client, after the counsellor has explained them. I will return to the process of contracting, confidentiality and self-disclosure in Part II, 'Managing the Process: Features and Practice'.

Counselling and the law

It is important to consider employment law in the context of changes in working patterns, e.g. increase in short-term and fixed-term contracts, delayering in organisations and privatisation of government departments. These factors, combined with an increase in flexible employment arrangements, will impact on the codes of practice in organisations. Current government initiatives in employment combined with the impact of directives from the European Union means that legislation will continue to change. Keeping up to date is desirable but not always realistic; therefore when in any doubt it is important to refer your client for current legal advice and clarify your own legal position.

Where legal situations occur the role of the workplace counsellor is to facilitate a process whereby the client can consider their options, clarify issues of disclosure and then facilitate an appropriate referral should the client choose to proceed by taking formal or legal action.

Counsellors have a professional responsibility to take reasonable steps to increase their knowledge of any current law which may affect their work. Where legal and professional conflicts of interests exist then it is good practice to discuss these with their supervisor or an independent person so that the counsellor can clarify their own legal position.

Developing the Counsellor's Role in the Organisation

It is easy for counsellors to forget that they have other valuable skills, which might help them develop their role in their organisational context. Previous work experience and networks can prove extremely useful. They are well placed to have an important input into policy documents and to make a very real difference by reporting current trends and concerns.

Influence and power

The tension between being proactive and reactive in staff counselling is much debated. As in the commercial world, tensions can exist between marketing and the product deliverers. Often the high moral ground and superiority is attached to proactive work because of its higher profile, minimising the value of the daily delivery of the service. This can leave caseworkers feeling valued by their individual clients but not by their team as a whole. Counsellors are human beings and require team building like any other work-group. Role specialism is possible where differences are respected and valued. Below are some anecdotal examples:

'I would like to be more proactive, but in reality I am a reactive person by nature.'

'I am so busy advertising the service that I haven't got time to deliver it!'

There is growing pressure to prove the worth of counselling services and despite statistics it can be difficult to prove their actual effectiveness. Issues around confidentiality limit opportunities to influence; nevertheless it is important to see where it is possible.

The counsellor may encourage people to address issues in the organisation, for example where staff are not being consulted regarding changing work patterns or relocation. The counselling service needs to establish relationships with the decision makers. Promoting the service is just one way of raising awareness about human resource issues in organisations and is an intervention in itself.

Sometimes the notion of having power is not attractive to counsellors even though in reality it does exist. Power is the ability to get things done, the ability to mobilise resources and to influence others. In that sense it can be contrasted with powerlessness. A powerful person is secure and can give others power. A powerless person tends to use what little power they have by being bossy and domineering, because of feelings of insecurity. The ability to influence events directly affects the individual's response and adaptation to change. The workplace counsellor has the potential for being a catalyst for change through counselling and organisational interventions. However, in order to fulfil this role they need to feel secure in themselves and acknowledge that they have power. Often they do not. When I invite participants on courses to consider with what and with whom they associate the word 'power', often negative examples of power come to mind and history offers many examples of the abuse of power to support these views. But the etymology of the word 'power' infers 'potency' and I associate potency with strength, energy and creativity – all qualities required if one seeks to make a difference in an organisation.

French and Raven (1967) distinguish between the following types of power:

Reward power	The ability to deliver positive consequences or remove negative ones, e.g. transfers, praise, thanks, time off in lieu and performance-related pay.
Coercive power	The ability to mete out negative consequences or remove positive ones, e.g. punishments, disapproval, not promoting, annual reports.
Legitimate power	Others accept that you ought to have power over them because of your position, e.g. your role, grade, official power, e.g. the police.
Referent power	Others identify with you or want to be like you, e.g. role models.
Expert power	Others see you as having some special knowledge or skill (doctors, counsellors).
Information power	Others believe you have resources or information which will be useful to them, e.g. messengers, networks and formal clubs.
Internal power	This is the power which comes from within the individual and is often called 'personal power'. It is perhaps one of the most important sources of power because others cannot take it away. Internal power can, however, be reduced by various forms of internal 'blockages'; for example, stress, illness, depression, refusal to use it, regarding the responsibility of power as too frightening, or low self-esteem.

The reason I am including 'power' at this stage is that at 'an organisational level' workplace counsellors can get into a mind-set of 'powerlessness' and forget that, as described above, they do have sources of power. As Fincham and Rhodes (1992) suggest, 'making it in an organization means learning to navigate in the subtle and dangerous currents that bring rewards'. Organisational politics exist and services can be at risk if counsellors are unaware of the impact politics can have on their ability to deliver a competent service. The interpersonal skills required to build good relationships are not to be underestimated, as they ensure that the counselling service is consulted, included in discussions and offered relevant assignments.

Exercise: power

- What kinds of power do you think a Counselling Service or Workplace Counsellor has?
- In what ways are you using the sources of power given to you in your role?
- What stops you using your personal power?

Publicising Services

Although over the past 15 years counselling as a term is used more frequently in the United Kingdom, there is still much myth, mystique and misinformation about the practice of counselling. I always ask new counsellors how many times they have personally used the service? Or what their impression of it is? It is important, therefore, to consider what messages a staff counselling service wishes to portray.

Because of the nature of the work, which is often done on a one-to-one basis in a private place, people in organisations are not necessarily aware of the expertise of their staff counsellors or the scope of the work they are able to cover. In many organisations publicising services consists of putting a poster on a notice board and nothing more. Many services have just evolved over time, responding to internal market forces, and only when under threat of 'takeover' or 'merger' do they really consider what they have to offer. In workshops I have facilitated, called 'The Changing Role of Welfare', I ask participants to consider the following exercise as a way of liberating their thinking about promoting the service.

Exercise: redefining and promoting counselling services

Imagine you are responsible for introducing a counselling service into your organisation. You have a blank sheet and there are no constraints. Try to imagine how it would be.

- What sort of service would you offer?
- What form would it take?
- What would the key elements of the service be and why?

Allow yourself to be really creative

You may like to consider the following factors when designing or publicising your service.

Issues to consider:

- Who are your customers and what are their needs?
- What type of service do you wish to offer?
- What message do you wish to get across?
- What is the degree of independence within the organisational structure?

Publicity might include:

- Scope and range of services available
- Access to the service
- Office hours or 24-hour telephone line
- Response time
- Number of staff and range of expertise
- Training and qualification of the counsellors
- Information Contracts including number of sessions offered etc.
- Confidentiality statements
- Ethos

Methods:

- Posters
- Visiting cards
- Attending policy meetings
- Office visits
- Talks and briefings
- Input on training courses (particularly induction courses for new entrants/new managers)
- Personal recommendation
- Articles in in-house journals on specialist topics
- Display boards
- Statistics
- Web pages and E-links

Summary

The typical dilemmas facing practitioners working in organisational settings will be those of knowing how to preserve confidentiality and when and how to manage the conflicts with other functions, arising from differing pressures and perspectives. The workplace counsellor needs to consider how the pressures on other functions – such as line managers and personnel officers – combined with the overall culture of their organisation, might influence their own thinking about the potential for counselling interventions in their organisations.

In order to manage the role, workplace counsellors need to take into account the following:

- Boundaries, confidentiality and its limits
- Legal requirements
- The opportunities and limitations within the role
- The necessity for impartiality in order to establish credibility in the role
- The potential for role confusion and overlap
- The range of clients and ways they present
- The importance of treating any interaction between the counsellor, an individual or client group with respect and integrity
- The fact that more than one client may be involved, including the organisation as a whole
- Their position in the organisation
- The interpersonal skills required to develop their role
- The ability to say 'no'

By the very nature of the work there is a degree of 'invisibility' in the role of the workplace counsellor. Counsellors need to believe that what they offer is of value to the organisation. Where they and the service they provide has a high and esteemed profile it makes intervention more feasible, particularly in difficult times. Where it is not, the workplace counsellor can be left feeling 'now I am like everybody else' and at risk of becoming demoralised and impotent.

Part II

Managing the Process: Features and Practice

INTRODUCTION TO PART II

Learning to be a counsellor is not the same as learning to be a doctor, psychiatrist or psychologist, where the training is almost entirely academic and you do not have to look at your own emotions and attitudes. One of the distinguishing features of counselling is the ability to relate to the client and to understand their problems without getting drawn into their emotional condition to the point where it serves neither client nor counsellor. This section of the book, 'Managing the Process', is divided into two parts to consider these issues.

The first section, Part II: 'Managing the Process: Features and Practice', focuses on integrating theory and skills to manage the process of counselling in practice. Quite naturally it produces further questions and therapeutic dilemmas yet to be answered. These will be addressed in Part III: 'Managing the Process: Issues and Dilemmas'.

To help you integrate these ideas with your own professional practice I would encourage you to bring to mind your own casework examples and make a note of them for your own personal development.

CLIENT AND PRACTICE MANAGEMENT

Introduction

In this chapter general concepts of counselling will be considered. These will include the distinguishing features of counselling such as the therapeutic alliance, the art of listening, and counsellor and client attitudes. It will then focus on the practical issues of client management.

Therapeutic Alliance

The counsellor's role is to facilitate the client's growth in ways that respect their personal values, resources and capacity for self-determination. The relationship between counsellor and client, known as the therapeutic alliance, is a collaborative one intended to be beneficial and generally helpful to the client.

This sounds relatively easy. However, upon closer scrutiny counsellors soon come to realise that the therapeutic alliance is filled with dilemmas. In order to practice effectively and ethically one of the first considerations is that of understanding the dynamics of the therapeutic alliance. Consider the following questions:

- What form will the relationship take?
- What should one do when co-operation is absent?
- What happens when the relationship doesn't appear to be working?
- Is there an agreement to be made within the organisational boundary?
- And if so, who will be responsible for ensuring such an agreement is adhered to?

There is also the question of boundaries and where individual practitioners draw the line. For instance, I would describe the counselling relationship as an intimate one in the sense that clients share extremely private experiences with me, often profoundly moving to us both. Nevertheless I do not consider my clients as friends, even though I hope to behave in a friendly manner towards them. Each individual therapeutic alliance is unique because it is a relationship between particular people within a certain context and at a given time, whether it is on a one-to-one basis, a group basis or at an organisational level. The quality of such a relationship can be therapeutic in itself depending on the counsellor's ability to be a real person.

It is widely accepted by practitioners and theorists that effective counsellors are those who can establish caring, non-threatening relationships with their clients in which both parties feel secure enough to interact as real spontaneous people. Perhaps the primary tool of the therapist's trade is the therapeutic relationship itself. This would then suggest that the responsibility for creating such a relationship lies mainly with the counsellor. If this is the case then counsellors will need to become familiar with this tool. They will need to hone and fine-tune it to the point that the power of the tool (the therapeutic relationship) can be used to good effect.

Counselling can retain a mystical quality and so I would like to simplify the therapeutic alliance by dividing it into three key elements:

■ **The Counsellor** – *oneself*
■ **The Client** – *the other person(s)*
■ **The Interaction** – what happens between them

What follows is a discussion of some of the features of these three elements.

The Counsellor

Counselling should provide a safe place where clients can release their feelings, attitudes, emotions, prejudices and problems without fear of abuse or of feeling that they are in danger of losing their dignity. To ensure clients' psychological safety counsellors need to know their level of competence, have access to a referral system and be committed to their own personal development. It is equally important that the counsellor's safety is assured, both physically and psychologically. Consideration needs to be given as to whether or not the staff counsellor is physically at risk, for example from a potentially violent or disturbed client, or psychologically at risk from case overload or lack of professional support.

Attitudes and motivation

A recurring theme across theoretical approaches suggests that therapists' attitudes are more important in the therapeutic relationship than are their techniques and procedures. If this is the case then considering the counsellor's motivation for doing this work is an important step in beginning to think about the counselling relationship (see Chapter 9). Managing the counselling process involves managing oneself, including attitudes, belief systems, experience, knowledge and existing skills.

A competent counsellor requires a balance of objective knowledge and subjective personal knowledge. Objective knowledge includes the study of theory and principles, including legal and professional codes of behaviour. It involves comparing research, discriminating between the various therapeutic schools and acquiring information about referral agencies and specialist subjects. In addition, workplace counsellors need to gain knowledge about the organisations and the settings in which they work. The latter requirement sounds perfectly logical until one addresses the question of impartiality.

Just how unbiased and independent are those who take their first steps as workplace counsellors? Only by addressing subjective personal knowledge, which involves a well-developed self-awareness, including intuition, perception and feelings, can counsellors obtain a clearer understanding of these issues. Through training, experience and personal development counsellors develop a sense of personal and professional identity in order to be available to clients' experiences. I describe this as: 'knowing where I begin and where I end, both personally and professionally, in order that the client can experience him or herself as a separate being'. However, counsellors are human and just as their clients' lives are changing, so are their own. For example, they may experience bereavement, illness, difficulties in personal relationships or even conflicts with their own line manager. As their personal circumstances change it is important for them to be committed not only to initial training but also to continuous personal development in order to remain an effective practitioner.

To help new counsellors strike a balance between objective and subjective knowledge I offer them a continuum showing two extreme positions that a trainee counsellor might potentially adopt. I then usually invite them to identify where they would put themselves on that continuum at that moment in time and why.

Objective knowledge----------------------------------Subjective knowledge
(Intellectual self)   (Emotional self)

A new counsellor may have an natural inclination towards one end of the spectrum rather than the other, or they may be spot on, right in the middle. In practice this simple exercise can be enlightening and helps counsellors set their own learning goals. To express their full potential and to be psychologically available to their clients it is important to have both sets of knowledge at their disposal, striving towards some semblance of balance between these two potential extremes.

Expressing a preference for one over the other is sometimes merely a question of previous methods of learning in education or at work. This is relatively easy to address through training and supervision so that the counsellor is better placed to make the necessary adjustment. In other instances the inclination towards the one, at the cost of other, could be because of a psychological defence mechanism against acknowledging intellectual abilities or the emotional self, the origins of which might be a little more complex and challenging. This may require a different approach in order to obtain the necessary balance. The following examples illustrate this.

Example: the enthusiast

A highly enthusiastic participant engaged quickly with clients and put them at ease quite naturally. He was an open man, ready to share his life experiences for the benefit of the group, the first to volunteer for practice sessions; however when it came to discussing theoretical concepts or how litigation might affect client confidentiality he just switched off. He couldn't see the relevance. In terms of the spectrum he veered towards the right-hand side.

Example: the thinker

A highly motivated individual, she had read all the literature she had been given prior to arriving on the training course. However it became clear from observing her interviews that she did not pick up on the emotional content of her clients. In group supervision she found it difficult to talk about herself. The challenge for her was to become more comfortable with expressing her emotions.

Objective and subjective knowledge needs to be combined with opportunities to develop the counsellor's techniques, competence and an awareness of their limitations. The ratio of counselling skills practice to theory and personal awareness is therefore equally important. If one uses video or peer feedback in training then how counsellors conduct themselves, perform and react to their clients can be identified. Micro skills training is particularly useful in helping counsellors practise, improve their skills and gain confidence.

Counsellor characteristics

Consistent themes of what produces a competent counsellor are like threads weaving their way through the literature of all therapeutic disciplines, including counselling, psychiatry, psychology and social work. Rogers (1961) placed great emphasis on the counsellor's attitudes regardless of theoretical orientation and believed that a therapist should show 'congruence', 'empathic understanding' and 'unconditional positive regard'. These are often referred to as the three core conditions of counselling; those of genuineness, empathy and respect. They mean being real, attempting 'to walk in the shoes of another person' and accepting others regardless of difference, e.g. of beliefs, attitudes, lifestyle or behaviour.

When interviewing prospective candidates for counselling training there are several desirable characteristics I hope to find, such as:

Warmth	Genuineness
Empathy	Respect for others
Open-mindedness	Acceptance of others
Self-awareness	Objectivity
Non-dominance	Non-judgemental attitude

When thinking about workplace counsellors I would add four additional qualities, those of assertiveness, flexibility, an ability to take initiatives and to negotiate. Not all workplace counsellors start from scratch. Some bring specialist training and experience in areas such as HIV, health counselling, debt counselling, couple and sexual counselling, bereavement or redundancy counselling.

The Client

Imagine someone who is wondering about whether or not they should seek help. It might be that they have heard the company is about to relocate, they are experiencing harassment in the office, or it might be that they are desperately trying to juggle being efficient at work whilst caring for an increasingly dependent elderly relative.

Client attitude

In general most staff try to keep their personal problems to themselves. An overall social attitude of keeping a 'stiff upper lip' exists, and people in the workplace do not easily seek counselling help. Only when the balance is tipped, between the fear they might be experiencing (in asking for help) and the rising level of their anxiety about their situations, do they present for counselling or respond to the suggestion of referral.

At this point they will start to look around for who might be able to help them. Nowadays there is no shortage of doors upon which to knock, each with their different signs saying 'staff counselling', 'bereavement counselling', 'alcohol and dependency counselling', 'trauma counselling', 'debt counselling', 'relationship counselling' etc. Individuals in emotional trouble, or in need of emergency help, may arrive in some bewilderment and this underlines the point made in Chapter 1 of how important it is for the counsellor to offer clarity about what type of help they can offer realistically, thereby not adding to the client's existing confusion.

There will be some clients who, just as customers in the retail world, simply 'shop around' cautiously looking at the 'goods' or asking around for 'recommendations'. Certain clients will be concerned with the 'quality of the merchandise', enquiring in more detail about the type of service the workplace counsellor offers. Others will seek out 'a bargain' and the issue of fees will play an important factor in their decision or they will have read about 'the latest fashion'. Some with low self-esteem may feel they do not deserve to go into the counselling shop at all, whilst others know that even though they cannot afford it, in financial terms, they realise that they cannot afford not to enter. The client's part in the counselling interaction starts long before the first meeting. Clients enter with their own private thoughts and feelings and each will require something different from the counsellor.

Example: 'Who can help me?'

Jenny is an administrative officer in a government department. Of late it has been noticed by her line manager that she has seemed more withdrawn in the office and there has been an increase in sickness absence. Jenny has a personal difficulty in maintaining an intimate relationship and is experiencing financial problems which she has tried without success to resolve. Her father died about two years ago and her current partner has just told her that the construction company for whom he works wants him to work abroad for six months.

If Jenny seeks help, from which source will it be? We can see from this example there are many doors through which this particular client could enter. She might self-refer, because of her personal distress, seeking out the help of her general practitioner or the workplace counsellor. Personnel might refer her because of her level of sickness absence or because of her line manager's genuine concern. There is also the question of attitudes towards asking for help. In an individualistic society where there are strong messages about self-reliance, asking for help can be distressing. In an organisational context many equate asking for help as a sign of weakness and dependence, and proof that they cannot 'cut the mustard'. The idea that they may require some support is repulsive and yet at the same time that is exactly what they need. There lies the paradox.

Common client needs

Having now acknowledged that there will be individual differences in what clients require I would like to return to the theme of similarity. Here are some common client needs:

- to feel safe;
- to be heard;
- to be accepted and recognised as a person of worth;
- to be seen as an individual;
- to be given permission to express how they feel without judgement;
- for confidentiality to be maintained;
- to be allowed to express confusion and conflicts;
- to have a response to expressed feelings;
- to make their own choices and decisions;
- to have the right to stay with those decisions or change them.

It could be argued that the above is what we hope to receive from a real friend, but in life this may not be possible. A counsellor fulfils these needs temporarily so that the client can live a more resourceful and satisfying life.

Client motivation

Background, cultural attitudes, norms concerning asking for help and upbringing, combined with the severity and the nature of the problem, will affect the process. If counselling is about bringing about some change in clients' lives then it seems to me that people change for three main reasons. Firstly because they are bored and therefore seek change in their lives, secondly because they have change foisted upon them (for example through redundancy) or thirdly because they discover they have the ability to change. Entering the counselling process itself could be a significant change in itself. Some of the factors to consider are the individual's motivation for change, their capacity to change and the opportunities afforded them.

Client ambivalence is normal and to be expected. The degree to which a client is motivated, their attitude towards change, their presenting situation, their expectations, degree of openness and their environment will all affect the outcome of the counselling. At the beginning of the relationship the counsellor might reflect on the following questions in an attempt to understand what motivates a particular client towards change.

- To what degree does the client actually wish to change?
- Why are they seeking change at this particular point?
- What is in it for them to change or to stay the same?
- To what degree will they be able to address and cope with painful past experiences?

Whilst I hold to the belief that change is possible for all and that even a small shift is significant, people do vary in their ability to change for reasons other than motivation. For those more severely affected emotionally and interpersonally (e.g. bipolar depression, schizophrenia or personality disorders) insight is at times limited. For these client groups change can be particularly difficult but not impossible in counselling settings, as recent research has shown (see Siebert, 2000). In practice the workplace counsellor's role might be limited to helping the employee maintain the best possible adaptation to their situation, with regular contact described as 'long-term support' as opposed to counselling.

Other examples are clients experiencing phobic conditions. Although they are motivated they may require an alternative type of help as practised by a clinical psychologist or cognitive behavioural therapist, e.g. anxiety management or desensitisation. Unless they are familiar with these techniques the workplace counsellor's role would be limited to providing a supportive link to the organisation. In addition there are individuals with varying degrees of brain injury who seek change but may experience cognitive difficulties. Some clients have well-developed defence mechanisms. They may try a variety of sources and methods of help, outwardly declaring that they seek change, yet finding it extremely difficult to achieve.

Even when a client is highly motivated it may be that the opportunities do not exist for them to go forward. Perhaps job opportunities do not exist in their area, maybe there are limited resources for long-term counselling or the specialist form of treatment they require has a long waiting list. Where clients present with debilitating or life-threatening illnesses they may not be afforded the time to make the necessary changes they seek. In such cases the focus of work would be on coming to terms with the limitations for change. In reality one cannot be of assistance to all who come through the workplace counsellor's door. There can be an enormous relief in realising the limitations of the counselling role, particularly when working with short-term contracts. I compare workplace counsellors with general practitioners. Both need to have a sound knowledge base of a variety of conditions and though they are able to help the majority, often they act as a referral service for specialist treatment.

A change in one person usually requires an adjustment on behalf of others within the system within which they live and work such as a relationship, family or a department. Even when the client is trying to make changes we should not assume that all those around them will afford them that opportunity. Others in that system might not like it, might find it threatening and may be unsupportive. If it is unwelcome or others are unwilling to accommodate change themselves the clients may not be supported in their efforts to change. 'Get back in role' is the implicit or explicit message: 'We knew how to cope with you before.' The client will need encouragement to continue if they are to sustain the gains they have made from the counselling process.

Resistance to Counselling

In general terms resistance is anything that hinders the counselling process. Often it is the client who brings resistance and as they attempt to enter into the therapeutic process they erect a barrier. However, words such as 'client resistance' are used even when it is not the client who is the cause of the barrier. For example counsellors can attribute blame to their clients for lack of co-operation and progress when maybe it is the counsellor who has not really engaged with their client. Perhaps what the client is trying to convey to them cannot be heard because of the counsellor's own difficulties.

Resistance can manifest itself in a variety of ways and I would regard a degree of ambivalence as perfectly normal (see the section in Chapter 4, 'Initial Referral'). Rogers (1951) says: 'It simply means that in every desire to do something there is also the desire not to do it, that every positive

59

feeling also has in it something of the negative.' As a rough guide:

■ when 55 per cent of the client wishes to change and 45 per cent of the client is resisting the change, it may take time but change is possible.
■ if 55 per cent of the client is resisting change and 45 per cent wishes to change, there is little hope of an effective outcome.
■ if 50 per cent of the client wishes to stay the same and 50 per cent does not, the therapeutic relationship becomes 'stuck'.

Counselling is not an exact science where these percentages can be measured accurately and so as counsellors we rely on our skills and awareness of how the relationship is progressing. Below are some ideas of ways in which the client might manifest resistance. They are offered with a cautionary note, as one needs to be careful about making interpretations too early or unhelpfully.

Behaviourally – by not attending, missing appointments or by a pattern of being late, remaining silent in sessions.

Mentally – by not thinking about certain areas, generalising, distorting facts or changing the subject and attributing actions, emotions and thoughts onto others.

Emotionally – by repressing or suppressing emotions, projection and introjection.

These manifestations are not exclusive to one-to-one counselling. For example, where teams are experiencing difficulties or where personality clashes exist, it is not uncommon that where one person suggests the possibility of counselling, then another will resist the idea and even sabotage it. This occurs frequently in couple or family counselling but is also applicable to workplace counselling. For example, where one employee is not committed to changing within a team structure they can sabotage constructive meetings with plausible reasons as to why they are either late or absent.

The Interaction between Client and Counsellor

Having considered the counsellor's and the client's contribution towards the therapeutic alliance, I would now like to focus on the therapeutic alliance's third feature, that of the interaction between them.

Counselling is a person-to-person form of communication marked by the development of an emotional understanding between client and counsellor. This is often technically described as rapport or empathy. Despite requests for answers, counsellors know they do not have them. Solutions, if they are to be found, evolve out of what transpires between client and counsellor. The counselling interaction is dependent, in part, on the nature of the person who seeks help and also on that of the counsellor and their particular style.

The psychodynamic theory of personality development suggests that all human beings are subject to emotional trauma. The structure of the character and personality is determined by the way in which each individual receives and deals with these experiences. Therefore, the counselling interaction will include the following:

- the personality of both;
- the life experience of both;
- the behaviour styles of both;
- the content of what is shared between both.

Understanding how the above impacts on the counselling process is fundamental, as awareness of the dynamics of the interaction is the key which

Table 3.1   Interaction between client and counsellor

Client's needs	Professional relationship
Need for expression of feelings.	Facilitated mainly through purposeful listening.
Need for understanding and response to feelings expressed.	Controlled emotional involvement with client through sensitivity, empathy and understanding.
Need for recognition as a person of worth and dignity in spite of faults, weaknesses or problems.	Acceptance of client as someone of worth and dignity as a human being.
Need for help as an individual rather than a case, type, category, etc.	Individualisation – recognition of each client's unique qualities and situation.
Need not to be judged, or condemned as a failure.	Non-judgemental attitude – not assigning guilt or innocence, but seeking to make an evaluative assessment of actions and attitudes.
Need to make own choices and decisions.	Self-determination – helping and allowing the client to make own decisions.
Need for assurance that personal information and expression of feelings will be confidential.	Confidentiality – preservation of client's private, personal information which is disclosed in a professional relationship.

unlocks the potential for a healthy therapeutic alliance. By noticing which interventions help or hinder the process, by being alert to issues of power and equality and observing how the client uses the counselling opportunity, the development of a professional relationship is enhanced. Table 3.1 is a way of summarising the interaction between client and counsellor, adapted from Biestek's work (1970).

The Helping Process

The helping process is one where counsellors enable or facilitate clients to function more effectively in their situation. It may produce a concrete observable change (for example a growth in confidence, a move to another division), or a change which is much more subtle such as the acceptance of the loss of a relationship. Or it may be the first step in a major reconstruction of their identity, which will require a long-term commitment to, say, psychoanalysis.

The art of listening

If there was only one skill I could emphasise in the helping process it would be the ability to listen, to really listen. To use a cooking metaphor, listening is the basic stock from which a hearty meal can be created. It is the foundation for any counselling recipe and once one has acquired the art of listening then other ingredients can be added. It is all a question of knowing your ingredients, their strength and how to combine them in appropriate quantities. My recipe for a basic 'stock' would be a good measure of listening with some accurate empathic responses. To the above I would add a sprinkling of thoughtful questions here and there and the odd pinch of confrontation just to add a little spice when required.

Active listening, which is the foundation of any therapeutic relationship, begins in my view with the counsellor listening to themselves, increasing their own sense of awareness so that they can then be available to hear their clients. Listening is one of the core skills of any therapist and by training themselves to monitor any tendency to selectively hear they can begin to really listen, without filtering the message their clients are endeavouring to impart. Counsellors are then in a position to respond empathically and appropriately. This is particularly important when a client presents material which either reminds the counsellor of their own life experience or contradicts their own value system. A relatively simple illustration of this might be a client presenting with a debt problem.

Example: 'I can't make ends meet'

'Well, you see, it's not just the bank, it's also all those credit cards ...
and then of course there are my friends who have helped me out from
time to time ...'

The thrifty counsellor thinks:
'How can you possibly have got yourself into such a mess!'

The overdrawn counsellor thinks:
'I know just what you mean, I can't resist a bargain, which reminds
me, I must reply to that letter from my bank manager sometime ...'

Neither counsellor in the above example is listening fully to the client. For
quite different reasons their focus of attention is on their own thoughts and
reactions. Active listening requires the ability to set aside one's own agenda
for the time you are with the client. When working as a marital therapist
I had an early-morning appointment with a couple. The night before my
husband and I had had 'a bit of a barney' which was still unresolved as we
set off for work that day. Although I went into the office in good time to
prepare I was still upset and found it hard to switch off from the way in
which we had parted. I began to question what right I had to be sitting in
the counsellor's seat after what had just happened in our own lives. This is
just one personal example which illustrates how challenging this work can
be and reminds us that counsellors are not robots.

Effective listening requires discipline and the naturally chatty or inquis-
itive person might have to work really hard to curb that aspect of their personality when occupying the role of counsellor. Silence is an important part
of the counselling process as it creates the space for clients to collect themselves and to share the more important and often difficult aspects of their
lives. However for some people sound is more manageable than silence and
so they may fill the space by talking. In a task-orientated society, a business
setting or organisation filled with activity, introducing the concepts of 'time
to reflect', 'to be' or 'to sit in silence' can be quite threatening. The challenge for the counsellor is to be able to tolerate the silence and not to fill
this valuable and potentially creative space. One of my favourite tips to new
counsellors is: 'If you can bear to hear then your client will be able to tell
you what they really need to say.' Another tip is to listen to the themes of
what the client is saying. When you listen to a piece of music, whether it be
classical, rhythm and blues, heavy metal, pop or rock, there is usually
a recurring beat and tune, which returns and is replayed. Clients are really

very good at letting us know what is important and give us more than one opportunity to 'hear the beat' of the message.

There are other barriers to good listening such as tiredness, illness, time pressures and anxiety about one's own ability to perform in the role, to mention just a few. Once you have become aware of them they can be managed and, when mastered, the art of listening can be an enjoyable experience. I will explore in more detail in Chapter 5 some of the dilemmas raised by the therapeutic alliance.

Some comparisons in the helping process

Given that there are so many schools or approaches to counselling and psychotherapy it will come as no surprise that there is a plethora of models to describe the helping process, including non-directive and action-orientated disciplines. In dividing them into three main streams Clarkson and Pokorny (1994) suggest that:

- An orthodox psychoanalytic approach would be 'to focus on the past and ask the question *why?*'
- An orthodox behavioural approach would be 'to focus on the present, including the immediate past, asking the question *what?*'
- And the humanistic-existential approaches would 'focus on the present, including past and future, asking the question of *how?*'

One example of a model which would fit into the latter group is Egan's (1977) model, as outlined below:

Pre-helping	Attending	Suspending the counsellor's own concerns physically and psychologically.
Stage 1	Exploring	Helping the client to explore their behaviour and examine their difficulty and where they are.
Stage 2	Understanding	Helping the client to understand what may be happening to them and helping them own the consequences of their current situation, including what may be keeping them there.
Stage 3	Facilitating	Helping the client to act upon any insights and to come to terms with these understandings.

Given its sequential approach I have found that as a starting point this model appeals to workplace counsellors who come from organisations where they are used to operating in a structured way. For those for whom counselling, in purist terms, is only part of their overall role, then Egan's model, when combined with counselling skills training, enables them to operate in a variety of situations.

Life skills

Many would argue that the interpersonal skills required within the counselling process are those that we need in life in general. The concept of life skills in that sense is nothing new and just another way of helping. Taking a down-to-earth approach, it is something that parents attempt with their children on a daily basis when they ensure their safety and welfare and generally try to be of some assistance in their growth and development.

> It may be learning something new or re-learning something one has forgotten; it may be learning how to learn or it may be unlearning; paradoxically, it may even be learning what one already knows.   (Corsini and Wedding, 1989)

Nelson-Jones (1993) takes the view that helping does involve learning and he offers a five-stage model called DASIE which teaches life skills as a way of helping in a variety of situations.

- **D**evelop the relationship, identify and clarify problem(s)
- **A**ssess problem(s) and redefine in skills terms
- **S**tate working goals and plan interventions
- **I**ntervene to develop self-helping skills
- **E**nd and consolidate self-helping skills

As Nelson-Jones makes clear, many of these skills can be usefully incorporated into counselling techniques and practice.

Practice Management

Having focused on the therapeutic alliance and features of counselling I shall now look more closely at the issues and dynamics involved in 'practice management'.

The setting

Earlier we identified the three main features of counselling as being (1) the counsellor, (2) the client and (3) the interaction between them. Each of these features can be – and often is – affected by a fourth dimension, that of the setting within which the counselling takes place. Counselling in general can take place in a variety of settings:

General settings	Workplace counselling
In an organisation	In a counsellor's office
In a specialist counselling office	In the client's office
In the client's home	In the client's home
In a social service office	In a third party's office
In GP's practice or hospital	In hospital
In the voluntary sector	
In private practice	

When working in an organisational setting consider how important it is to the client where the counsellor's office is located. It may be that the client is reluctant to be seen entering a welfare officer's or staff counsellor's office. It might help the counsellor to be aware of and to acknowledge the potential difficulties. It can also elicit much about clients' attitudes towards counselling or the importance of privacy in their lives.

I have also known some workplace counsellors agree to choices of location and settings which in my view were far from ideal and initially involved them using unconventional settings, e.g. meetings in coffee shops or public parks. Upon enquiring why they had agreed to such an arrangement they would usually present casework where either the client was fearful of being seen in the office or where the client's motivation was so low that the counsellor felt that the only way of engaging with them was, in the first instance, to visit them in such places. Whilst acknowledging the argument for flexibility, I think such situations suggest blurred boundaries and are open to misinterpretation. In these instances the counsellor will need to consider how they wish to work and how to maintain the necessary privacy required to do some effective counselling work. In my view on-going counselling contracts do not lend themselves to such settings and are not advisable.

A safe place means the provision of a quiet space without distraction. The counselling room should be relaxing and informal with privacy assured. You may like to consider whether the décor is warm and inviting or whether the seats are comfortable. It is also a good idea to make sure telephones are switched off. Managing the 'physical' boundaries with the outside world is part of the counsellor's responsibility. With a busy schedule it requires discipline on behalf of the practitioner and usually requires negotiation with others in the organisation, for example if there is a shortage of interview rooms.

Example: 'Engaged'

A counsellor went into the room she had booked for her counselling sessions only to find a meeting taking place. Here we have an example of how competing needs in the organisation and hierarchy can influence the counselling process. The counsellor's patience was tested; in the short term she decided she needed to find an alternative space and then decide on how to deal with the organisational issue of communication and power.

Domiciliary visits

In many organisations it is standard practice for personnel or staff counsellors themselves to write to clients offering them the opportunity of a visit from a staff counsellor. With domiciliary visits there is the potential for confusion in the role. For example, is it clear in what capacity they are seeing the client? Perhaps there is an expectation on behalf of the client that the appointment has been made to obtain a medical or personnel report as opposed to an offer for counselling. Then there are overlaps with other professionals – for example, the general practitioner, the community psychiatric nurse or the health visitor – which could influence the expectations of the client.

By entering clients' physical space the counsellor is also entering their 'internal psychological world' and their perception of what this means for them. Perhaps their home is thought of as a sane and safe haven but, on the other hand, it might be experienced as a prison (Noonan, 1992). Although fraught with distractions, seeing the client in their home can have advantages in that much can be gleaned from working with someone in their own environment. A positive example of this was the client who had been suffering from depression for some time, who on the fifth visit greeted the staff counsellor with an offer of refreshment saying: 'You know, this is the first time I have felt like making a cake.' The counsellor was immediately able to identify and acknowledge the shift in the client's progress in dealing with their depression.

Natural politeness and social norms, for example endless offers of cups of tea, or the intrusion of the television and other family members, all need to be managed by the staff counsellor if the therapeutic relationship is not to be minimised. In addition the staff counsellor has to manage their own feelings about entering situations over which they have little control, like pets or unhygienic environments. On occasion counsellors might feel 'captive', unable to get up and leave. In such situations it is important to maintain boundaries, reminding themselves of the professional role they are fulfilling. In my experience the more distressed or disturbed the client is the more they respond positively to the reliability and consistency of a relationship that has clear boundaries.

Another factor is that the workplace counsellors may find themselves isolated and potentially vulnerable. There are the issues of personal safety for the counsellor in the sense of location, time of day, nature of the problem and assessment of risk. Some organisations provide counselling staff with mobile telephones or personal alarm systems when counselling in isolated environments or when seeing a client alone in the building after office hours. If the counsellor feels they are at risk then letting a colleague know where they will be and agreeing to telephone them after they have left is one practical approach to such a situation. Although domiciliary visits are not ideal, and may be full of constraints and pitfalls as described, if handled with skill they are a useful and viable way of working.

First contact with a client

Most clients telephone to make an appointment. The first point of contact therefore is usually with an appointments secretary, receptionist or member of a help line. The role of the person at the client's first point of contact is key to the intake process as the individual, having summoned up the courage to make the call, might be anxious or even desperate. A warm, friendly and calm approach is very important.

For the person taking the call it can be frustrating when they are not able to offer immediate help to a distressed caller. A basic knowledge of counselling skills can help them to offer some comfort to the client and to do a 'holding operation' until the client is able to get an appointment with a trained staff counsellor. This requires a degree of skill which, sadly, is not always recognised by organisations. Being able to explain how the service works and listening to a client's concerns at this stage is a valuable part of the overall process. For instance it may be that such a person gleans important information as to the level of urgency or who might have referred the client and why.

People in distress need human contact and, with the increase of the use of answerphones, often the first point of contact with a counsellor may be via an answerphone or voice-mail. A clear message ending with something like: ' ... and please be assured your call will be treated in confidence' can be very reassuring. It is imperative that the staff counsellor responds in person as soon as possible. As this is sometimes difficult it is also important to offer alternative telephone numbers in case of emergency.

Monitoring the Progress

Monitoring progress depends on being clear about the various stages in the process. It involves the initial assessment, agreed contract, focus of work and the methodology used. Monitoring progress requires reviewing and evaluating at regular intervals, using, for example:

- personal reflection – case notes, professional logs, developmental diary;
- record of attendance, indicating frequency, number of sessions and cancellations;
- supervision;
- case discussion groups;
- audio or video tapes, with client's permission.

An essential part of counselling is for the counsellor to be able to assess where they are in the process at any given moment. Self-observation through written process comments from audio-visual tape recordings helps counsellors confront their own practices (Kagan, 1980). These can deepen their understanding of the client and also help the counsellor not only to appreciate areas for self-improvement but also to recognise their own abilities.

Here are some reflective questions which help link the counsellor's thoughts, feelings and actions with the client's behaviour:

Reflective questions
- What did I hear my client say or see my client do?
- How did my client react to my interventions and me?
- What was I thinking and feeling about my observations?
- What were my alternatives?
- How did I choose from among the alternatives?

Self-monitoring, peer feedback and supervision are useful in helping counsellors recognise their individual stage of development and their own level of competence and skills.

Evaluation

Evaluation is a normal part of organisational life. Accountability, assessment and appraisal are familiar terms to most employees. However, evaluating workplace counselling can be challenging for several reasons. It poses questions such as who, what and how is the evaluation to be implemented, and what are the objectives and how do they relate to organisational needs? Time constraints, workloads and respecting client confidentiality often means that the keeping of statistics is not seen as a high priority. The benefits of providing the statistics necessary for effective evaluation may be insufficiently valued. Through monitoring casework, records can assist the process of providing management with vital information regarding trends, which could lead to preventative interventions being made in certain areas. Stress-related illnesses, bullying and discrimination are just a few examples. Furthermore, monitoring the service can firstly fit the purposes of quality assurance, secondly collect data to justify the provision, and thirdly increase the acceptability of the counselling service to those who have not as yet made use of the service.

Two of the main dilemmas are how to preserve confidentiality whilst gathering data and how to maintain credibility with the client group and the organisation as a whole. Management information systems have been designed which do record statistics such as initial presenting problems, source of referrals, grade, method and location of counselling, whilst not disclosing personal details. Durkin (1985) examines various methods of evaluation which are applicable to counselling, and rigorous economic analyses such as McClellan (1989) demonstrate the value of workplace counselling schemes.

When discussing the task of clinical supervisors, Carroll and Walton (1997) are helpful in considering the role of evaluation within the supervisory relationship. Finally, for those of you who are setting up a counselling provision or who are interested in evaluation of a service, I would recommend the findings of Highley and Cooper (1995).

Record Keeping

Record keeping and the law

Counsellors are not exempt from an increasingly litigious world. For some time now a situation has existed whereby client records might have to be disclosed either during litigation with a client or if summonsed by a court to give evidence. The Data Protection Act 1998 means clients can ask to see their paper-based or computerised records during their course of counselling. It is important therefore to consider the possible consequences of clients gaining access to their records – both for the client, and for the counsellor, their supervisor and the agency or employing organisation.

Counsellors and their organisations have a responsibility under data protection law to ensure the security of records, whether computerised or manual. They are also responsible for keeping records in a safe place, e.g. locked filing cabinets or the use of encryption in computer systems and passwords. There is no set time limit regarding how long therapeutic records should be kept. It falls to each individual organisation to devise its own policy on an appropriate time limit for keeping records, prior to organising their safe and confidential destruction. BACP (2001a) says that 'there is a responsibility to destroy records on their expiry in a way that continues to prevent unauthorised access'.

Summary

Whichever definition of counselling one chooses to use, the therapeutic alliance is central to the counselling process and involves understanding the dynamics between client and counsellor. Furthermore, counsellors need to be aware of the variety of settings in which counselling takes place and their impact on the therapeutic relationship.

Counselling is centred upon one or more problems of the client and should be free from authoritarian judgements and coercive pressures by the counsellor. Client and practice management begins with self-management, which entails:

- a commitment to taking responsibility for personal development;
- balancing objective knowledge, subjective knowledge and the development of counselling skills;
- considering methods of monitoring progress;
- ensuring systems are in place for appropriate and ethical practice.

Considering how clients are received and treated at the point of entry is also part of the counsellor's overall responsibility, as is giving thought to the use of relevant statistics and meaningful evaluation.

THE PROCESS IN PRACTICE

Introduction

I will now address in more depth the counselling process and professional practice. In this second chapter of Part II: 'Managing the Process: Features and Practice', I will focus on how to begin, develop and end counselling relationships, what I call the 'nuts and bolts' of counselling.

Beginning the Relationship

Diagnosis and assessment

It can be helpful to see the first meeting as a two-way assessment. The counsellor makes it quite clear at the outset that neither party is under any obligation to continue beyond the first meeting and that together they will come to a decision during their time together.

Clients present with a range of problems and some may bring issues not overtly concerned with what is really troubling them. Some will 'test out the water', initially presenting a fairly practical problem or a request for information – just to see how they will be treated. Having done so they may go on to talk more explicitly about underlying and important concerns. It is important, therefore, to listen carefully and to take seriously the level of the presenting problem, whilst providing opportunities for clients to say more about other areas in their lives.

> **Example: 'I just need some information'**
> A client makes an appointment to see the staff counsellor and seeks advice on her pensions rights. Having addressed the client's immediate

concern the staff counsellor wonders, given the client's facial expression and tone of voice, whether there is something else she wishes to discuss. The counsellor could continue saying something like:

'We have talked about how you might be able to get some more information about your pension rights. I'm just wondering if there are any other areas you might find helpful to talk about?'

Picking up the emotional content of the client's request for information on pension rights might, for instance, enable the client to express concerns about a recently diagnosed illness which perhaps they are having difficulty acknowledging. At that point, using their contracting skills, the counsellor can offer further opportunities in the form of a counselling contract.

Pincus and Dare (1978) suggest that diagnosis does not help if it ends up placing distance between the helper and those seeking help. Most people feel uncomfortable when they realise that someone is trying to label them or put them into a box without trying to understand them thoroughly. It is, therefore, important to balance the need to be systematic and scientific with the desire not to dehumanise people. Diagnosis or assessment, if done skilfully, offers the client the opportunity to clarify problem areas and to understand what is realistically being offered. An effective assessment has a therapeutic value in itself as it provides the client with the opportunity to identify their needs. Working in collaboration, the counsellor and the client can discuss the most appropriate intervention to maximise the latter's chance of having their needs met and decide whether they wish to continue.

Although many clients arrive with a general and all-pervasive sense of being unhappy, some clients have measurable goals: for example, they may wish to gain sufficient confidence to give a public presentation, or manage to express their anger towards a particular individual. Bearing these goals in mind and reviewing goals with the client on a regular basis is probably one of the most useful indicators of progress. What may not seem a significant shift to the counsellor may be regarded quite differently by the client.

Contracting

Managing the role and the process of counselling carries with it responsibilities that include establishing contracts with clients and terminating the therapeutic process at an appropriate point. Although for some clients a clear treatment plan will be the answer, for many counselling is a process of exploring new horizons and the journey is the aim rather than the arrival. Although approaches to contracting may be different and terms may differ, there are certain basic elements. A counselling contract is an explicit agreement, written or verbal, to work in a particular way and indicates commitment between two or more parties.

Sometimes the contracting process begins before the client actually meets the counsellor, for example when a help-line takes the initial call. Some counsellors will begin to contract over the telephone whilst other practitioners prefer to meet with the client to discuss arrangements face to face. Other questions will arise. For example at what point does the counsellor introduce the idea of a written contract, consent forms or disclaimers? Some counselling services insist that these be signed at the first meeting. If this is required then the preamble may take longer than one would like and can set the tone for the relationship. Keeping it brief and being clear at the outset leaves the way clear to getting down to work, for if the counsellor leaves it until the end, the client may have already said something which needs to be disclosed by the counsellor. In a risk-averse world I think a balance needs to be struck between protecting both clients' and counsellors' rights. Practical solutions are already being found, such as having codes of ethics and information sheets visible in waiting rooms or sent with confirmation of appointments. Some counsellors ask clients to sign a written consent form for the service to hold written counselling records, right at the beginning of the session.

Ultimately it is a question of judgement. I personally would find it very hard to say to a distressed client, 'Stop, before you say another word, or sob another tear I must tell you that ... ' Remember, the first contract is the one you have with yourself, including how you wish to practise in the light of these factors. Clarity and confidence within the counsellor will help the client.

Key characteristics of a contract

When designing a contract, a good starting point is to consider what a client will need to know at a first meeting so that on a conscious level they are better informed to decide whether or not to make a commitment. Common to all therapeutic counselling contracts are the following:

- the counsellor's method, background or ethical code;
- the boundaries of confidentiality;
- clarity regarding availability, with contact telephone numbers (including any back-up service);

- venue, duration and frequency of sessions;
- fees including cancellation fees;
- length of contract;
- how the contract can be changed;
- goals of counselling (the extent of this will depend on the particular theoretical approach);
- the unspoken and often unconscious expectations of both parties.

Some counselling services provide clearly written information for all clients to see prior to committing themselves. Counsellors also need to be mindful of their position in relation to the law and company policy.

Project- or process-based models of contracting

A project by definition is goal-orientated behaviour. Project-based contracts have clear objectives right from the start, particularly where the therapeutic alliance is seen as one which is curative, corrective or remedial. Contracts are future-orientated with a clear treatment plan, and emphasis is on the achievement of a specified goal.

A process-based model of contracting is different in that it has no final goal. It is developmental and every part is a natural outcome of what has gone before. A general goal may emerge, e.g. to feel more confident, but that may change as the process proceeds into, for example, 'having a more satisfying career'. The following illustrates, rather eloquently, a process-based approach to considering goals and solutions:

> What matters is how life is led rather than where it is leading to, since life itself is a process and needs no solutions. (Kfir and Slevin, 1991)

Some clients are quite definite in limiting what they are hoping for and are precise about the area of their lives in which they wish help. Others have less specific goals and may not realise the full significance of the change they seek or the time it will take to achieve. The counsellor needs to respect this and decide whether or not they can work with the client in this way.

It is important not to mislead or to collude in offering unrealistic expectations of the potential of counselling. In recent years there has been criticism of the psychotherapeutic world with reports of clients feeling a sense of being misled or misinformed. Extreme examples have been reported of well-functioning individuals setting out to find someone to help them with a restricted problem, such as a career choice, only to end up several years later having entered three-times-weekly psychoanalysis.

Given the various approaches to counselling it is not surprising that contracts differ in their provision and focus. What counsellors have in common is that each will spend time in the first session(s) helping their client decide what they wish to achieve and whether or not they are able to provide the appropriate form of help.

Group contracts

Contracting is a two-way process, but where more than one person is involved, for example mediation, couple counselling, or teamwork, then contracting is done at a group level. The latter involves the use of group facilitation skills. Weiner (1993) has described a group contract as being: 'An explicit, non-coercive, mutually agreed-on statement of the tasks each is to perform and the ends to which those tasks are a means.' Once a contract is drawn up it can serve as a reference point, particularly if and when the group gets into difficulties.

Length of contract

The issue of length of counselling is really a question of how long is a piece of string? A client may consult a counsellor on a one-off basis, for a limited number of sessions, or may commit themselves to several years of therapy. In a crisis situation one potent intervention can have a profound effect on individuals. Often it is not possible to know in advance how long the process will take and some counsellors make an open-ended contract with their clients.

In the current economic climate the task of providing the best and most cost-effective source of help in the workplace is complex. The tendency in organisations nowadays is to offer short-term contracts for approximately four sessions. An average number of sessions in Employee Assistance Programmes is five, after which it is common practice to encourage referral. Whether the provider is internal or external, financial pressure on managers means that they try to keep to four or five sessions but in practice negotiation is possible for special circumstances. If agreed, the counsellor is free to make a clinical decision whether or not more sessions are required. Where they are, the staff counsellor seeks permission to extend the contract. The extent of their autonomy will vary according to their individual organisation and contract. There can be resentment at having to seek approval from people who are not clinically trained and yet have the power to make these decisions.

Frequency of sessions

Common therapeutic practice offers a weekly one-hour session that is sometimes known as 'the 50-minute hour', where the counsellor allows ten minutes between clients for reflection and making notes. Some counsellors allow an hour and a half for an initial assessment session, to include the contracting process.

I have found that staff counsellors who are required to travel long distances to see a client feel they need to justify the journey and expense by spending several hours with them. I still question the value of such lengthy sessions, as there is an optimum time after which concentration dissipates.

The debate about the weekly session continues in counselling circles. In my clinical experience, for a counselling contract to be effective a fortnightly session seems too long a gap for real progress to be made. When the gap is too great the client often feels the need to 'fill you in', giving a detailed account of what has happened since they last saw you. This is relevant to a point, but leaves little space for unresolved issues to be raised and worked upon. Fortnightly intervals are useful for maintenance purposes, e.g. keeping contact with a client who is returning to work after a long absence.

The First Session

'Why', said the Dodo, 'the best way to explain it is to do it.'
(Lewis Carroll, 1865)

There is no substitute for practice. However many manuals one reads about driving there is no substitute for getting behind the wheel and actually doing it. The experience of panic, joy, frustration, sense of movement and at times getting stuck is similar to the counselling process. Let us discuss the first sighting and greeting. The manner in which people arrive at a first meeting with a counsellor is crucial in establishing the relationship. Sometimes they will just walk in, unsure of how much time you have to give them and what you can offer them. There is much to consider. For example, should the counsellor sit behind a desk as opposed to a more informal seating arrangement? What are the potential implications for the relationship?

The client's contribution

Bearing in mind the three features of counselling as outlined in the previous chapter – the client, the counsellor and an awareness of interaction – I would like to develop further what clients bring to a first meeting:

- the immediate problem as they see and experience it;
- a degree of ambivalence (part wanting, part resisting help);
- feelings, hopes and expectations of how the counsellor can help;
- underlying problems which are not immediately apparent;
- their life experience;
- inner defences which have enabled them to cope and function;
- attitudes towards asking for help;
- a degree of motivation;
- strengths and resources;
- needs as outlined previously;
- the journey that they have made in order to arrive at this point;
- realistic and unrealistic expectations;
- some information about the service, but not always.

The counsellor's contribution

The counsellor too brings many of the above features, such as motivation and life experience, and inner defences. Although at one level the client and the counsellor are simply two human beings, they do occupy different roles. The differences in the counsellor's contribution are outlined below:

- training and knowledge of counselling;
- experience of other clients;
- ability to differentiate between client's world and own;
- ability to manage a degree of involvement;
- an awareness of the dynamics;
- techniques and skills;
- ability to communicate;
- motivation for helping people;
- belief that change is possible;
- value of the healing relationship;
- an understanding of their working method;
- containment of any unresolved current problems.

First impressions

A process of observation and unspoken questioning begins from the first moment. Both client and counsellor immediately begin to size each other up. The appraisal is reciprocal and the internal dialogue might go something like this:

Client	Counsellor
Can I trust him?	*He seems rather reticent*
He reminds me of ...	*His voice sounds depressed*
Not what I expected	*He is not how I imagined him to be*
What is that pad and pen for?	*Is he tense or on the defensive?*

There are many subtle negotiations that occur which are not part of the formal contract. This is a natural part of the two-way process and it is important to stay with the client and put them at their ease. In order to shift from a problem-solving or advice-giving approach to a counselling approach two questions – 'Who is the client?' and 'What is it like to be in their position?' – are useful. They help new counsellors, in particular, stay focused on the client's experience and not their own anxiety!

First impressions can be useful as a basis for monitoring future progress. When reviewing a case after several sessions the counsellor should then notice any changes in behaviour: is the client more relaxed? Has their physical appearance changed? It is often said that a picture says a thousand words. Relaxing sufficiently to really observe their demeanour, degree of movement, physical appearance and posture can be helpful but beware of making assumptions, e.g. that a shivering person is frightened when they might just be cold. One could assume that body odour means unwashed when it could be that there is a medical condition.

Opening words

Often in the bustle of ushering the client into the room, the anxiety – sometimes panic – of meeting a new client means the 'moment of the meeting' can get lost. How easy it is, as a human being, perhaps still relieved at managing to be physically there, to miss those first vital words from the client. Those few words can tell us so much about the client's state of mind, their expectations (or not) of how they can be helped. For example:

'I don't know why I have come.'
Perhaps the client is saying: I am confused, I feel hopeless or unsure.

'I shouldn't be here, I really can't afford the time off and yet I must ...'
Perhaps the client is saying: I am really desperate.

'I don't expect you can help, but as I'd made the appointment ...'
Perhaps the client is saying: nobody has ever been able to help me in the past.

The client having arrived begins to tell their story. Some have rehearsed what they wish to say and arrive with a semi-prepared script. However, not all clients are able to identify or articulate their problems and often the unspoken word speaks volumes. They may seem tentative, vague and even elusive. The first stage of counselling might be helping them to clarify their needs and expectations. They will want to feel that the counsellor has the ability to see their situation as they do. They will wonder, can I talk to this person, can I tell them what I need to say, and will they judge me? A warm and trusting relationship needs to be established as a foundation if change is eventually to take place.

The counsellor's words, posture and manner all provide invitations for clients to talk. Sometimes clients begin to talk quite freely straightaway. Others may wait until invited by the counsellor. Despite different approaches there are no hard and fast rules of whether the workplace counsellor initiates conversation or waits for the client: it comes down to the counsellor's personal style and judgement. One point, however, is not to fall into the trap of social exchanges, such as the weather or traffic, from which it can be difficult to extricate oneself and can then dictate the level at which the client will work.

The Initial Referral

When receiving a referral it is important to think about how much information you actually need or want to know before seeing the client. Sometimes too much information can get in the way of the first meeting, leading to preconceived ideas about the client, based on the referrer's views. On the other hand, if the counsellor is experienced enough to set aside these views, others' perceptions and prior knowledge can assist in the process of engaging with the client. Sometimes clients are referred by others because of poor performance or prospective disciplinary action and they clearly do not wish to be seeing the counsellor. I shall refer to this group as 'sent' clients. I have found it helpful to acknowledge that such tensions exist in the client and to 'normalise' them by saying something like: 'I sense part of you really wants to talk about what is troubling you and yet part of you is finding this difficult ... ' or 'It seems clear to me that you are angry that it has been suggested you see me ...'. Counsellors need to leave plenty of space for the client to respond, but in the latter example I found the client only too willing to let me know just how angry they were. I will leave their responses to your imagination. Being able to handle strong emotions right at the outset makes it possible to renegotiate an acceptable contract with the group of sent clients.

Recognising that ambivalence in the client is normal can be enormously helpful. There is often an inner turmoil between the part of the client that wishes to be helped and the other part, which is resisting the help. It is as though the parts are battling to see who will gain supremacy (see Chapter 3: 'Resistance to Counselling'). One of the lessons I have learned is that when a client is 'sent' or not wishing to be there, speak to the part of them that longs to be helped. When a client is voluntary and is eager to work, don't be surprised when you reach a stage which I call 'the wall of resistance' – in other words, the part of the client that is finding the process difficult at that point in time.

To illustrate the first point I recall a time when I was working with social workers who had statutory responsibilities towards children and therefore many of their client group, the parents, were 'sent'. Parents referred because of concerns picked up by schoolteachers, hospitals or GPs were initially defensive and often hostile but in subsequent sessions these parents spoke with enormous relief that the situation, which they knew existed, was finally being addressed. Somebody had picked up their distress which they, at the time of referral, were unable to express directly.

Expectations at a first session

The client might have arrived expecting the counsellor to be a kindly parent figure or hoping that they will, like a magician, solve their difficulties easily. They might seek practical help from the staff counsellor but also long to talk about more personal issues. Perhaps they expect the counsellor to be a therapist who will dig deep into their mind against their will, causing them great pain. On occasion clients have a determination to prove counsellors wrong or to prove that they are beyond help. Enabling the client to verbalise their expectations and adjusting any misconceptions clears the way for a useful therapeutic alliance to be entered into.

Clients' expectations might have been based on hearsay, what others have experienced, or are based on their own previous contact with the staff counselling service. This might have been a negative experience for the client or, alternatively, a positive experience where the previous counsellor was held in high regard.

Example: abandoned

A referred client had seen a staff counsellor on a previous occasion. They had been working successfully on a difficult relationship problem when the counselling had to be terminated because the staff counsellor was taken ill and was subsequently medically retired.

How might this affect the client's expectations? Parkes et al. (1991) and Bowlby (1988) emphasise the importance of early patterns of bonding and adult relationships. Sometimes not being cared for stimulates previous experiences of being 'abandoned' in some way. Perhaps the client felt let down by the previous counsellor because the relationship was cut short, and feels angry. Perhaps they wondered, just as children do when their parents become ill or die, whether they were responsible in some way, perhaps experiencing a feeling that they had been too burdensome or difficult.

These feelings are not always easy for a client to acknowledge and so they may be rationalised or totally denied, so that the client is not aware of just how important the counsellor had become in their life. Here I am describing a psychodynamic approach to this situation but whatever theoretical approach you use in your work, some enquiry regarding the client's previous experience of counselling can clear the way, should any barriers exist, for the client to fully engage with their current staff counsellor. In practical terms this means encouraging the client at the first meeting to talk about their previous counsellor and to say what helped them and also what did not help them in the previous relationship. This provides an opportunity for the client's experience to be expressed and increases the chance of a balanced view of the former relationship being integrated. It is useful to be aware of how a previous counsellor can be idealised but also that they may be criticised by the client who is all too keen to say how useless they had found them. In the former instance it is easy for inexperienced counsellors to be left wondering how they can possibly measure up to their predecessor who clearly got everything just right, and in the latter instance to gratefully collude with becoming the counsellor on the pedestal.

The new staff counsellor is not responsible for what has gone before, but they are responsible for how they manage their therapeutic relationships. During a first session some of the testing out of reality will be done and that is why it is important to try to 'depersonalise' oneself from such negative or positive preconceptions and attempt to be one's own unique self. At this point one hopes the client will be able to disclose the nature and extent of their problem and the counsellor, together with the client, will be able to make some kind of assessment of the way forward. This might include agreeing a contract to work together, making a referral to another agency or the client going away to think further.

Ending the first session

Even when a time limit for the session has been made very clear at the outset it can be very tempting when the client is in full flow to continue beyond the agreed finish time. There exists a hope that if one continues just that little bit longer it will make all the difference. This is quite common and it can be helpful for counsellors to remind themselves that most situations presented to them have not come overnight and therefore they will not go away overnight. Shared openly with the client, this thought can have the effect of reducing pressure on both parties.

Aside from the limitations of what the counsellor can offer within their role, there are also limitations on time, energy and concentration levels of both parties. Sooner or later the session needs to be brought to a close. Counsellors often ask me: 'What should I do about my watch?' or 'Should I have a clock?' My own thoughts on this are that having a clock or watch clearly visible between counsellor and client helps to foster an atmosphere of mutual respect and equality in terms of power. If the counsellor prefers to keep the watch on their wrist then I would recommend an open approach rather than surreptitious glances, which can be unnerving for the client. The counsellor can even point to their watch and say something like, 'Let's see how much time we have left for today.' Done in an open and honest way this then signals the reality of the situation for both parties.

A useful tip is to agree an end time before you begin, stating clearly how much time you have on offer at the outset and checking any time constraints that the client might have. In this way both parties can settle down to the business in hand. The ending of a first session, which might be used for the purposes of assessment, needs to include an offer of a further appointment – it is all too easy in the workplace to assume that staff only desire one session. Reminding them of what you have on offer is part of the closing stage of a first session. Elements that characterise the ending stage of a counselling session are:

■ summarisation;
■ agreeing the next step;
■ checking the contract is understood by both parties;
■ refocusing;
■ ending.

The counsellor can initiate summarising by offering their view of the session. Alternatively, inviting the client to summarise for themselves can be illuminating and a useful process in itself. Clients quite naturally talk about their expectations upon arrival, what they have talked about and their overall experience. Either way, summarisation offers opportunities to check inaccuracies and adjust perceptions.

Exploring the client's initial expectations is a useful way of drawing the session to a close. Here are some ways to enter the ending phase of the session:

'We're coming towards the end of our time together, I'm wondering what you hoped for when you made the appointment to see me?'

'What has the experience of coming to see me been like for you?'

'What do you feel we have achieved?'

'How are you feeling now?'

'We have come to the end of our time for today. Given what you have said, how would you like to proceed?'

Notice I said 'enter the ending phase'. Endings take time if a satisfactory point is to be reached and therefore should not be left till the last five minutes and then rushed.

Usually the client will refocus quite naturally on where they are going or what they are doing after they leave the counsellor's office. They might, however, be returning to their office and be concerned about how they appear as they walk out into the corridor. Time needs to be allowed for the client to gather themself, particularly if it has been a very distressing time. In some counselling settings there is an anteroom or secretary's office into which they can be ushered to do this, but most counsellors have just one room. If they are expecting another client within the next ten minutes this aspect has to be managed so that both clients are treated with equal respect in terms of time management.

The door handle

Sometimes the client is reluctant to leave and offers an interesting piece of information just as they are going out of the door. This is often referred to as the 'door handle' syndrome. It is tempting for the inexperienced counsellor to invite the client to continue and perhaps even sit down again. However, experienced counsellors realise that the client has purposely left this information until a time when it cannot be picked up and it is therefore safe to disclose it at the end of the session. Whilst resisting the temptation to enquire more, it is important to acknowledge what is said, perhaps by saying: 'This is clearly important to you, perhaps we can talk further about this area when we next meet.'

Managing time boundaries is a perennial challenge for new and experienced counsellors alike. The inexperienced counsellor might have been thinking at the beginning: 'I do hope the interview lasts more than twenty minutes.' Now they are wondering: 'How shall I get them out of the door?' The mature counsellor, if tempted to continue, looks at this dynamic with a different perspective and wonders: 'What is it about this client and our relationship that makes it difficult for them to go and for me to be firm with them about finishing the session?' Sometimes it reflects the depth of need that the client is experiencing at the time, sometimes they are just not used to having so much attention and, having begun to receive it, they find it hard to stop. Of course the very opposite could be true and the client is extremely used to getting a great deal of attention! The point I am making here is the need to reflect on the dynamic in order to further your understanding of the client–counsellor relationship.

When the client leaves

Earlier I emphasised the importance of active listening. What I did not say was just how tiring it can be to give someone your full psychological and physical attention for, let us say, one hour. So when the client leaves it is all too easy to rush off to another appointment, or just slump in the chair, put the kettle on and not make the time to review the experience. It is tempting to go from one client to the next and counsellors need to be firm about appointments and resist pressure to fit in more clients, because this will reduce their own time for reflection. Apart from preventing the case from continuing to occupy the counsellor's mind, assigning time to reflect can serve several other functions. It can help to debrief the counsellor or catch ideas for the next session. It can provide a useful on-going record for evaluation of progress and act as an *aide-mémoire* for supervision. The counsellor may also identify areas overlooked by the client or notice particular phrases they used.

Self-observation is a form of self-supervision, which is a professional way of managing the counselling process whilst at the same time being practical.

Note taking

In practice many counsellors, particularly when new, are scared that they will not remember everything the client has said. This anxiety can lead to an expressed need to make notes during the session. This concern can and does get in the way of paying attention to the client and having an overview of the whole therapeutic process.

Taking notes during sessions is for the most part distracting for both parties. Clients in the early stages of a counselling relationship want to know that they matter and that their concerns are being taken seriously. I have found that once rapport has been established very few clients will object to necessary notes being taken of important facts, particularly in cases of debt, legal or medical conditions. A useful way of dealing with this is to wait until the latter stages of the session and then to be open with the client and say why you feel the need to make some notes, explain their purpose and who is likely to see them. Finally, check with them as to how they feel about this and gain agreement by saying something like: 'Look, there seem to be a lot of facts that we will need to consider. I'd like to jot them down … is that OK with you?' Naturally a closed question could just elicit a 'yes' from a rather passive client, but this is where your awareness of the interaction between you comes into play. If you notice any diffidence, pick it up and work with it.

Being honest about the purpose of notes is part of behaving ethically. Counsellors use them as an *aide-mémoire*, for the basis of a medical report, in order to take mutually agreed action or for their own professional supervision and so on. At the contracting stage I also make it clear that it is part of my standard practice to ask for the name of the client's general practitioner and then obtain their agreement to contact them should it be necessary. Usually one does not need to use it, but there have been occasions where it has been crucial.

Setting aside time to reflect after the session requires self-discipline, but if one has really been paying attention I find that the main themes are easily recalled and the information floods back. I would like to make the following points regarding case notes.

- They are principally for the counsellor's own use or, where agreed, that of the counselling team or service.
- They can offer insights into the counsellor–client relationship.
- They can be used for their own professional development.
- They may be used for supervision internal or external to the organisation.
- They form the basis for summaries which could then form part of a report if required.
- The counsellor may be asked to disclose them in certain legal situations.

- They need to be recorded and kept in a way that supports the client's right to confidentiality (Data Protection Act 1998).
- The counsellor should be mindful of the client's right to privacy and any legal implications.

Process recordings and notes used in training/supervision

An appropriate distinction can be drawn between the case notes kept by the counsellor, to which access may be granted, and other notes made by the counsellor for their own learning and supervision needs. These are written process recordings and supervision notes, which could be deemed to be the private working tools belonging solely to the counsellor and therefore not available to anyone else. Such notes would be destroyed as soon as possible after they have been used for their immediate purpose.

Process notes are also useful for effective supervision; however, counsellors may be influenced by recent legislation and its implications to the point that they make very limited notes. I personally think it would be a pity if new legislation inhibits best practice. A balance needs to be struck between maintaining professional competency and adhering to the law. If case notes are to be useful for developmental purposes then counsellors need to be free to record their observations, reactions, transference and countertransference issues (see Chapter 5), hunches and even opinions. A useful discipline is to review them regularly and write as objective a summary as possible, just keeping core relevant information such as:

- client's details;
- original contract;
- summary of appointments kept;
- number of sessions;
- initial assessment;
- outcomes as appropriate;
- any contact with other professionals, e.g. GP;
- risk assessment (suicidal, self-harm, or potential threat to others);
- personal circumstances as relevant.

You might want to consider how much sensitive information is relevant at this stage, e.g. sexual orientation, HIV status, and history of illicit actions or substance abuse.

For an initial 'assessment' you may be given a standard data control sheet or you may be left to create your own format based on what you think would be helpful to you in your work. What form might it take? You might use genoagrams to show relationships, or mind maps or simple questions. Figure 4.1 shows a very simple example of an intake sheet to be used following an initial interview. Have a look at it, then design one that would be appropriate for you in your particular setting.

Reports

Up until this point there is an assumption that communication, whether oral or written, is confidential between client and counsellor. However, workplace counsellors, as part of their role, may be required to make a report to

---

INTAKE SHEET

Client (reference code for client confidentiality)   Age: Sex:
Department: Job:
Relationships: Children:

---

1 First impression of client (appearance and manner).

2 Client's concept of self.

3 Client's attitude towards counsellor.

4 What is the immediate problem as seen by client?

5 Reason for referral.

   (Why do you think client came now?)

6 When did client first experience the situation as being difficult?

7 Who else is involved in the situation?

8 How does client appear to react to significant others?

9 Matters left out or avoided?

10 Any areas of emotional conflict in the client? Any themes?

11 What will you aim at in the counselling? (Focus for work)

12 Agreed contract.

13 Number of sessions agreed.

14 Any agreements to contact others (e.g. GP)?

15 Comments (other current professional help, medication).

Note: Identifiable information to be kept in locked or secure place.

Figure 4.1   Sample intake sheet (adapted from Relate).

personnel or an occupational health service. When this request is made it requires the ability to balance the interest of the individual with that of the organisation, particularly if the staff counsellor is in the middle of a counselling contract. Sometimes the focus is totally on a particular individual and the organisation as a client can be forgotten, even when the staff counsellor's role is defined as providing an independent and confidential counselling service to the whole organisation. Even when confidentiality has been clearly negotiated counsellors can be manipulated by either party and they need be able to maintain their individual professional boundaries without being unhelpful. If asked to write a report, asking yourself a few simple questions might help: why am I writing this report and for whom? and what specialist or relevant information do they require from me?

Establishing sufficient rapport is essential if the client is to feel comfortable about disclosing their condition or situation. Reports are clearly more public and obtaining a consent form or permission to disclose that information to a third party, in the context of a counselling relationship, involves skill and honesty. In such circumstances clear contracting is vital so that the client realises the purpose of the session or visit and they are given the opportunity to see and to adjust the final report.

Here are some general ideas about what to include in a report:

- name, date of birth, duties;
- name of person who requested the report;
- reason for the report;
- if sick say what is the absence, nature and length;
- health history;
- medication and current treatment;
- personal circumstances;
- any concerns of client;
- note whether client is happy to have contact with others;
- underlying problems or concerns;
- client's views and wishes.

In general, occupational health doctors do value staff counsellors' comments and they often form part of final medical reports and recommendations. Under the Access to Medical Report Act (1998) patients have the right to see a copy of any medical report.

Developing the Relationship

Fairbairn's phrase 'the moment of real meeting' describes the moment when the counsellor truly connects with the client: a moment which transforms the relationship so that the client is able to tell, and the counsellor is able to hear, exactly what is meant. It is only inside a good relationship that deep insight occurs. This can be during a first meeting or over a longer period of time (Fairbairn, 1952).

At the second meeting the counsellor could just greet the client and let them begin where they wish to start. More active approaches would be to invite the client to say how they are feeling on that particular day or to ask them what they 'took away' from the last session.

The time that a client actually spends with a counsellor is minimal compared with the combined hours and occasions when they interact with colleagues, friends or family members. The gaps between counselling sessions are 'intervals', as in the theatre. Viewing counselling in this way can help the counsellor to realise that the client leaves each session with plenty of time to reflect on what has happened between them both. Returning for a further session, the client might wish to share what has been happening in the intervening time. However, if too much time is spent on this activity, the agreed focus of work can be avoided and the session is then used on catching up rather than progressing. On becoming aware of such a trend the counsellor can offer this observation back to the client.

In terms of ending subsequent sessions, once an ongoing contract has been established a subsequent session can be closed with an acknowledgement of the work that has been done, such as: 'We've covered a lot of ground today and there is much to think about … '.

Client disclosure

Take an enthusiastic counsellor who has just experienced their first training experience and tutorial. They approach their first meeting with the client with a mixture of anticipation, trepidation and excitement. They begin by listening and doing all that they have been taught and yet the client still cannot speak.

It is important to remember that the client has not been on a training course to be a client and that relationships take time. Some people have held onto their problems for so long that they literally cannot 'let go'. It's a bit like travelling on a motorway where there are no public services for 20 miles and you are in some physical discomfort. When you finally stop, the brain says 'OK, you can relax now', but perhaps the body cannot. It takes time. Once trust has been established the client is able to say whatever is necessary without it needing to make sense; they feel accepted for who they are and what they bring to the session.

There is often a rhythm and flow to the counselling process. Sometimes everything comes out very quickly with lots of facts and feelings. The client begins to flounder a little and the counsellor wonders, 'Where should we go from here?' Using imagery such as a stream, river or ocean can help to identify the size of the presented problem and the pace of disclosure. In counselling there are times when the work reminds the counsellor of Niagara Falls and they feel the need to protect themselves from the force of the gushing waters. At other times a slower pace of disclosure occurs which seems more like the gentle trickle from a river's tributary. Even though counselling at times feels like a gentle stroll (to use another metaphor), it is important to remember not to force the pace. At other times it seems more like a jog, a canter or even a gallop and then again it suddenly can come to a halt. Discovering a mutual pace is all part of the two-way ongoing therapeutic contract between counsellor and client.

In the early stages the client gives the counsellor a picture of their life. After a while perhaps the counsellor begins to question whether the picture that is portrayed actually fits. Take the following example:

'My father was bit of a disciplinarian, the salt of the earth you know, fair mind, he would give me a good thrashing ... ', he said as he smiled.

The client displayed no pain or distress as he was disconnected from the pain of the event. The client in this case was defending himself from the pain of the memory of his childhood.

For memories to be healed they need, to some extent, to be re-experienced, not just recounted. Telling the story is not enough. In order to reach a shared understanding of what is happening perhaps the counsellor can comment on the way the client is telling the story and enable them to explore the particular area a little further, eventually leading to a discharge of emotion. This is often possible within a developing relationship of liking, trust, respect and mutual commitment.

The wall – defence mechanisms in practice

Psychological defence mechanisms exist for good reasons. They are there to protect the individual from high levels of anxiety caused by current or previous psychological threats, as in a traumatic event. Some find it too painful to change ingrained behaviour patterns or to use their existing personality resources for growth. Perhaps these clients' defences are so strong that they will resist entering the therapeutic relationship until external factors have an impact, such as a major life crisis or the fact that they can no longer function. Only then will they face change.

I would like to use the metaphor of 'a wall' to describe defence mechanisms in practice. A client may have erected a wall to protect themselves for very good reasons many years ago. Even though the original threat no longer exists and the wall is no longer needed they might still be hiding behind it.

Case example: 'I can't get close'

A man in his late twenties presented for help in making relationships. During the counselling it became clear that it was difficult for him to allow himself to get close to women, including the counsellor. As a result of our work together he was able to talk about an event which he had almost blocked out, the fact that his mother had died as a result of an overdose when he was twelve years of age.

Even though at one level he wished to have relationships, at another level he was ensuring that he was not going to be hurt again. Clients, as in this example, might be lonely, longing to come out from behind their 'wall' or to let someone come a little closer, but they are scared. Even with the best will in the world the caring counsellor, wishing to help, can at times find this frustrating. The client plays a cat-and-mouse game of 'now you hear me now you don't', letting the voice be heard and then going silent. Frustration can build to anger and there maybe a desire to 'smash the wall down' and to destroy it. After all, we might reason, isn't this what the client really wants? We need continually to remind ourselves that the client erected the wall and even if we know a lot about 'construction' or 'reconstruction' it is the client's wall to dismantle. If we have established a contract for reconstruction then counselling is about helping the client to take down their wall, their defence mechanism, brick by brick. As counsellors we are there as their supporters to enable that process. To continue the metaphor, we should be neither 'bricklayers' nor 'demolition experts'. Psychodynamic counselling in particular is about providing a climate where the client himself can dispense with defence mechanisms that he no longer needs.

A simple but important point to be restated is that it is the person in the room who is our primary client. Another defence used by the client may be to spend time talking about everyone else but himself. The client presents with: 'I am worried about my son ...'. After spending an hour trying to sort out the son's problems we might usefully remind ourselves that our client is the person actually in the room. Perhaps they are not yet able to say: '... and I am worried about my relationship with him.'

Cancelled appointments

The practical arrangements of cancelled appointments should have been made clear in the initial contract. However the cancellation of an appointment by a client can evoke a strong reaction in the counsellor, such as rejection or frustration. It might also be one of relief in the midst of a busy schedule, or because the work was not going too well. More often the reaction is one of concern, wondering why the client was unable to attend. Was the reason genuine or not? Has it a deeper meaning? The counsellor may wonder whether the client has reached a point they wish to avoid or whether the client is angry with them. Sometimes clients just don't turn up. This prompts clinical decisions about whether to telephone and 'chase' the client or whether one allows the client, if they are acting out patterns of behaviour or ambivalence towards being helped, to do just that. Supervision of casework can be extremely helpful in such situations. In my experience the counsellor, through discussion, can then decide whether to address these issues in the next session.

Where safety is an issue (if the client has been severely depressed, or there is a history of abuse), then ethical consideration needs to be given as to whether or not to telephone the client's GP. This underlines the importance of obtaining the client's consent to contact their GP at the initial interview. These are ongoing issues of boundaries and ethics, which are part of professional practice (see Bond, 1993).

As a counsellor, being in the right place at the right time is one of the ways to minimise anxiety in the client, and therefore cancelling an appointment with a client should not be done lightly, mainly because the counsellor represents reliability and consistency in the client's uncertain world. Similarly holidays and breaks should be handled openly and with sensitivity, as it can restimulate other experiences of separations or abandonment.

Goals

'Would you tell me please which way I ought to go from here?' asked Alice.
'That depends a good deal on where you want to get to', said the Cat.
(Lewis Carroll, 1865)

93

I cannot think of a better way of describing a counsellor's approach to goal setting. Where does the client actually wish to get to? And what is their motivation for change at this point? Alice points out, 'I don't much care where', to which the cat replies, 'Then it doesn't matter where you go' but Alice continues by way of an explanation: '– so long as I get somewhere.'

Inviting the client to use their imagination to rehearse their desired change can help them set realistic goals and think about what might get in the way of their achieving what they want. For instance, asking the client what they might do to sabotage their plans can be enlightening. Perhaps they will be able to relate to New Years' resolutions, which have never proceeded past February.

The initial stages of counselling, those of exploration and understanding, often give the client a very useful insight into the sources of their problems. Your use of the core counselling skills of active listening, summarising, questioning and appropriate challenging by this stage will have helped the client considerably. Problems will have been clarified objectively, emotional reactions will have been explored and various alternatives and their consequences will have been considered. For some clients such help may be enough and they exit the relationship. Relieved of their distress, they may feel ready to make plans, are clear about what they wish to do and ready to take new steps without further help.

It could be argued that a Rogerian approach emphasises the exploratory stages of counselling and sees them as sufficient for change to occur. However, some clients continue to express their goals in vague general terms. In such cases the counsellor can help by facilitating and promoting action towards some form of constructive behavioural change on the part of the client. Approaches that are particularly suitable at this point are solution-focused or cognitive behavioural therapies. Cognitive behavioural techniques can be incorporated at this stage with person-centred approaches if this is mutually agreed within the therapeutic contract. Using a cognitive approach to elicit and challenge assumptions or self-destructive inner dialogues can be very useful at this point.

Making plans and taking action

John Lennon wrote: 'Life is what happens whilst we are busy making plans.' Moving from making plans to taking action is what this stage of the counselling process is all about. Those who find this difficult will need help in focusing on specifics, not only in terms of the desired change, but also in terms of how, where and when they will actually go about making these alterations in their lives. A behavioural approach might look something like this:

Client's task	Counsellor's task
To examine own goals and resources	To teach problem-solving techniques
To make constructive behavioural changes	To facilitate and reinforce

The counsellor will be in a better position to help in developing action programmes if they have some knowledge of problem-solving techniques and methods of helping people change, such as desensitisation or role playing.

Remember that at the contracting stage a project-based contract would only focus on the goal, whilst a process-based contract would seek to ensure that any planned action is that of the client and not shaped by the counsellor. 'You seem to want to move on ... Now that we have reached this point how would you like to proceed?' With the client's agreement the counsellor can still incorporate other techniques by being direct and by recontracting. You could say, for example: 'I have some ideas that might help, which would involve us in working in a slightly different way ....'

Hypothetical case example: where shall I start?

A woman is suffering from recurring backache, which distresses her, her family and her boss. She has a husband who is depressed as a result of being made redundant, a son who has been in trouble with the law, and mounting financial difficulties. For her the 'solution' may involve a satisfactory resolution of all these different problems. But there is no cure-all in counselling. Having laid out her table, so to speak, at this particular stage of the counselling process she will need to set realistic goals and establish an order of priority in terms of which problem she will tackle first.

Let us suppose that she decides to tackle the financial problems and sets herself a goal of settling the debts the family already have and not incurring any further ones. She will need to explore ways of paying off the debts, reduce overall expenditure, possibly increase the family income and create and maintain a budget.

Sometimes the path towards such a goal can be perceived quite readily once it has been established as a priority. Where problems are complex many different approaches may have to be explored. Force-field analysis is a structured exercise designed to enable the client to identify and overcome the strength of the forces holding back action in order to find a way forward.

The idea is that by reducing the negative forces holding an individual back, the positive forces for change come through. In this case the family might be identified as one of the negative forces as well as the client's own money management. The counsellor might then enquire: 'In what ways could you involve your family in achieving your goal?' Often the client is able to pursue their plan and take action quite quickly, but often the problem has arisen because he or she lacks certain skills or habits. For example, the client in the scenario above may take too much of the burden upon herself and lack the skills of assertiveness and communication to successfully confront her family. At this point there is more counselling work to be done in exploring her attitudes towards these issues. Perhaps anger and resentment have built up and she will need help in dealing with this before moving forwards.

Clients such as these will require help with planning how to acquire new skills or change old habits. The counsellor should be supporting them through a gradual process of encouraging and helping them to think of how they could reward themselves as they take small steps towards their final goal. To establish an action programme the counsellor and the client between them need to:

- determine the client's goals;
- determine an order of priority for those goals;
- decide how to reach the first of these goals using problem-solving techniques;
- establish a detailed plan of action with a built-in time framework and rewards;
- make some contract to include the above.

Visualisation is another technique, which the counsellor can use to enable the client to imagine what it would be like for them to have attained their goals (see Lazarus and Fay, 1975). Let me illustrate this by way of a structured exercise using visualisation, which might go something like this.

'In the discussions we have been having over the week what kind of changes would you like to make? Think of one personal change you would like to make.'

'Imagine seeing yourself having made this change.'

'Where would you be?'

'Anyone else there?'

'If I were to walk in what would I see? What would I hear? What would you tell me you feel? What would you be thinking about yourself and thinking about others?'

In discussing the visualisation the counsellor would explore the client's goals and suggest manageable and realistic steps towards the desired state, encouraging them to identify specific changes they could make in terms of their own behaviour. It is all too easy to cling to the hope that others will do the changing. Knowledge of transactional analysis is useful in enabling the client to recognise the pay-off they might get for not changing. It is important that the client has ownership of the plans they make; otherwise they simply will not act upon them (Berne, 1975).

In moving towards the final stage of counselling it sometimes seems necessary to go back to the beginning again, with the client needing to explore their feelings about taking action. This is only to be expected since if there were no difficulty in taking appropriate action they would have done so already without seeing a counsellor. Even though an action plan may have been worked out, because of different life experiences of change, attitudes and feelings towards it will inevitably vary. Some clients will eagerly embark on change whilst others will avoid and postpone it. Where there are fears connected with taking action, these need to be explored and sometimes challenged at the same time as acknowledging the importance of overcoming them. The client will often require encouragement and support from the counsellor to continue to implement change and reach the goals they have set themself.

Ending the Relationship

The aims of the ending process are to help the client to review and take forward an integrated experience of both the positive and negative aspects of the counselling experience; and, moreover, to have a balanced view of the work that was done, recognise the depths of the therapeutic relationship between counsellor and client, and to say goodbye.

The counsellor needs to be clear about the agreed contract and its boundaries and handle this stage in a calm manner without feeling guilty. Here are some ideas: 'We have two more appointments' or 'Well, here we are today, this is our final session. I'm wondering how you would like to say goodbye?' Some argue that one should end with reassurance, saying that 'The door is always open'. Others believe that to do so confuses the ending process and undoes the work of helping the client to be self-reliant. In an in-house occupational setting the 'door' is literally still there, either physically or in terms of seeing the counsellor around in the building.

When disengagement has taken place do not assume that clients will regard you as 'an old friend' or even wish to recognise you should you meet again by chance. Do not be surprised if you should you meet your client in the supermarket and find they do not wish to acknowledge you. Often the counsellor is associated with a particularly difficult time in the client's life, which they would prefer to forget. Or it can work the other way around – as it did to me when someone whom I could not immediately recognise came up to me in a motorway café on the M1 motorway!

Endings of whatever kind are important and clients require time to adjust to them. Whilst being mindful of the strong feelings that can exist, it is helpful to balance these with the sense of it being a liberating experience for the client.

Types of endings

In a sense – because of the contracting process – both client and counsellor agree an ending before they begin. However, as in life not all endings are ideal and in some circumstances it will not be possible to complete the original focus of work. Various types of ending are discussed below.

Agreed ending

This is probably the most satisfactory way of ending as both the counsellor and client agree that the work has been completed and the client can cope with their life on their own. Parting and ending the sessions for good can be emotional for both parties. Counselling is an intimate relationship and people often trust the counsellor with aspects of their lives they have never shared with anyone else before. The counsellor's task is to prepare the client in advance and encourage them to end the sessions.

Client does not return

Sometimes endings are forced upon the counsellor because the client does not return and does not give a reason. It could be that the client has experienced rapid relief of their situation or that there are negative reactions to the counsellor, which I shall discuss in further detail in Chapter 5. Whatever the reason the counsellor is left not knowing and this can feel very unsatisfactory and lead to feelings of frustration, concern or even guilt.

Counsellor chooses

When the counsellor feels they are unable to do any more for the client, perhaps because they feel their level of knowledge and skills is insufficient, or because they think the client is not ready to fully engage in the process, it is important to be direct with the client and explain why they feel this is the situation. In the latter case modify 'open door' reassurance to include the proviso that should the situation change they are welcome to return.

Recognising one's own limits of competence is part of professional practice. Perhaps the client has made significant progress but may require additional specialised help, which is beyond your competence. In this situation the client, having begun to make a relationship with you, might experience a sense of apprehension, reluctance and even rejection.

Enforced ending

In an organisational setting endings may be imposed for a variety of reasons such as the medical retirement of a client, geographical job changes or if either one dies. Where it is the counsellor who is leaving then consideration of how to 'hand over' is beneficial for all concerned. For the counsellor withdrawing from the case there may be the question of to whom they feel they can entrust their clients and they may wish to have some say in who might be most appropriate. For the person taking over, it can be enormously helpful to have the co-operation of the outgoing counsellor, as long as they are being constructive and not undermining. This is particularly so when the counsellor who is inheriting the casework is a novice.

Phased ending

This involves gradual withdrawal of the counsellor. For example, instead of meeting weekly, the final sessions could be fortnightly or monthly. This can be helpful where there has been long-term involvement, for example an employee who has been suffering from depression and has been on sickness absence.

Handling Endings

It is important to be honest with the client as soon as possible, offering them the fullest possible range of options to help them make a decision. They may decide to continue in counselling or agree to be referred to another staff counsellor or external agency.

Counselling work is often about loss of one kind or another. It might be a loss of a relationship, a job or self-esteem and the work often entails dealing with previous endings that have not been satisfactory. Therefore when it comes to the end of the therapeutic relationship the loss of that relationship requires acknowledgement. One needs to prepare the client, particularly where there is a hand-over to another counsellor.

Counsellors become central people in the lives of those experiencing a crisis or personal difficulties. Clients often arrive in a vulnerable condition and the counselling experience can restimulate the client's dependent nature; and as part of the transference process the ending phase may evoke memories of previous losses and unfinished mourning. Therefore if handled well perhaps for the client who has experienced a bereavement in their lives where they were unable to say goodbye, acknowledgement of the loss of the counselling relationship offers them an opportunity for a different experience of an ending.

Disengaging from an intimate relationship can be emotional, as clients can grow fond of you and you of them. Some clients are very demanding, needy and dependent. Some humble you and you can underestimate the value you have been to the client or the bonding that has occurred. Some may be full of joy while others may feel rejected. Just as some clients cannot bear to think about a relationship lasting for very long, others cannot bear to think of it not lasting forever. It is important to guard against the client becoming dependent on you or you on them, with one of the parties not wanting to let the other go. It is also important to demonstrate respect for the client by acknowledging their strength to manage on their own and by not reinforcing their dependence on you.

This final stage of the counselling process offers rich opportunities for any unfinished business to be addressed so that the relationship can be concluded. There may be unspoken words that exist between the client and the counsellor and the ending process offers them both the opportunity to minimise regrets by expressing these. Being able to talk about the good and the bad and to take forward a whole picture of the relationship will be valuable to both.

Summary

This chapter has offered a sequential approach to how to manage the counselling process. In the early stages of their careers trainees often shun the theories of counselling as having little or no relevance to the demands that confront them daily in the workplace. Like any other scientific tool, theory has little intrinsic value – its real worth is in its usefulness. I hope therefore that this chapter has offered you some practical ideas that you can incorporate into your counselling relationships.

In offering myself as a 'guide', I am aware that inevitably, as stated at the outset, my own experience and beliefs come through. I would encourage you to read other people's views on the subject and ultimately design your own 'route' through the intricacies of the counselling process in practice.

Part III

Managing the Process: Issues and Dilemmas

INTRODUCTION TO PART III

In Part III, the chapters on 'Therapeutic Issues and Techniques' and 'Working with Diversity' (Chapters 5 and 6) combine to address some of the more complex therapeutic issues that arise out of the counsellor–client relationship, and consider how practitioners might deal with them.

In this second section on 'Managing the Process' ('Issues and Dilemmas'), I will attempt to address some of the familiar situations and dilemmas that occur in counselling practice. The practice of counselling takes place in a maze of ethical questions, moral considerations and choice points for intervention. In highlighting these, it would be easy to allow them to provoke unhelpful anxiety in the counsellor. This would in my view be a great pity. Unencumbered by our own concerns we are much more likely to help our clients through their own maze, be able to hear their sounds, see their sights and experience being with them during their counselling journey. Whilst I am not advocating irresponsibility, remember that too much circumspection can mean the counsellor can become immobilised, fearful of taking any risks at all.

Hand Notes:

PL Intellect. Level	Adult
Order Date	07/06/2007
PL Category	General
Site / Location	p
Budget/Fund Code	dcobk

Customer Number: 33628001   **ISBN:** 9780333922552

Sheffield Hallam University

P00GK7BCG

Processing

5

THERAPEUTIC ISSUES AND TECHNIQUES

Introduction

For most practitioners counselling is an activity that takes place privately but for workplace counsellors it is a little more complex. In practice the workplace counsellor emerges from what could be considered a private session only to be catapulted straight back into the organisational dynamics in which both client and counsellor work. For instance, they are often faced with a list of answerphone messages or requests to attend meetings where they will need to operate at a different level.

Sometimes the counsellor is able to switch off quite easily and refocus on the next job, but at other times, for some apparently inexplicable reason, this does not seem possible. Building on the idea, mentioned in previous chapters, of making time to reflect, I shall in this chapter focus on the issues of involvement, the counsellor's own feelings and managing boundaries when working with a client over a period of time.

Subjectivity and Objectivity

Managing ourselves in the counselling process at times seems quite precarious. We need to be aware of our footsteps and be sure-footed in order to stay balanced and effective. Sometimes the question of how close to get to a client is a delicate balancing act. Having both feet in the world of the client may lead to the counsellor becoming over-involved and feeling swamped. However, if there is too little involvement – no feet in – we become 'clinical' to the point of being detached and the client may perceive us as aloof and unapproachable. If the degree of involvement is too great it is possible for this type of work to drain any kind of emotional commitment to others such as family members or partners. Somehow we need to establish a balance.

A particular stimulus can cause the counsellor to react in either of the ways described above. The client, during their session, might remind the counsellor of an unresolved previous experience, or an issue that is current for the counsellor. For example:

Client speaking of her son's gambling debts says:

'You just don't understand what it is like.'

Counsellor whose daughter has recently been in trouble with the police for taking drugs thinks:

'No, I don't.' (*detached*)
'Oh, don't I – you have no idea!' (*identifies*)
'Oh, you poor thing.' (*sympathises*)

Awareness of these 'parallel processes', once identified, can free the counsellor to be able to respond more objectively. In the situation described above one counsellor might react by trying to help the client's family a little too eagerly, whilst another might just 'switch off'.

It requires courage to enter the client's world and discipline to remember to ensure that we keep at least one foot firmly placed in our own world. The key to being fully effective is a heightened awareness of your own inner life. Moreover, we do not have the right to 'steal' and take on our clients' problems as if they were our own. Try to imagine the following:

Case example
A client is distressed by the fact that their partner has recently died. In the session they describe what it is like each time they return home and open their front door. Their anguish is deep and raw. When the client left, the counsellor felt a deep sense of loneliness and literally was 'in pain'.

Counselling is an intimate business where getting close means taking risks. As we attempt to enter the client's world we risk getting submerged in it to the extent that we experience their problem as our own. Their distress can become ours. 'Stealing' is taking something you want from another person. Do we, as counsellors, really want to pocket our clients' problems, their depression or their pain? A balance needs to be struck between empathy – being moved by the client's situation – and becoming overwhelmed to the extent that it belongs to us.

Counsellors can be caught out in the act of acting by pretending to possess qualities that they do not actually have. Sooner or later the client senses this and it diminishes the relationship. Whatever theoretical knowledge and skills counsellors are acquiring I have always sought to get across the following message: 'Don't forget that one of the most important gifts you can give a client is yourself.' What we can do is to be there for clients as fully as possible. Rogers explores the tension that exist between the scientist in him and the non-directive therapist risking himself in order to deepen the relationship between himself and the client:

> I launch myself into the relationship having a hypothesis, or a faith, that my liking, my confidence and my understanding of the other person's inner world, will lead to a significant process of becoming.   (Rogers, 1961)

Yes, we can risk ourselves but we can also ensure that we develop strategies to help us maintain a sense of equilibrium. Self-monitoring and the use of imagery (using creativity to describe how a counsellor perceives a client and their relationship) can be effective techniques that individuals can incorporate into their practice. Talking through situations with colleagues and supervisors can help to disentangle the client's world from the counsellor's. This process not only improves the quality of casework, but it is equally important in that it keeps counsellors psychologically healthy. If you do not have enough support you absorb more disturbance, distress and dis-ease from your clients and patients than you are able to process and let go of and then you become overburdened by the work (Hawkins and Shoet, 1989). Support and external supervision are particularly important when working in an organisational setting where the counsellor, in addition to client distress, needs to consider the nature of the organisational culture, potential projections, their impact on them and their work.

Counsellors need to assess how emotionally invested they are with their clients, as it is quite possible for counsellors to lead most of their emotional lives at work leaving little time for their personal lives. They also may be faced with personal predicaments and will need to ask questions of themselves, such as 'how realistic for me to counsel my friend?' and 'can I be a friend to my client?' I find Kennedy succinct and delightful:

> Perhaps one of the chief dangers, especially to people who are just starting in on their counselling work, is not that they will be friends with clients but that they will act like therapists with their friends.   (Kennedy, 1977)

How easy it is to sit with a friend and try and use one's new found skills. My tip is 'don't'. I well recall falling into such a trap and responding to the anguish of a dear friend's mother who begged me to intervene when she knew her daughter-in-law was having an affair. 'You can help now, I know you can.' She left the husband and children anyway despite all my efforts to help the couple talk, for she had already made up her mind to do so. What happened was that the plea for help hooked straight into my newly found 'perceived wisdom'. Now I just try to be a good friend and friendship happens to involve listening.

Whether it arises from enthusiasm, fascination with the subject or a genuine desire to be of help, it is not ethical to use counselling techniques where the other person is not party to a therapeutic contract. Yet certain counsellors do transfer counselling attitudes into their social lives. They look serious, use reflections and at times offer unwanted interpretations – much to the distress of their friends who might prefer ordinary social conversation. Although listening to family and friends is an important interpersonal skill, behaving like a counsellor can lead to the erosion of the individual's spontaneity and personality. This potentially destroys the mature use of self, which is essential to effective therapy.

Setting limits

According to my supervisor it was Foulkes (1975) who remarked 'the first duty of a therapist is looking after him or herself'. In other words, we need to be healthy for our clients by respecting our own needs and taking good care of ourselves.

Supervision example: being human

A staff counsellor in a supervision session was concerned about how he was managing his time. The counsellor, who already had a full diary, said to me: 'I had allowed just enough space in the following two weeks for catching up with paperwork when the telephone rang with a referral from a line manager and I found myself saying "yes" even though I knew I really didn't have the time.'

Clearly he was stretched and feeling quite stressed. Having acknowledged his emotional condition we went on to explore why he found it so difficult to say 'no' to the referral. It emerged that he always felt he 'should be there for others' and found it difficult in other situations in his life to be realistic about his own needs. This acknowledgement and insight was the first step in his taking responsibility for how he could change this pattern.

Naturally there are many other ways of helping the counsellor in this situation. A cognitive-behavioural approach to dealing with the above example would focus on changing his thinking and behaviour Beck (1976). By helping the counsellor challenge his perception about the demands of his job it would assist him in managing his boundaries. For example: 'I must always be available for my clients' could be changed to 'I will do my best to be available for my clients' or 'I will set aside time each week for ongoing counselling.'

One of the most sensitive tools a counsellor has at their disposal is their vulnerability to clients' needs. In terms of sensitivity towards the client that is fine; however, managing stress and self-doubt and being able to say 'no' without feeling guilty is equally important. There is a delicate balance to be struck here as the following example illustrates.

> **Case example: 'Will she cope without me?'**
>
> A bereaved client had formed a trusting relationship with a staff counsellor. The counsellor was about to go to a conference followed by a week of annual leave, when the client disclosed that they were going through a really difficult patch and was feeling like 'ending it all'.
>
> The counsellor began to feel that in no way would it be possible to leave the client at this stage, even if others were alerted to the client's state of mind. At one level it was clear that the counsellor was concerned for the client and did not wish to leave them, it but at another level there was an element of self-sacrifice – putting the client's needs before their own.

Putting clients' needs before one's own eventually diminishes the ability of the client and in so doing disempowers them. This is counter-productive to what counselling and therapy is all about, which has to do with developing autonomy, self-esteem and self-reliance in the client. If the counsellor in reality actually allows the relationship to be changed from counsellor–client into mother–child relationship, it in some way perverts the process. It can also lead to resentment in the counsellor. In supervision the transference and countertransference issues in the case were picked up and the counsellor, although still concerned, was able to go on holiday no longer being the 'abandoning mother' or the 'mother who could make it all better'.

By addressing our own emotional needs first, I would suggest that we are less likely to interfere in the process of helping others on their individual and personal journey. Released from the need to be omnipotent and needing to have answers, we can truly share that journey with them. Incidentally, picking up on the theme of holidays, how many times have we heard the safety instructions to put on our own life jackets first before trying to go to the aid of another?

Transference and Countertransference in Practice

Two particular terms – 'transference' and 'countertransference' – are often bandied around in the world of counselling. Some counsellors find it fascinating and are enthused, whilst others struggle with these concepts to the point of dismissing them as not being applicable in workplace counselling. Personally I have found an understanding of transference and countertransference invaluable in my work with organisations. Whilst they are complex concepts to grasp I think it is worth the effort for two reasons. Firstly they help when working directly with clients and secondly they offer creative opportunities in understanding interactions in the workplace. Even if as workplace counsellors you choose not to work with transference I think it is important to know what it means and to be in a position of informed choice. In this section I will address these terms so that you can decide for yourself if and how these concepts relate to workplace counselling.

From all my reading and my experience of the various approaches to psychotherapy and counselling it seems to me that where there is agreement is that transference and countertransference do exist. What is different is whether or not they are addressed within the therapeutic relationship and if so how. There is also general consensus that it involves unconscious processes and therefore a level of self-awareness is required in order to be in a position to understand transference. Counsellors need to be prepared to find ways of acknowledging and accessing their own unconscious processes.

When I realised how many pages were being devoted to these concepts I stopped writing and began to question why? what was this was all about? The process was in some way reflecting what happens in the counselling room with regard to transference and countertransference, for example the potential for confusion, complexity and divergent views. It can take on an 'elusive quality': one minute you think you have grasped something important, at another you feel quite uncertain, and sometimes what one thought was there in the room suddenly disappears.

Transference

Transference is a term to describe the transfer of old relationships onto a new one in a way that doesn't take into account the 'moment'. It endows the other person with qualities one had experienced in childhood relationships. One of Freud's most valuable discoveries was the phenomenon of transference. The word transference comes from the German word 'Übertragung', meaning to carry over. The process can be described thus: 'in the transference, infantile prototypes re-emerge and are experienced with a strong sensation of immediacy ....' (Laplanche and Pontalis, 1988: 455).

Most counsellors, whatever their theoretical orientation, agree that people do recreate old relationships in counselling as they do in other everyday situations. A classical definition of transference in psychotherapy would be that the client unconsciously projects or imposes on to the therapist attributes that belong to somebody in their early experience. This discovery at first seems a little disconcerting but, as we shall see, if appropriately used working with transference presents opportunities for insight and for misperceptions to be corrected.

Transference and countertransference in everyday life

Transference occurs in all kinds of relationships, as it is a human experience. Perhaps you can relate to the following:

> **Case example**
> Arriving at a party you are introduced to one of the guests. Immediately you think you know them and that you have met them before. There is something, which you can't quite put your finger on. Quite suddenly you find yourself thinking they are dismissive of you or that they do not want to talk to you.

In this vignette there is no need to look for reality: the experience is immediate and feels very real. In his lectures Kelnar (1975) described this particular psychological process as happening as soon as two or more people come together. It is not something that is created, but it is simply set in motion. The important point here is to recognise the importance of the unconscious and to realise that early wishes or fears can be there without the person being conscious of transferring inappropriate ideas, motives and feelings onto a new person. An event, a stimulus, triggers off a reaction.

We do not see new people as if they were empty canvases; rather we respond to every new relationship based on patterns we have learned from our pasts. In their book *Families and How to Survive Them* Skynner and

Cleese (1983) talk about what goes on 'behind the screen' in families and how that affects choices in partners. Marriage and close relationships provide clear illustrations for us to see the concept of transference in action. Take a couple called Jane and Tom. When Jane sees her husband Tom not as himself, just being fatherly, but so like her father that Tom begins to respond to Jane as if he were her father, then we have what is called transference and countertransference. Metaphorically they are like a teacup and saucer in that they go together but for clarity's sake I shall look at each concept separately.

Transference in the counselling relationship

Transference takes on a special form in the therapeutic relationship. Within the therapeutic relationship feelings become intensified and the intimacy of the relationship restimulates these unconscious processes. By looking at transference relationships, the psychodynamic counsellor seeks to help the client by helping them understand how the past is linked to what they are experiencing today. In many instances the immediacy of the experience with the counsellor enables the client to rework what has gone wrong in the past by allowing it to surface, by experiencing it and then at the right time seeing it in action.

In working with transference, the counsellor firstly enables the client to feel safe enough to re-experience these feelings. Secondly they help them to understand that whilst it was a perfectly natural and appropriate way to react at an earlier stage of their emotional development, it is now a fixed way of responding, which does not allow for change. This provides the opportunity for change.

Example: real feelings, wrong person

If an employee persists in experiencing their boss as a punitive tyrannical father, the relationship is static, unchanged and inappropriate as an adult. The point about transference is for the client to realise that even if the boss is a bully he is *not* his father and the employee is no longer a child. It is out of place in the workplace.

Acceptance of early feelings can be of enormous relief to the client and one visually sees the burden they have carried for so many years lifted from their shoulders. By helping the client realise that it does not have to be that way now or in their future relationships the counsellor facilitates a deep and lasting change. This is the essence of therapy.

Positive and negative transference

The therapist, by providing an environment of care and attention where the client might feel secure, encourages the client to experience negative as well as positive feelings, based upon their previous experiences. Clients may bring both positive and negative feelings into the therapeutic relationship. They might expect to be loved, cared for, to rid themselves of pain or expect to find someone to help carry the burden.

In terms of transference, these expectations towards the counsellor would come from the original successful early relationships and one would hope to work with what is called positive transference. However, there might be negative expectations: for example a client may expect to be ignored, dismissed, blamed, punished, abandoned, rejected or hurt. This can be seen as negative transference originating in a flawed early relationship and this can prove trickier for the counsellor to manage. Bowlby describes negative and positive transference as follows:

> At the same time he (the therapist) is aware that because of his patient's adverse experiences in the past the patient may not believe that the therapist is to be trusted to behave kindly or to understand his predicament.
>
> Alternatively the unexpectedly attentive sympathetic responses the patient receives may lead him to suppose that the therapist will provide him with all the care and affection, which he has always yearned for but never had. In the one case the therapist is seen in an unduly critical and hostile light, in the other as ready to provide more than is at all realistic.   (Bowlby, 1988)

In other words the client turns the counsellor into somebody else, perhaps idealised or even denigrated, and reacts and relates to them as if they were somebody else. In a counselling setting transference happens (to a lesser or greater degree) often before clients have actually met us. Clients have preconceived ideas, they might long for a more satisfying resolution to some unfinished business in their lives. For example, perhaps the client hopes that this time around they will be so good and fully accepted by the counsellor that this person will love them as their own remote parent had not or that this time around they will not be rejected even if their behaviour is difficult.

Longing for attention one has never had or expecting to be seen in a hostile manner is also relevant in understanding transference in organisations. An illustration of this is employees who had expectations when joining their company or institution that they would 'have a job for life' or that in some way they would be 'looked after' as they had been in the family. In workshops on change management I have noted that whilst some were quick to adapt to new ideas and accept the reality of delayering, others struggled and were left feeling quite betrayed and abandoned. I wondered why they felt it so acutely. Could this be a transference reaction? Organisations are groups of people interacting, providing a situation ripe for transference to occur. What about an employee who does not feel heard by the organisation, as they were not in childhood? These experiences can restimulate strong feelings and unresolved issues, particularly in a paternalistic or hierarchical structure. The important point here is that the organisation is not the individual's father but that the employee might relate to those in charge as if they were their parent and vice versa.

The process of transference

By drawing on Kelnar's lectures (1975) I present the following as a sequential way of describing the process of transference up to the point of interpretation.

The client presents with their personality and their presenting problem and the counsellor is drawn into their internal world. Within the internal world of the client there is some kind of conflict or unresolved issue and as the counsellor is now part of this internal world, they have a role to play in it. The particular pattern of relationships in this internal world now therefore includes the counsellor. There is a projection onto the counsellor endowing the counsellor with emotional fears and attitudes, which are part of the client's internal conflict. The counsellor becomes the recipient of these unconscious emotions and they can hold, for a time, the projected emotions. The counsellor through self-awareness attempts to accurately understand the transference situation. Throughout it is important to hold on to the fact that the transference is unrealistic in that it is not an emotional reaction to the reality of the relationship, for example when the counsellor becomes the 'good mother' or the 'negative mother'.

If one were to use interpretation then the next steps in the above sequence would be that the counsellor, using the therapeutic alliance as a vehicle, would point out to the client what they are doing. This information then enables the client to change his behaviour. The aim of interpretation is to make what is unconscious accessible to the client so that it becomes conscious. The client then discovers that they have motives, anxieties and fears of which until now they were unaware, and which perhaps are contrary to values of which they approve of in themselves. The thinking behind interpretation and insight is that it is beneficial to uncover and be as aware as possible of unconscious motivations, anxieties and fears so that the client has more control over their actions and life can be lived as kindly and agreeably as possible. No individual can control their unconscious (it just 'leaks out' in behaviour) but they can control what is conscious.

Of course there is a dilemma with offering clarification in the form of interpretation. Whilst the counsellor seeks to be helpful in offering an explanation for the benefit of the client one needs to be quite clear with whom these feelings originate, the client or the counsellor. To help another person in this way, the counsellor must be as aware as possible of his own unconscious motivations. This is where personal therapy and supervision are so important. The counsellor's own therapy concentrates on freeing the counsellor from the repetitive nature of their inner drives, emotions, old habits and thinking patterns. This is the responsibility of any counsellor. If one chooses to make an interpretation the counsellor needs to take notice of it and decide whether it is positive or negative. The counsellor must decide when it is appropriate to bring it to the client's attention.

If one chooses to use interpretation, which in a sense is a form of con frontation in that it helps the client face themselves, then the timing is crucial, as is the counsellor's motivation. For instance, when is the client most likely to pay attention to the interpretation? At which stage in the process will they be able to hear what is being offered? In my experience they are not likely to accept an interpretation until a relationship of trust has been established and the client feels accepted and understood.

I would like to emphasise at this point that in my view it is not necessary to interpret. In my own work I have often found it sufficiently helpful just to understand the dynamics of the relationship, alerting me to what might be happening for the client. The counsellor, therefore, if sufficiently aware, has choices perhaps just to take note of transference situations without putting it into words to the client, to just be aware of its existence with no active intervention. That in my view is an intervention in its own right. I think it is important to remember that interpretation is only one form of response. When clients are in distress they long to hear the spoken word and to be offered some words that will ease their plight. When these words arrive they will listen to how they are expressed, and the emotional message is in many ways more important than the exact form the interpretation takes.

I would imagine you are asking yourselves whether you use this knowledge in workplace counselling or short-term work? One does not have to be an analyst to relate the concept of transference to workplace counselling relationships. Firstly I would say that an awareness of the dynamics between client and counsellor deepens the counsellor's understanding even when it is not interpreted. Moreover, transference is a random, non-selective repetition of the past and can pop up anywhere in the workplace. As it can ignore and distort reality it can therefore lead to inappropriate behaviour at work. I would suggest that awareness of transference and countertransference offers counsellors a deeper understanding of the dynamics in the workplace, e.g. between two colleagues in dispute, and once recognised can assist the counsellor in choosing an appropriate intervention. All too often I have heard it put down as 'a personality clash' in the section and the solution is to transfer one of the parties to another office. The situation is resolved short term, but it can recur at a later stage. In a smaller organisation where transfer is not an option, tensions build up until one or other might be forced to leave.

Properly used, transference allows counsellors to get closer to clients and in so doing they are the recipients of important information, which can assist the client to change. Perhaps the value of working in this way is that one has a deeper insight into what the client is talking about. What is happening for them in their lives can be addressed in what is described as 'the here and now'. Both counsellor and client can experience the issues and are then in a position to look at them and talk about them in a very meaningful way.

Saying the words out loud in the form of an interpretation names the client's experience and by picking up what is in the room it makes the counselling relationship into a whole experience rather than just an intellectual exercise. An understanding of what is being experienced and has been experienced in the form of an interpretation provides a chance for insight, the precursor of change. For example, a client who is rigid and has unrealistic expectations is given an opportunity to experience the reality of the counselling relationship and its limits. This first shift can then be seen as a hope for change in other relationships.

Other approaches to transference

One of the main differences between the three major traditions, psychodynamic, behaviourist and humanistic approaches, is not that transference does or does not exist, it is regarding the necessity to interpret it and how to use interpretation. Reality Therapy, for example, knows it exists but chooses not to include it in the counselling process. The psychoanalytic approach would actively work with the transference and try to understand the past through the relationship that is formed with them in the present for the purpose of the client's learning. They will use interpretation at the appropriate time making links such as: 'Perhaps right now I have become your father with whom you were very angry.'

A humanistic approach such as the client-centred approach, would explore what is happening in the 'here and now' between the counsellor and the client as something that is actually happening, without interpreting it as something from the past. They may say something like: 'I am sensing hostility in the way you asked me that question.' Client-centred practitioners emphasise self-realisation and where transference occurs the counsellor's reaction to the transference is the same as to any other attitude of the client. By being there as themselves, aware in the relationship, the counsellor believes that through exploration of the attitudes involved this will lead to recognition by the client that any projected feelings are within the client and are not in the therapist or another person.

Assuming the counsellor has the core attributes required for client-centred counselling then the client only experiences understanding and acceptance with no evidence to the contrary. Eventually they recognise that their reactions of, for example, fear and shame towards a projected image of a judgemental counsellor were as a result of judging themself. (See Rogers' *Client Centred Therapy* (1951) for comprehensive examples.)

Proctor (1978) advocates that even when working in a behavioural way anyone is bound to become involved in transference, be it positive or negative, since people seek approval, love and support in all kinds of accustomed ways.

I would like to emphasise at this point that a commonly held view is that only psychoanalytic therapy would actively encourage working with the transference. However Rowan (1983) when discussing transference and interpretation challenges this assumption:

> The brute fact of the matter, as it seems to me, is that humanistic therapists do as much interpretation as psychoanalytic ones do – may be even more – but they have ways of disguising from themselves that they are doing it. (Rowan, 1983: 103–4)

It seems to me that whether or not humanistic, behavioural or psychoanalytic practitioners favour interpretation is less important than whether or not they are aware that they are working with transference and therefore potentially in a position to abuse the use of it.

Responding to Mr Jones: alternative approaches

Mr Jones is discussing the problem he has approaching his line manager, to whom he refers in very deferential terms. He says he 'doesn't wish to bother her'. Here are several possible alternative interventions.

Psychoanalytic approach
'When you speak like that it is as if you were talking about your mother.'

Person-centred approach
'You seem worried about upsetting her.'

Gestalt approach
'Imagine in this other chair sits your line manager – try telling her how you feel.'

Bioenergetics approach
'You seem angry. Here is a punch bag – why don't you have a go and really hit it.'

Behavioural approach
'This behaviour doesn't get you where you want to be. How else could you handle it?'

Cognitive approach
'What thoughts do you have when you approach her, what do you feel and what do you do?

In the above example the transference issues picked up are between the client and his line manager and not between the client and the counsellor.

Countertransference

Another important part of transference is countertransference, the other half of 'the teacup and saucer' I described earlier. Countertransference exists whether we as counsellors are aware of it in our work or not. We all carry over into adult life some residual issues from childhood which can become 'live', restimulated at any time. This is as true for the counsellor as it is for the client. That is why counselling training stresses the importance of self-awareness and supervision. There are two concepts involved in counter-transference, one, which I shall refer to as 'the classical', and the other which I shall call 'the message'.

The original view of countertransference – 'the classical'

The term 'countertransference' was invented to indicate feelings which the counsellor transfers from the past and inappropriately applies to the client and their problem. Freud, whose original view was that countertransference was a neurotic impediment which stood in the way of the treatment process, rarely referred to countertransference. It was, therefore, thought to be counterproductive and an inappropriate reaction to patients.

'Classical' countertransference manifests itself by the counsellor projecting their own material, unworked neuroses or 'unfinished business' or emotional preoccupations onto the relationship with the client at any given time. In countertransference any strong feelings that the therapist might have about the client represent the counsellor's own unresolved conflicts and problems from their past or their present life – for example, strong dislike of features in the client, likely to arouse powerful feelings, which would get in the way of the working relationship, as of course would positive loving emotions.

Example of 'classical' countertransference

A student in a university presented for counselling. The client was dyslexic and as she talked about her difficulties with her studies, the counsellor began to feel indignant that not enough was being done to help her client and suggested all sorts of possibilities: for example, how to apply for extra help, obtain a grant for computer equipment, methods for helping her face exams. This went on for several sessions until she realised that the client's material was hooking into her own life experience where she had had a son who had dyslexia and she had been a very strong and helpful mother. Once she recognised what was happening in the countertransference she realised the client did not need her to be an active mother because she had her own mother who was perfectly capable. This freed her to concentrate more on the client's frame of reference and then other issues arose such as her sense of isolation and lack of boyfriends.

Here the counsellor's residual feelings emerged and she began to inappropriately treat the client as if she, the client, were the son. This is 'classical countertransference' and would have been seen as an obstacle to effective therapy. Until the counsellor was able to respond to the client as they really were, without contamination from the counsellor, the client was not free to explore their own material. In order to do this the counsellor needed to be made aware of her own processes, set her own experience aside and see the client as someone with their own unique experience.

How can one be sure that it is the client's transference and not our own? To discover what the counsellor might be putting into the relationship, they need to be as sure as possible by continually checking out where they are psychologically and in their relationships. This is where keeping case notes and monitoring one's own performance through supervision is ethically good practice. If the counsellor still feels that they are being misattributed it is worth considering it in countertransference terms. Whilst there seems to be a general shift towards valuing therapy and supervision there is still a considerable variation in the way they are viewed, depending on theoretical schools and the recruitment or selection process. When counsellors do not avail themselves of the opportunity of accessing their own unconscious residual and unresolved conflicts they are in danger of attributing these to the client. Unless we are aware of what is happening we are not in a position to respond appropriately.

Two hypothetical examples

- An aspect of a client might unconsciously remind me of my father. Unaware of that fact I could behave towards the client as though he were my father. Perhaps I might feel like a little girl, unable to help this adult.
- Two people at work are in dispute. I might side with one rather than the other, just as a child I might have tended to favour one parent's view over the other's in an argument. Alternatively one of the parties might remind of a sibling with whom I had a particularly good relationship.

Countertransference as a message

Classical countertransference is still a valid concept but over time an additional concept has emerged, that of 'countertransference as a message'. Countertransference is now viewed increasingly in the context of a relationship and can now additionally be seen as a useful, often powerful tool, albeit an unconscious form of communication from the client to the counsellor. In psychodynamic counselling this is extremely valuable in understanding clients. To do so, however, requires counsellors to be in touch with their own processes, free of their own concerns, relatively calm and able to weather the storm.

This second concept is a way of the client sending an unconscious message before they can verbalise it. The client sends an unconscious message, which is initially received by the counsellor in their unconscious, but the behaviour can become apparent in the counselling room. Clients have a way of letting you know what is important to them if you let them.

The personality of the client, the material being presented, or the manner of presenting it can be blocked when it disturbs unrecognised or unresolved inner conflicts in the counsellor.

Countertransference in this sense describes the response set off in the counsellor as a result of being receptive and open to the client's transferred feelings. Something in the client's presentation triggers off in the counsellor personal memories, feelings and associations of past experiences. So long as the counsellor pays attention to the source of these responses in themselves, then feelings experienced can provide vital clues as to what the client actually feels about themself but may not yet be able to express. These emotions, if they correctly replicate the client's, are a helpful guide in understanding what perhaps the client cannot yet express for themself. Three main features of countertransference as a message are:

1 The counsellor's reaction towards the client is influenced by the personality, the behaviour and the problems of the client.
2 The counsellor responds according to the behaviour of the client as if they were that person (perhaps a mother, father, sibling, manager) and not as themself, an individual who perhaps has qualities like that person.
3 The client sends an unconscious message of what is important to them and this message is then picked up as an unconscious association or feeling experienced in the counsellor.

I suspect that some of you are thinking that this makes sense, but wondering if it relates to what you do in your everyday practice. Some ways of recognising that this is happening is if you are behaving in a way that is not your usual style, such as being over-protective, over-anxious or over-controlling. Further indicators are if you are responding to your client by being completely passive, or are being manipulated by them. Another pointer might be when no negative feelings are mentioned or even if they are, they are not being dealt with.

Working with countertransference

[A]ssuming that the therapist comes to the relationship relatively calm and free from his own concerns able to listen, then what the therapist feels is part of the client's communication whether it be conscious or unconscious. (Brown and Pedder, 1993)

Let us say that the counsellor does come to the relationship free of any transference towards the client. Here are some examples of countertransference where feelings, associations and attitudes are evoked in the counsellor as a result of the client's unconscious communication.

Case example 1: 'Who am I?'

I remember a client whose father had left her when she was young and who been brought up by her mother. She made me feel quite inadequate in that I could never live up to her demands. Even though I became much more personally involved than was my usual practice, somehow the client was never satisfied. Through the use of supervision I realised that I was being made to feel like the mother who had tried to compensate for the rejecting father, who in her fantasy was an all-perfect father. Once clarified I was then able to be more realistic with my client and she in turn was able to see the father in her mind in a more realistic and mortal way, as up until then she had idealised the absent father. Unlike the rest of her family I had not colluded with her demanding behaviour. Understanding what this was about freed her to have a more balanced view of her own mother, her father and more realistic expectations in her relationship with her husband.

Case example 2: 'Will she, won't she?'

A woman in her mid-twenties was always late for sessions. Early on in the relationship the counsellor was left feeling nervous and uncertain not knowing if she would turn up or not. Sometimes the client would leave notes to say that she couldn't make the appointment. The counsellor even changed the times of the sessions in order to try and accommodate her. Eventually the counsellor became rather irritated with the client and challenged her behaviour. What then emerged was that the client's mother was changeable, inconsistent, prone to irritation and temper outbursts. Somehow the counsellor had picked up projected feelings from the client.

In both these examples the clients' unconscious messages tuned into the unconscious of the counsellor, who then reproduced features of their clients' mothers. By realising this was not her normal way of treating clients it provided the counsellor with important material to be fed back to her clients. But how should one do this? Here are some, and I stress only *some*, ways of responding.

Counsellor intervention: example 1

'You know, I have noticed when we are together I experience feelings that are not usual for me, I feel I want make sure all goes well for you, I try to accommodate your needs and yet I am left feeling inadequate. I wonder whether this is a way of you letting me know how it was for you with regard to ...'

Counsellor intervention: example 2

'You know, I have noticed when we are together I experience feelings that are not usual for me, I feel unsure, uncertain and a sense of irritation. I wonder whether this is a way of you letting me know how it was for you with regard to ...'

In both these examples the counsellors began to realise what was happening. Through self-monitoring and supervision they were able to use their own awareness and resisted the pressure to act like somebody else. As such they were able to understand their clients better and, with skilful attention, help the client understand what they were doing. They were clear that what was happening was not some unworked aspect of their own lives and that it was something their clients were trying to tell them, a way of letting them know what was really important. Here is a slightly different example.

Case example 3: underlying fears

A client who worked in the oil industry, was being asked to relocate to another country. He began to question whether it was worth the upheaval that the whole family would have to undergo in order to relocate. In particular he was concerned about the effect on his wife to such an extent that he was considering changing his job. At this point an old memory was aroused in the counsellor, and she experienced feelings of loss and abandonment. She recognised the feelings evoked in her – those of her own sense of abandonment at an earlier time in her life – and was quickly able to refocus on the client. It sensitised her to the issues that might lie beneath the surface in her client and she wondered whether he too was struggling with a fear that this temporary posting would in some

> way make his wife leave him. Listening to him carefully she realised that at this point the client was only talking at a rational level and any underlying deeper fears were quite unconscious for him but made conscious for her. The client was not in touch with the basic fear that lay beneath all his concern for everybody else in the family, but the counsellor received the real reason through the client's unconscious message.

The counsellor could respond in the following way:

> **Counsellor intervention: example 3**
>
> 'I'm wondering if in addition to what you are telling me about your concerns for the family, there is also a fear that your relationship will be altered in some way.' Or more directly the counsellor could say: 'I'm wondering whether you fear losing your wife.'

The point in this illustration is that the receptive counsellor was immediately aware of her own reactions to what the client evoked in her. She was able to note them, knew their source ('this is what I feel and why') and held onto them in case they were the client's projected unconscious anxiety which had surfaced in the counsellor's association with her earlier and resolved experience. Now in a position of conscious choice, she was able to decide at an appropriate point to put to the client what he might be unaware of. Her connection with a past event was checked out with the client to see if indeed this 'association' of feeling was really a message from the client's unconscious. This then freed the client to express any underlying concerns of anticipated loss or fear of abandonment he might have about their relocation. In this example the use of the counsellor's life experience was used constructively rather than allowed to become an obstacle. I was taught that the more the counsellor's own inner conflicts have been recognised or resolved the more flexible, tactful, alive and free-moving it is possible to be to the client.

Counsellors' life experiences can be a creative source of insight and empathy, so long as they are used with awareness and skill. Even if you have a contract with the client to work in this way, any interpretation needs to be done with great sensitivity as it can arouse feelings of shame in the client. A counsellor hopes to get in touch with countertransference reasonably quickly so that they can be aware of how their feelings and actions are being affected by the client's transference. Recognising it and understanding a little more of what is happening makes the work much easier.

With a strong negative transference, where you pick up the wish to reject, confront or be aggressive, a counsellor might need to reassess whether or not they can work with this client. They may decide to terminate the relationship before the client, whose unconscious agenda is to have their earlier life script affirmed, rejects the counsellor – having once more proved how unlovable they are and how bad a parent you (the counsellor) are, just as the original parent was.

With a positive transference, the counsellor may seek to nurture the client who might be very needy and wanting them to be the idealised mother who is always there for them and tuning into their every need. One indication of this is when the counsellor keeps the client for too long. A positive therapeutic alliance is helpful as long as it is does not become collusive to the point of a cosy relationship, which continues without any real shift in the client's situation. A situation like this needs to be challenged. A common example of collusion is when the counsellor is 'put on the pedestal' by the client as being 'the only person that they can possibly talk to'. Idealised in every way, how easy it would be to think that one really is 'the only one', the admired, wonderful, healing counsellor. However, if one starts to believe one is actually on the pedestal, one is also vulnerable to falling off, particularly if you dare to challenge or take a holiday!

Self-monitoring in countertransference

The counsellor learns to read the psychological climate between self and others through observation of their interaction in the 'here and now' and the detailed knowledge that emerges of the client's early psychological history. Psychodynamic counsellors use countertransference all the time as an important and impressive tool for understanding their clients, but it is sometimes uncomfortable, as described above, as they may feel something they might not otherwise wish to feel, e.g. depression, loss, guilt, and fear of death. If the counsellor has picked up strong feelings, which do not belong to them, or the countertransference has to with the counsellor's own unresolved problems, the question is what practically and ethically can we do about it?

As ever, the first thing is to become aware of it, for if we are too defensive we will never even notice it. Salzberger-Wittenberg (1970) suggests we ask the following questions:

- What does this person make me feel like?
- What does that tell me about them?

- What does it tell me about the nature of the relationship and the effect they have on others?
- Is this a valid intuition?
- Am I responding in terms of what the client is communicating?
- Am I reacting in terms of what I am putting into the situation?

Such questioning can lead to a greater understanding – of oneself, of the client and of the nature of the 'here and now' relationship. When this occurs the counsellor, with awareness, can see the client as someone in his or her own experience and help the client understand what he or she is doing in their relationships. Rowan (1983) suggests that we notice it and put it aside for supervision or personal therapy: allow it to sensitise us to issues that may be floating beneath the surface within the counselling and put it back to the client to check it out. Regarding the last point, as with interpretation and transference, a good level of trust is required to intervene in this way. All of the above strategies would be considered a non-pathological use of countertransference, but one could also act it out pathologically by falling asleep, switching off or not turning up for the session.

What makes a counsellor react in the above manner? Is it a strong indication that the relationship is one of indifference, no longer 'alive', perhaps needing to end or is the client trying to convey something more fundamental regarding their own life?

Making Sense of Transference and Countertransference

Recognition of the importance of the unconscious is essential in understanding transference and countertransference. In that respect, as one colleague put it to me, 'the unconscious makes sense of non-sense'. I have witnessed many situations where counsellors are involved in transference without understanding the concept. There is a world of difference between doing nothing because you choose to do so and doing nothing because you do not know what to do. The point I am making is that, once recognised, transference and countertransference can be used for the benefit of the client.

Earlier (in Chapter 3) I emphasised the importance of listening and said I would discuss in more depth barriers that might occur in a therapeutic relationship. I hope you can now see that whilst there can be a simple external explanation as to why it can be difficult to hear – building construction noise, tiredness, a bit of hangover etc. – there might also be more complex reasons, as in transference and countertransference, which interfere with the listening process. Understanding these concepts has helped me enormously to understand why counsellors selectively hear or have strong reactions to what they are told.

Projection

> *A little girl had been told to stop rushing around the sitting room but she did not. She bumped into a chair, which knocked the table, and as a result a precious vase was broken. Looking at the pieces on the floor she turned to the toppled chair, wagging her finger as she said: 'Naughty chair, you got in my way.'*

Children are just wonderful at illustrating concepts. Projection is a defence mechanism whereby qualities, feelings or wishes the individual refuses to acknowledge or rejects in him- or herself, are excluded from the self and positioned in another person, object or group.

In this scenario the little girl rid herself of any guilt by projecting it onto an inanimate object – the chair. In a society there are many examples – minority groups, cultures or famous politicians – whom we can unfairly hold responsible for all our difficulties. We can project unacceptable feelings on to them, but at a safe distance. In workplace situations, just as in families, there are many instances where projection can occur.

A workplace example

A client might be unaware of their own angry feelings towards someone else. They expel this feeling perhaps onto the counsellor or line manager, whom they then perceive as persecutory, the one who is 'angry' with them.

Projection is just one form of psychological defence mechanism. Defence mechanisms exist for very good reasons, to defend the 'self' against threatening inner conflicts. It is important to remember that they occur when anxiety levels are very high. This information in itself is helpful to the counsellor. Here is a subtler example of projection involving a rather stressed individual.

Examples of projections in counselling

Client to counsellor: 'I am sure you think my situation is a hopeless one.'
■ Projected feelings of depression in client

Client to counsellor: 'I am sure you have many more urgent cases to deal with than me.'
- Projected feelings of unworthiness in client

Client to counsellor: 'I feel I am wasting your time.'
- Projected feelings in client of lack of satisfaction in the relationship

Projective Identification

A special and complicated type of projection has been given the name of projective identification. It was introduced by Melanie Klein (1952) to describe a mechanism that rids the client of these unacceptable feelings and locates them in a significant person (partner, child, counsellor, therapist, colleague, manager) who then carries or contains that feeling and unconsciously experiences what has been received. The reason for this is that the client evacuates themselves of what is experienced as 'dangerous' feelings. It is a very strong unconscious message and the sending is in the unconscious, which then experiences it, holds it and feeds it back.

Projective identification, as opposed to projection, occurs within close relationships and the recipient's role is to unconsciously identify with what is received as though it were their own. Whilst the projected feelings are usually 'too destructive', 'too bad' or 'too good' to be contained, at the same time they must not get lost. They must be preserved, for they need to be identified with and related to and so the projector manages this by 'putting them' into someone close by or into an intimate group. These feelings represent what we call 'a split-off' part of their personality, for example the love, the hate or the envy they cannot contain. In counselling the recipient is often the counsellor.

Unlike repression, which is the internal suppression of emotions that cause conflict, with this process the client pushes the unwanted feelings out of their mind and into someone else's. For the counsellor, this means that he or she starts to feel, think and behave in a way that is uncharacteristic. The counsellor may experience something of the client's unbearable and unacceptable feelings as if they were their own. In that sense they are vulnerable to penetration by their client's mental pain and made the carrier of it. Once identified, the counsellor can contain these feelings and, by demonstrating that they are not overwhelming, the client may be able at a later point take them back and internalise them. (Note: In transference the counsellor understands it is not them, whereas in projective identification they do not.)

Such psychoanalytic views suggest that clients are continually involved in unconscious interactions, which in some way enlist the help of others to enact scenes from their internal worlds. Ogden (1982) reminds us that it is only in retrospect that we begin to understand that we have been playing a particular role in the enactment between two people. He goes on to say that a therapist who allows themself to be influenced by the process of projective identification and is able to observe these changes in themself has access to a very fertile source of data. He offers a clear personal example of the therapist suddenly 'losing interest' in the patient who was then understood by him as having deeply unconscious death/suicide feelings yet the patient was unaware of feeling suicidal.

In her paper 'On Identification' Klein (1963) makes the point that this process leaves the 'projector' impoverished until the projected part is successfully reinternalised. In other words the client is the poorer for having given us their projection. It is part of them and whilst we might, as therapists or counsellors, see the value of holding the projection (an indicator of the client's unbearable pain) for a while, the unwanted aspect does not belong to us. Eventually we must return it in a more mature, modified, acceptable way.

Containment

Bion (1961) suggests that the client, finding his anxiety, aggression and despair is accepted and contained, is enabled at a feeling level to realise that someone exists who is capable of living with the feared or rejected aspects of themselves. This in itself is very reassuring to the client because it means that these parts of them are not all-powerful and therefore they become less frightening. The process is one of:

- unbearable feelings being contained by the mature personality of the counsellor;
- an experience with an understanding, concerned and caring counsellor who is not overwhelmed by the client's feelings;
- the client absorbs within him- or herself those containing aspects of the counsellor;
- anxiety is altered or modified;
- the client is enriched, more stable and manageable.

In addition to the capacity to contain mental pain, there is the ability in the counsellor to think about, clarify and name what is often a vague feeling in the client. For example, the client might present with 'pressure so great I feel I want to explode'. By being able to understand, these feelings can become more manageable instead of being all-pervasive.

Open to influence in this way, the counsellor can then become a changed person in the mind's eye of the initiator. Balbernie (1999) described such a case in his paper 'Inadmissible Evidence'. He gives an example of projective identification from his work with a six-year-old adopted boy, where he found himself 'almost completely unable to function for several sessions'. A traumatic past experience belonging to the boy, which he could have had no conscious knowledge of, had been pushed out of the boy's unconscious and lodged into the therapist who in turn acted out a version of that experience. This transferred data will ultimately benefit the client, but it underlines the need for personal awareness, supervision and objective theoretical models as a way of decoding these out of ordinary experiences.

In psychodynamic work counsellors might 'hold' clients' feelings over several sessions until the latter are mature enough within the therapeutic relationship to be able to receive back these powerful, unconscious feelings. In my work I try to think about being the custodian of something valuable that the client has left with me for a while. In that sense psychodynamic counsellors are like the pawnbroker who is the keeper of something precious – we wait until the clients can emotionally afford to come and reclaim them. It is then that we give them back.

Even if you choose not to work with a psychoanalytic model, these concepts might help you make sense of the times you are left feeling confused, angry, fearful, puzzled or just disliking your clients, or, as Ogden (1982) describes it, being the unwitting actor in a role you have not chosen.

Giving experiences back

The idea of being receptive to what the client communicates by projection is another way in which the client communicates the type of feelings they want us to have. They could be happy ones but more frequently what they are communicating and leaving with us are their feelings of fear, depression and despair, those which they find so hard to bear. Perhaps this helps you to realise why this kind of work can be so exhausting.

It is important for us to discover ways in which we can give back to the client the feelings which they have deposited with us, their problems, the right to own their experience. It is not ours, it does not belong to us, and we have no right to them. Let us consider the following illustration from my own clinical experience, based on Jung's (1969) ideas of imagery, spirituality and symbols.

When a client comes to see me it is as though they bring, in the form of the presenting problem, an object that belongs to them. Perhaps, symbolically, it is a 'wrist watch'. Metaphorically they take their watch off, they show it to me and together we discuss the way in which it works or not, we feel its weight, they tell me how long they have had it, their feelings about it, attachment to it etc. At the end of the session it is important for me to remember that this watch does not belong to me. I must give it back to the client, or at least remember to put it down on the table between us so that the client may pick it up again at another time. If at the end of each day we do not do as is suggested above, by the end of month we would have a sizeable collection of watches on our arm of all shapes, makes and sizes, and where would we put them all?

Sometimes a counsellor, in the face of a client who feels hopeless, unlovable and untreatable, begins to feel that they and the counselling are worthless (that 'the watch' is irreparable) and that there is no point in continuing. This option, to terminate the counselling, would reinforce the client's view of themselves. A psychoanalytic approach would be to say nothing and to bear such feelings for a time, without actually acting on them by prematurely terminating the counselling. However, the pressures of the culture in which the counsellor works, in combination with the counsellor's level of training, may not allow for this method of working.

Another approach might be to discuss the client's opportunities to have 'the watch' repaired, or replaced and an alternative strategy would be to enable the client to adapt and live with the 'damaged watch'. To continue the use of the metaphor, if they were always 'running late' because of their damaged watch they could try setting it five minutes early, thus ensuring that they arrive for appointments on time.

Let us use the focus of relationships with and at work. One client might seek to 'repair' what is wrong and wish to discover what has caused 'the damage' so that restoration can take place. A second client might say that there is no hope and that the relationship is 'damaged beyond repair' and they wish to leave. Then the work would be about discovering ways to adapt to that reality. In the last example a client could present with a phobia regarding being on time for work and then the focus of work would be about helping the person change their behaviour patterns.

It helps to remember that counselling is about helping clients to own their situations and that it should be an empowering process. When we treat clients as responsible people it is amazing how their prospects for growth are increased.

The deliberate use of symbols is very compatible with a humanistic and spiritual approach to counselling (see Rowan, 1983). Another image which I use with students is that of the 'winter overcoat'.

Example: winter overcoats

A client brings you their anxiety about job uncertainty. They work in an organisation in which redundancies are about to be announced. Think of the number of clients who might present with similar concerns to that of the first client. How heavy this would be. Can you imagine the weight you might end up carrying by inadvertently holding or 'stealing' all of these overcoats?

What is being described here is not only that which is 'absorbed' from an individual client but also that which 'can be absorbed' as a result of the current issues in the organisation in which the counsellor works. It could be, for example, that an organisation is 'delayering' and the counsellor has information in advance that redundancies are about to be announced. The counsellor's own job might be under threat and then they will, in addition, have their own 'overcoat' to wear. The practitioner in such a situation will need to decide how much of the anxiety belongs to the client and how much to their own situation. Perhaps they will experience what is described as 'a double dose' – a bit of both. This underlines the importance of having effective strategies and support systems to be competent in this work.

Getting stuck

Sometimes counsellors experience a feeling of 'stuckness' and describe situations where they feel that they are stuck and getting nowhere. It can be helpful to share these feelings with the client by simply saying: 'I wonder what is happening here, we don't seem to be making much progress.' It is surprising how often the client will say: 'It's strange that you say that because that is how I have been feeling and ... .' In this situation the counsellor has picked up what is happening for the client and by addressing the dynamic the process moves on. Reviewing the therapeutic contract, which was established in the first session, can remind both client and counsellor of what they set out to achieve.

At other times the counsellor 'unconsciously' is holding the client's experience and by sharing it within a supervision session or 'off-loading' it within a case discussion group the counsellor is then able to stay with the client's non-progress a little longer. In my experience it is remarkable how often it happens that, having done this, in the next session the client 'miraculously' shifts.

Perhaps we cannot know to what extent the client's early life experience and his inner feelings affect his outside behaviour. He might reproduce patterns of his earlier life, as described earlier in the sections on projective identification and transference.

Case example: 'I must not upset her'

Mary's mother died when she was ten years of age and she had lived with her father and stepmother, with whom she had a volatile relationship. She presented in an extremely distressed state following job appraisal. In counselling a situation developed where each time the counsellor offered a gentle challenge Mary would get upset to the extent that the counsellor felt stuck for fear of 'upsetting her'.

After several sessions the counsellor shared directly with Mary what she felt was happening between them. She said that she felt a little like her line manager and was apprehensive about offering her anything that challenged her view of the situation. As a result of this 'here and now' intervention Mary went on to talk about how her stepmother had 'always put her down' and how rows would erupt in the family with her father threatening to send her to stay with relatives.

From this point on the focus became Mary's difficulty with dealing with criticism and her constant need for approval. By confronting the situation in the therapeutic relationship, the client was able to see things in a different way and the process moved forward.

Confrontation

Confrontation is a term that is often used to describe this stage of counselling where the client comes face to face with him- or herself. It is where they take on different perspectives, looking at their situation in an altered way. Sometimes the result of effective empathic listening, as in a client-centred approach, is that the client *self*-confronts and they say something like: 'I've just realised that ...' Confrontation is an important part of the counselling process for if the client is seeking change, whether it is in terms of altered behaviour or an acceptance of a life situation, then the client needs choice and control over their lives. If clients are able to challenge themselves by seeing repeated patterns of behaviour, querying relationships and how they cope in certain situations, it then offers them a wider picture from which to consider change.

In the above example it was the client who naturally moved into this phase, but sometimes it is the counsellor who will need to be more active and use their challenging skills. At this point the counsellor often senses a need to 'move the process forward'. Sometimes not being able to withstand the client's rejection of the counsellor's considered perceptions, or the risk of the client leaving the relationship, can hold counsellors back from using challenging skills at an appropriate stage. Issues to consider are motivation, timing and the counsellor's fears. The following questions may provide a useful guide.

- Why do I wish to challenge this client and what do I wish to confront?
- Whose need is it to confront and will it help the process?
- Does the client feel sufficiently understood?
- Have I spent enough time attempting to appreciate their situation?
- Is there sufficient trust in the therapeutic relationship?

Case example: challenging projection

Bill was discussing with the counsellor a decision he had to make as to whether or not to relocate or take voluntary redundancy. He talked in a flat and unemotional way about how he had been treated very shabbily by his previous employer. As the details of the story unfolded the counsellor began to feel extremely angry about Bill's humiliating experiences and to wonder how he could have put up with the way he had been treated. The counsellor began to feel frustrated and irritated to the point where he felt he wanted to challenge him for his passive attitude. Bill remained calm throughout without a trace of resentment being expressed.

Here the induced set of thoughts and feelings experienced were vivid and alive – to be used in the counselling or not. The counsellor could challenge the projection by saying: 'You are telling a very distressing story and yet you say it in such a calm way ... '.

Self-disclosure

The question of self-disclosure is an important one to address early on in the counsellor's training. Sometimes it seems that it would be reassuring and supportive for a client to hear that the counsellor has experienced a similar situation and discover what they did to cope with it. How should we address this?

Let us for the moment consider two extreme views on self-disclosure. At one extreme there is the traditional psychoanalytic view that therapist self-disclosure is not recommended and should be treated with great caution. Storr (1979) has this to say about self-disclosure:

> In fact, revealing things about himself is, for the therapist, nearly always a form of self-indulgence, however much he may try to believe that it is for the patient's benefit. ... Therapists want acceptance and understanding from people just as do their patients.

Clearly he would urge caution and goes on to explain why:

> When therapists reveal themselves to their patients, the situation changes from therapy into a mutual exchange: an ordinary relationship of the kind which exist between friends and therefore one in which the therapist is obtaining the kind of gratification which occurs in mutual exchanges between friends. The therapist's job is to understand his patient, not to obtain understanding from his patient.   (Storr, 1979: 65)

Rowan (1983) suggests that psychoanalytic counsellors adopt this position because they take the view that 'the ideal therapist is a mirror, freely playing the client's unconscious fantasies'. This is based on Freud's early ideas of the analyst as a mirror onto which the patient could project his problems, previously described as the 'blank screen'. At the other extreme is a position taken by a traditional existentialist, described here by Rowan:

> That the whole value of the therapeutic encounter lies in the real meeting of real people in a setting where it is made hard to evade these realities. (Rowan, 1983: 45)

In other words, the humanist existentialist would welcome self-disclosure as it emphasises the 'real relationship', which could include 'transpersonal dialogues'. Most counsellors place themselves somewhere between the two positions described above.

From clinical experience I would argue that the use of personal examples takes the focus off the client and distracts them from their own thought processes and from their feeling of being the most important and central in the relationship. However, I would suggest that each situation deserves consideration on its merit, remembering the uniqueness of each therapeutic relationship. Let us consider what this might mean in practical terms. Sometimes the client will put you on the spot by asking a direct question such as:

'Are you married?'

You can throw it back to the client by saying:

'It seems important to you to know this.'

This probes for the reason why this is important and picks up the message behind the request. Sometimes the client will put it in a different form:

'I don't suppose this has ever happened to you.'

In this instance the implicit message is:

'... And you don't understand and cannot understand what it is like for me.'

The counsellor could pick up the hostile tone and say:

'You seem rather angry.'

Or they could respond in an empathic way to the implicit message:

'It seems that nobody can truly understand what it is like for you at the moment.'

Or answer the question directly and minimally:

'Yes, I am married, but tell me more about why that seems important to you right now.'

In this last example the counsellor discloses, in an open way, and quickly gets back to the client. Take another situation where the client says:

'I just can't face the thought of another promotion board ... I get so nervous, I can't speak.'

To which the counsellor replies:

'Yes, I know that feeling well. I used to be so frightened of groups it almost kept me from becoming a counsellor. I hope together we can help you overcome your fear.'

In one way the client could be reassured by the fact that the counsellor too has had difficulties and has overcome them, but on the other hand there is a danger here that they could see the counsellor as being even more capable than before, thus reinforcing the client's sense of inadequacy. As Clarkson and Pokorny (1994) describes:

> The counsellors' reply to a client who asks 'how are you' will be determined by the specific needs that did not receive an appropriate response by the clients' caretakers in childhood.

Take a client who as a child was always taking care of others and overburdened with their parents' difficulties. The counsellor says:

> 'It is not necessary for you to worry about me, right now I am here to take care of you and I am ready to do that.'

Or, to the client who as a child was never allowed to show her care or love for her parents, and is always enquiring after the counsellor's health:

> 'I am fine, thank you – it's really kind of you to enquire about me, I appreciate that.'

In attempting to be genuine without taking up the client's space, the counsellor considers how much of oneself to disclose and how to be real without distracting the client from their own agenda.

Touch

We have been considering balancing judgement with spontaneity regarding verbal interventions, but how should we behave physically? There is physical touch when one offers a hand out to comfort or help the client during a session and then there is 'psychological touch'. One can be touched deeply by words, emotions or caring. Whether to touch physically is a perennial issue for counsellors. The traditional psychoanalytic view is that such reparation or re-parenting is an avoidance of the client experiencing their original pain. Unless the client actively seeks this from the counsellor, most counsellors will err on the side of caution.

Humanistic therapists, on the other hand, tend to be much more flexible in considering touch. Touch on greeting and parting needs to be distinguished from touch as part of treatment. Biodynamic massage, Rolfing, rebirthing, primal screaming or bioenergetics use systematic physical methods, such as massage, to provoke emotional discharge. Lowen (1976) suggests that actively giving the client permission to touch the therapist in turn allows the client to get more in touch with themselves. This would be particularly relevant where a client who had a need to touch their therapist experiences this as a taboo.

A more common use of touch in therapy is when the client is crying and seems to need encouragement to continue or to go deeper. A light touch to the upper back or shoulder can offer great comfort without stopping the flow of emotions. At this point some argue that it is important not to hold the client as it can prematurely stop the client discharging. By allowing the emotional discharge to build up to a peak it can resolve itself through catharsis.

Does withholding touch when a client is in great pain compound the original lack of care or sense of isolation? Or does it deny the client their experience and in that sense intrude? For many counsellors this area is one of considerable professional concern and they may withhold touch not through choice based upon theoretical understanding but because of fear of being misunderstood. The counsellor's own inhibitions, attitudes to cross-sex or same-sex touching are areas which can be explored during training and supervision. Touch as a technique in counselling needs to be considered in the light of good professional practice and used with discretion.

Power

Human beings have an enormous capacity to cope with extraordinary circumstances. The purpose of counselling is to help clients gather their own strengths so that they can confront and deal with issues in their lives. It is all too easy just to see the vulnerability of the client in distress and veer towards unhelpfully protecting them. We as counsellors have no right to rescue them. Like the child who grows up with overprotective parents, this just reinforces their sense of powerlessness or inadequacy.

Case example: rescuing the client

Take the client who decides not to have treatment for their alcohol problems despite the fact that management say they will lose their job if they do not get specialist help. Add to this the knowledge that management have invested a great deal in this employee, whom they know they will be hard pushed to replace because of their specialist skills. Knowing that they may not have a job and there are children to support, and appreciating management's views, we might believe that the client must at all costs seek treatment. We decide that this would be a good outcome for all parties and go to great lengths, which might include stepping outside the boundary of the session. We might spend time finding out more about treatment centres and 'arrange' for the client to receive information, even making the first appointment.

What we are doing here is decided by what *we* think is best for the client and because we wish to be perceived well by management. Having a large investment in the client getting better we 'get busy' on their behalf. It is not surprising that when the client, who has less of an emotional stake in the outcome, doesn't do what we think is best for them we are left feeling let down, even angry.

If counsellors suffer from a deep need to rearrange others' lives and to provide happy endings, then they are in danger of colluding in a rescue fantasy which ultimately will help none of the parties concerned. In the previous example the omnipotence of the counsellor takes precedence over the client's capacity for autonomy and growth. By pushing too hard it diminishes the client, implying that they are helpless. This reinforces any self-destructive patterns. The role of the counsellor is to step back and point out what the client is doing. At the point of losing his job the organisation has been sensible enough to offer some help but because at this moment in time he lacks motivation, he is in a sense helpless. Due to the destructive aspects in his behaviour, he has made himself a victim.

Author Alice Miller (1990), a former psychoanalyst, writes movingly about the destructive consequences of the abuse of power as experienced in childhood. She talks of the parent–child relationship, which is by its very nature one of power, authority and great influence. As counsellors we do have power and we need to be aware of using it responsibly, not becoming 'a parent-counsellor' who might commit a 'second abuse': that of the abuse of trust.

Earlier in this chapter we saw how clients come with positive and negative expectations with regard to the counsellor's power. Whatever approach we as counsellors choose to use we need to consider the potential abuse of power in counselling. In the instance of touch, for example, the abuse of power would mean that touch was for the gratification of the counsellor.

> Practitioners must not abuse their client's trust in order to gain sexual, emotional, financial or any other kind of personal advantage. ... Sexual relations with clients are prohibited.   (BACP, 2001)

Counsellors must maintain appropriate boundaries, for example by not taking sexual advantage of a vulnerable client who may as part of the transference 'fall in love' with the counsellor. Another abuse of power would be to use interpretation as a defence against our shortcomings in the face of a challenging client. Perhaps the client is correct in what they have to say about our behaviour.

A relationship of power is implied when anybody seeks help from another person. The recipient is likely to feel vulnerable, perhaps even helpless. Kareem (2000) suggests 'we cannot escape from the fact that our profession and livelihood depend on the availability of distressed human beings'. Whilst it is natural for the client to want to progress sooner rather than later, minimising expense or the cost of time out of the office can be issues. Of equal concern is that for some counsellors it may not be in their interest for clients to get better too quickly if this means a decrease in personal income or departmental statistics.

Other specific power issues exist in counselling in general, for example, counsellors have the power of knowledge about the therapeutic process and etiquette to which clients may not have access, but issues of power are of particular significance when working with clients coming from any minority group. In this context the relationship can become a microcosm of society, for example, where the counsellor is white and the client is black then the client may feel particularly 'powerless'. Reflecting the imbalance in society, the client might perceive the counsellor as particularly 'powerful'. Clients might be disadvantaged in communication, perhaps because their first language is other than English, making it difficult to communicate outside their own community.

Masson (1989) highlighted the abuse of power by psychotherapists. I think it is healthy to be challenged and it is a debate worth having, but as yet very little has been written about the positive use of power within the therapy, for instance, the ability to empower and to influence lives for the better. As mentioned earlier, one meaning of the word power is potency. Power can be used for good or evil as history clearly demonstrates. Just as there is the power in the surgeon whose knife when used with skill can save life, so there is the power for therapeutic healing within the counsellor–client relationship. Ghosts can be laid to rest, distress can be discharged, and unresolved relationships understood, allowing clients to go forward with their lives.

Summary

In today's world workplace counsellors in their professional roles are faced with many therapeutic issues and techniques to consider. In this chapter I have chosen to include some of the more complicated and controversial concepts, in particular transference and countertransference, in the hope that they will help you to make 'sense' of what often seems 'non-sense'. The potential for projection in organisational settings is substantial and when this is not understood it not only causes distress to the counsellor but also renders them less useful to their client base.

One final thought. Although understanding complex ideas is enriching, I believe we should never allow ourselves to become distanced from our clients and sacrifice our counselling relationships in the name of 'therapeutic techniques'.

6

WORKING WITH DIVERSITY

Introduction

In this chapter I seek to acknowledge issues of diversity, to address what the workplace counsellor's role is in this and how it affects the counselling process.

> If you belong to a culture which is at odds with the predominant one in which you live, you may wish to consider carefully whether you wish your cultural values to be challenged, respected or upheld.   (Dryden and Feltham, 1995)

My personal belief is that one can retain and respect one's own culture, have it challenged and still learn from and make a contribution to the predominant culture. But in order for that to happen I think one needs to consider and respect both cultures, even in the face of intolerance.

I have experienced this at first hand. As a small child I recall the playground taunts, bullying and extortion that were visited upon my brother and me, along with our incomprehension as to our alleged crime. Whilst we as a family did not deny our heritage, the need to belong and to be like everybody else was very strong. 'Why didn't we go to our parents?', I hear you ask? Perhaps we did not want to upset them or feared that if we did they would act and take it up with the school authorities and that could lead to further trouble.

Perhaps this is how people in the workplace feel who are on the receiving end of discrimination and harassment. I am reminded of clients who do not go to their line managers because they fear complaints backfiring on them, thus increasing their sense of isolation. Perhaps there is also a mindset in the workplace which says, 'Let's keep our heads down, don't make waves and let us just fit into the predominant culture', and another, which says, 'Let us stand up and be counted.'

In my experience there were mixed family messages – one, which said, 'We are different and live in a different way', and the others which said, 'fit in' at school. As I grew older there were messages from teachers, who said 'Remember you are an ambassador for your religion.' What a pressure and a burden for a teenager. How difficult it was to be naughty without 'letting the side down' and being labelled. Perhaps here too there are parallels for adults in the workplace. Being different in the group for whatever reason can bring with it similar messages and pressures to represent 'one's group'. What is it like to be 'the token' female, male, black or disabled person on a committee?

As an adult, racist remarks made within my hearing, when the individual did not know that I came from a particular ethnic group, were both hurtful and challenging. It takes courage to stand up and be counted when one is in a minority, particularly when others in the group seemed to accept what is being said. Although I learnt how to deal with such situations it was not always easy. To balance the bigotry I also encountered decent, fair-minded individuals who influenced my life for the better. Perhaps I am an optimist but I believe them to be in the majority, belonging to a group which doesn't necessarily have a formal voice or political platform.

Historical context

There was a major shift in awareness of racism, sexism and other forms of discrimination in the 1960s and 1970s with key landmark legislation and the establishment of commissions for equality. After generations of discrimination the need for equal rights for all was beginning to be recognised. Then in the 1980s there was the backlash against 'political correctness', followed by the Stephen Lawrence enquiry in the 1990s. Equal Opportunities is about reducing or removing all forms of unfair discrimination by:

- breaking down barriers for people in particular groups;
- ensuring that people are treated in a non-discriminatory way;
- challenging any behaviour which could be regarded as inappropriate or unfair;
- ensuring that systems and procedures do not discriminate unfairly against individuals or groups.

Traditionally this has been done through legal means. For example, current legislation makes it unlawful for an employer to discriminate directly or indirectly on a number of grounds including race, ethnic origin, nationality, sex and disability. But as yet there is no specific legislation regarding discrimination as a result of age (Chartered Institute for Personnel and Development, 2001), sexual orientation, political belief or religion (other than in Northern Ireland). The current government is proposing to introduce legislation in relation to religion but this is proving quite controversial. Whilst the law goes some way to protecting minority groups in that it makes discriminatory behaviour illegal, it is limited and does not necessarily change prejudicial attitudes and feelings. And so 'managing diversity' has emerged as a way of enhancing equality of opportunity.

Some organisations go further than legislation requires and have specific policies, which not only take into account race, colour, sex and disability but also guard against discrimination on grounds of religious belief, sexual orientation, working pattern, gender reassignment or age. Others go still further and provide effective equal opportunity training or act positively to address under-representation in particular groupings.

Harassment and discrimination are problems for many organisations. They can be some of the most offensive and demeaning experiences an employee can suffer and can have a serious effect upon health and well-being. Initiating formal complaints procedures can be embarrassing and fraught with further problems, both real and imagined. In the absence of any simple recourse against it, employees who are suffering from discrimination or harassment for whatever reason may lose time at work through illness and generally be less productive. If the situation is not resolved satisfactorily, they may leave to find another job. Discrimination and harassment, therefore, can have adverse effects on both employer and employee.

Managing diversity, productive diversity and valuing diversity have become shorthand terms for good human resource and business practice. Done well, it encourages employees to maximise their contribution and encourages and supports employees who wish to develop and improve their skills and abilities. It values and respects different opinions and perspectives; it is open to flexible ways of working and is about 'inclusion' rather than exclusivity. Put this way it both makes good business sense and is a commitment to social justice, filled with optimism. However the rhetoric does not always match the practice and well-intentioned initiatives are often dismissed as having politically driven agendas.

The extent to which diversity is or is not being managed in the workplace will have an impact on the nature of workplace counsellors' casework. Where organisational policy does not match practice, employees are afraid to raise issues for fear of retribution, ridicule or no action being taken. This leads to a cycle of discrimination, harassment and workplace bullying. Although progress is being made and many employers are genuinely committed to equality of opportunity, there still exist levels of denial regarding prejudice and diversity.

Workplace counsellor's role

Many organisations have clear policies and grievance procedures specifying the steps staff should take if subjected to discrimination or harassment. Some even appoint harassment officers specifically trained to deal with complaints. However in practice many staff do not make formal complaints and workplace counsellors may be the first port of call in dealing with the distress caused by discrimination or harassment. In this respect workplace counsellors have much to contribute to the well-being of staff and the organisation as a whole (although first they need to explore the impact of their own race, culture or religion and acknowledge their own prejudices). They can ensure that victims know how to raise concerns and feel confident in taking action should they choose to proceed with a formal complaint. The staff counsellor can help employees address and resolve their situation, regardless of whether or not a complaint is taken forward.

A team might be struggling with diversity issues and finding it difficult to work together. Here the workplace counsellor can act as a facilitator by helping the team raise issues that are difficult to talk about. Unspoken questions can be addressed, for instance, 'Why is this colleague choosing to or being isolated from their workgroup?' 'What terms are considered offensive?' 'What are your customs and traditions?' 'What are the significant religious dates in your calendar?' By openly identifying tensions and addressing difficult questions, perhaps knowledge can be shared and myths dispelled, making better teamwork possible. It is challenging work, reminiscent of the work done with families in conflict where certain individuals hold great power, others feel powerless, some are scapegoated and others live in fear. It therefore requires knowledge of group dynamics, skill and confidence.

Workplace counsellors may become involved in specific cases that have organisational implications. In terms of assisting 'the organisation as the client' effectively implement policy they may have a role working with line managers and staff who are feeling quite anxious about diversity issues and what this means for them. They might require support in taking forwards policy in a meaningful way and the counsellor can be extremely useful in helping them to process their own feelings about confronting and dealing with sensitive situations. In order to do this the workplace counsellor needs to stay calm in the face of organisational anxiety or pressure and not get lost in the rhetoric of policy.

Counselling individuals who face discrimination and harassment can evoke strong emotions and views and one of the challenges facing the counsellor is not to project their own values onto the individual but to allow them to take make their own decisions. The workplace is an ideal arena for the 'Karpman Triangle' to be acted out, where individuals perceive themselves and others as taking on the roles of 'victim', 'persecutor' and 'rescuer ' (Mavis Klein, 1980) and alternate between them. When working with discrimination or harassment counsellors need to be particularly aware of this dynamic.

I think it is worth recognising that counsellors are often a 'minority voice' within the organisation and just like any other minority group may feel vulnerable and fear alienation if they stick their heads above the parapet. Alternatively they may take a fighting stance to ensure they are heard. However, workplace counsellors have a lot to offer by holding on to the core values of counselling: honesty, respect, genuineness and understanding. They are uniquely placed to provide a safe place where employees can be treated with respect and not be subjected to discrimination or abuse.

Race, Culture and Ethnicity

For some time now the United Kingdom has been a 'multi-ethnic society' but it is questionable whether it is a 'multicultural society'. These terms are often used interchangeably but what do we mean by them and how will they affect the counselling process? Words and their meanings have a whole history and are continually evolving. Counsellors with cultural sensitivity will know the significance attached to language when working cross-culturally. Fernando (1991) defines the above terms as follows:

■ race – as relating to physical aspects;
■ culture – as a sociological construction;
■ ethnicity – as a primarily psychological state.

Race usually refers to a group of people who see themselves and are considered by others as a group of people who are joined together by inherited characteristics. It could be a tribe, a clan, an ethnic group or a nation. 'Race as a term is often used to define a group of people who have the same skin colour, hair shape and colour, eye colour and blood type, and a common ancestry' (Eleftheriadou, 1994). An historical perspective of race says that 'race is a term that has largely been discredited in biological science, but was particularly prevalent in the nineteenth and early twentieth centuries' (Moorhouse, 2000). Where race was used as a term it assumed that humans could be clearly 'divided in to distinct populations based on biological characteristics derived from their genetics, usually together with the belief that this also determined behaviour and institutions' (Littlewood, 1989). What is clear is that in the United Kingdom there are an increasing number of people who are of dual heritage and so long as people perceive others as being from a different 'race' so racial discrimination will continue to impact on people's lives.

Culture refers to a way of life, particularly the beliefs and customs of a group of people at any given time. It is seen 'as inter-subjective, as the process of transmitting conceptual and social guidelines to the next generation through the use of symbols, language, art and ritual' (Helman, 1985). Culture is based on a psychological need for a sense of belonging and collectiveness but it is also flexible, disposed to social influences and the environment in which people grow up. It is therefore potentially changeable and assimilable.

Ethnicity is increasingly being used to replace the concept of race and culture. As Eleftheriadou (1994) suggests 'ethnicity refers to a group who share a specific history, background or origin and who have common culture'. It is important to be aware that there are variations within any one ethnic group just as there are between different ethnic groups. Whereas culture can be seen as dynamic, ethnicity can remain a relatively static concept for individuals unless they are born of relationships between groups. Dictionary definitions help to a point but in my experience how individuals perceive a word is more important. In terms of culture, race and ethnicity how might you describe yourself in each of the following scenarios? Supposing you were born in Malaysia but you have lived most of your life in Germany, or your grandparents were of Irish Catholic descent and you now live in America, or your mother is a white atheist and your father is of African–Caribbean descent brought up as Christian and you now live in Glasgow? Questions like these can be helpful in raising awareness of the multicultural backgrounds of our clients. Of course your family could have been born, raised and brought up in the same village for centuries.

Culture as a word has many meanings and is used in different contexts. For example we refer to a global culture, the culture of a society, of a particular race or religion, but we also refer to the culture of a profession and of an organisation as discussed in Chapter 1. Diversity is often associated with discrimination but culture may emerge as an issue within a counselling session. I think the following case highlights what an integral role culture plays for people.

Case example: 'Didn't realise'

Hussein was from a Turkish background but had lived in England most of his life. He presented just after having separated from his wife. He described a turbulent relationship filled with arguments. Events came to a head when his wife smashed the frame that contained a photograph of his late mother. This was the final straw and his grief broke forth. It was as though the frame that was broken literally contained all his grief. He not only mourned the potential loss of his wife but also spoke profoundly of the hitherto denied loss of his culture, which his mother represented. She was his link to the past and it had been broken.

Cultural barriers are not just limited to race and sex, they apply equally to other areas of society by way of disability, religion, sexual orientation, education, class and geography. The culture of an organisation can reinforce stereotyping with the use of labelling and oppression of certain groups. One might deny one's ethnic group, dislike it or choose to move away from it (consciously or subconsciously) but one cannot change one's history, background or origin. It is still part of you even if it is open to influence from other cultures. As each culture has its own belief systems, and the need to belong and be accepted as part of a group or subculture is very strong, prejudice can be culturally determined.

I recall a very dear colleague with whom I trained as a supervisor who always prided herself on being 'working class'. One day she emerged from a video playback of her giving a tutorial looking distinctly shaken. When I asked her 'What on earth is wrong?', she turned to me and said in a very forlorn voice, 'Loretta, I can't believe it. After all these years I've just realised I am now middle class!' Until that moment she had been unaware of how her social and work environment had influenced her and now her personal identity, in terms of class, was threatened.

People who interact with others with different practices and beliefs may be influenced by them just as my colleague discovered. People are influenced throughout their lives by the socio-cultural messages they receive. The individual and their culture are intertwined and one naturally influences the other informing the individual's identity. This sometimes brings up generational conflicts in families where the next generation do not wish to adhere to the rituals of their ethnic group, caste or its cultural norms.

Case example: 'Which path shall I follow?'

A British-born Asian woman of the Muslim faith was suffering from 'stress'. She was being forced into an arranged marriage and presented as feeling depressed and in fear of losing her job. The counselling focused on the conflict between her duty to her family and its belief system and the freedom of choice, with which she also identified, and had witnessed in the country in which she had lived since birth.

With regard to organisational cultures, race, sex and cultural norms may have developed as a result of a certain group in power defining and determining what is 'normal'. If the individuals in power are white, Anglo-Saxon and male these perspectives are likely to be reflected in the cultural norms within an organisation. At the Civil Service Racial Equality Launch in 2001 the Civil Service Diversity Champion, Sir Nicholas Montagu, said:

> It is all too easy for those of us who are white, male and middle-aged to pontificate about the need for change. Until we understand better how it feels not to be a member of that group – which has been comfortably dominant for far too long – our strategies, however well-intentioned, can be no more than theoretical.

Prejudice

Any difference can lead to assumptions, preconceived ideas and personal prejudice. There are some differences, which are obvious, such as colour, physical disability age or gender, whilst others such as religious beliefs, mental disability and class are subtler and less clear-cut.

When difference is obvious people can use politically correct language and behave outwardly in a non-discriminatory way whilst underlying prejudice goes undetected. Some would say that prejudice can still be picked up through non-verbal behaviour described as 'leakage' or 'vibes', but without the concrete evidence it can be difficult to confront: for instance, sexist or racist remarks may not be made overtly to women and black people as frequently any more but they can still be unfairly overlooked for promotion.

With less obvious forms of difference, prejudice is free to emerge and people may make overt discriminatory comments. When work colleagues collude by not challenging such behaviour they contribute, perhaps unwittingly, to the development of a cultural norm and this can be extremely hurtful and reinforce feelings of isolation within the work-group. Whether prejudice is hidden or overt it is distressing and can leave colleagues as well as recipients wondering whether to say anything and what to do.

The events of 11 September 2001 and the public's reaction to the terrorist attack on the World Trade Center show how cultural and religious prejudice is deeply embedded worldwide. Whilst prejudice will never disappear completely its effects can be – and need to be – minimised if people are to live and work productively together.

Working with Difference – the Counsellor's Role and Responsibility

Ethical and legal responsibility

Some counsellors would argue that there is too much talk about diversity. 'After all,' said one, 'isn't counselling all about valuing and respecting people as individuals?' Yes, of course it is. As counsellors we work with difference every time we meet a new client because each client is a unique human being, but I question whether this is sufficient. I wonder whether counsellors are sufficiently trained to acknowledge their own cultural backgrounds, prejudices, preconceptions and stereotypes.

Acknowledging that one has prejudices is an uncomfortable experience and it is particularly so for counsellors who are expected to be and think of themselves as being 'non-judgemental'. However, there are unconscious processes that affect conscious thought and behaviour in the counselling room regarding diversity, which are not always addressed. We live in a pluralist society in which there are many myths and misconceptions surrounding diversity. By familiarising oneself with different philosophies and developing personal awareness regarding diversity, prejudice and discrimination, we are not only being 'genuine' but also demonstrating 'respect' towards our clients.

As part of their professional and ethical responsibility, counsellors need to explore their own racial, ethnic and cultural identity, belief systems and prejudices. I believe counsellors have a personal obligation to commit themselves to the necessary training to enable them to work with difference. I would go further and say that as a profession, in terms of equality of opportunity, we can learn a lot from public- and private-sector organisations in terms of training in diversity.

Implementing policy decisions to deal with diversity, and in particular sexual, racial or disability discrimination and harassment, requires commitment and sensitive handling. For those subjected to any such situations it can be challenging to take forward a complaint through the relevant procedure and an informed, independent staff counsellor can be enormously useful. As employers are responsible for the behaviour of their employees while at work this includes workplace counsellors. I cannot stress enough that the counsellor must take into account their own position with regard to the law. They need to be aware of their own legal obligations within their organisation and to be clear about what is expected of them with regard to discrimination, victimisation, disclosure and their contract of employment.

Apart from their ethical duty to act professionally, workplace counsellors need to act within the law. In an increasingly litigious world, whether counsellors are internal or external, they need to keep up to date with information. From a legal standpoint they have the same responsibilities not to discriminate as other service providers, employees and employers. Legislation is there to support managers and staff but the law in this area is often complex and, if in any doubt, I suggest that counsellors contact their own professional bodies for codes of ethics or any of the relevant organisations such as the Disability Rights Commission or the Commission for Racial Equality.

Cross-cultural Perspectives

One of the factors that have contributed to the development of transcultural, intercultural or cross-cultural counselling is the increase of mobility across the world, which means that now we live in a society that has increased in cultural pluralism. More recently there is the effect of the European Community (EC) merger (1992) and its effect on legislation. Although little research has been done to date, there is a noticeable increase in awareness of cross-cultural issues, books and training courses.

Transcultural counselling (Eleftheriadou, 1994) is about the practitioner being able to recognise their own culture, acknowledge differences in other cultures and see beyond them, whilst Kareem (1978) believes that it is essential to address both conscious and unconscious assumptions, in the patient and in the therapist, if the therapy is to be successful. Fostering an atmosphere where difference of culture or observance of rituals can be freely expressed is an essential component of transcultural counselling.

We can quite easily identify with difference in culture and attitude if we think about how counselling as an activity is viewed in two countries. Whereas the whole notion of counselling is part of the culture in the USA, here in the UK counselling, although on the increase, might be considered as something one would have when there is a 'serious' problem. In the USA client-centred counselling is very popular and emphasises the importance of the individual. Other cultures would find this difficult because of the cultural norms of valuing the communal more than the individual. The Western approach emphasises the individual whereas in some African cultures the group takes precedence over the individual. Whilst in the West individuals are encouraged 'to disclose', in other cultures, such as the Middle East, this is discouraged. Japan practices introspection therapy originating from Buddhist philosophy, whilst China discourages ambition and aggression, and encourages conservatism. Then there are different attitudes towards women and the elderly. In Middle Eastern cultures it is rare for a man to feel comfortable discussing his personal difficulties with a woman. Islamic beliefs, for example, could inhibit or even prohibit cross-gender counselling. This could also be true with ultra-orthodox Jews. In some cultures attitudes towards seeking advice could inhibit men.

When a client brings the issue of bereavement the counsellor needs to be aware of not making assumptions about the bereavement processes for that individual. This is true of bereavement counselling in general (Parkes et al., 1972). However, in addition, when working cross-culturally understanding different rituals of mourning, beliefs regarding death or afterlife and cultural variations in the emotional reactions to loss is very important.

In terms of emotional expression one just has to visit other countries in Europe, such as France or Italy, to see how emotions expressed in the form of gesticulation are common, in contrast perhaps with Scandinavian countries. What is considered as appropriate emotional discharge is another area for consideration. There are differences in cultural emotional expression and one must beware of labelling clients as 'overemotional' or 'cold'.

Then there are differences regarding physical distance and touch. For example in most Mediterranean cultures the custom is to shake hands when you first meet, whereas in other cultures this would be considered 'forward'. Misunderstandings between counsellor and client can result in lack of early rapport, leading to early termination. For some, direct eye contact would be considered impolite whereas in Britain we would expect the opposite. As I mentioned earlier, how the counsellor's and client's cultures interact affects how they behave and relate to others. Let me offer you a personal example.

> **Example: the meaning of time**
>
> Carmen was a counsellor who came from an African–Caribbean background and was prone to turning up late for supervision sessions. I wondered how she managed time with her clients. When I raised the issue with her she had difficulty understanding the importance that the organisation, for which we both worked, placed on time keeping. She explained that in her culture time took on a different meaning. Unconsciously she had been challenging the rules and it was not until the subject of her ethnic origin was discussed that she was able to talk about what it was like for her to live and work in a predominantly white culture. As I began to learn more about Carmen, the 'difference' in our cultural backgrounds was acknowledged and the supervision sessions became more productive. Not only did our relationship change but also so did Carmen's with her clients and the organisation. Through choice she consciously moved over to our values of time keeping in the counselling culture without denying her own culture.

Lack of knowledge of culture and language can result in misunderstanding. We live in a diverse world and effective counsellors need to be sensitive to how their clients refer to themselves and their own communities. Some terms will immediately give offence if they do not accurately reflect the client's identity. When a client uses a language other than their native language, some of the subtleties of meaning get lost in the translation and words are open to misinterpretation. Use of words, phrases and names for relationships may have different meanings. (For further reading see Hall and Moodley, 2001.) In the case of transcultural counselling, D'Ardenne and Mahtani (1989) suggest that counsellors have to work through and across the cultural differences and that in so doing they bring a heightened sensitivity to the counselling process.

Sexual Orientation

Speaking about sex remains for many one of the most difficult areas to address because of its intimate and private nature. When meeting a person for the first time one of the first distinctions one makes is whether they are male or female. As with any difference it is easy to deny sexual variation and its degree of importance for the client. Gender identity, sexual preferences and sex role stereotypes are important areas for counsellors to explore. They need to feel comfortable personally if they are to enable their clients to speak freely.

Some would argue that racial discrimination is more important and place it higher on the agenda, whilst others see this as a convenient avoidance of tackling this intimate area. Yet again the counsellor needs to be self-aware, to understand clients' sexual identities and personal choices in order to be able to work, for example, with gay men and lesbians irrespective of whether or not they are gay or lesbian themselves. Counsellors need to be clear about terminology yet mindful of labelling people unhelpfully. To the extent that homosexual clients are breaking from traditional norms they will require their counsellor to have considered these areas. In practice clients may be concerned about how they will be treated by a counsellor of a different sexual orientation and it is argued (Davies, 1996) that gender or sexual orientation matching is essential in gay counselling.

Case example: 'Treading on eggshells'

One counsellor described a case where she was working with a 24-year-old man who presented with a debt problem. In the first session he also mentioned in passing that he had recently come out as being gay. She avoided picking up the clear signals that the client was giving her regarding his sexuality and focused on the debt problem. She felt inhibited in some way and described the experience as 'treading on eggshells' even though in her personal life she had many gay friends with whom she felt quite at ease.

The counsellor, through discussion, was able to acknowledge how difference had actually influenced the process. Initially she was aware of 'not wanting to say the wrong thing', fearful that her usual language was not appropriate She felt it took until the third session for her to relax, be herself and pick up what the client really wished to talk about.

When allocating cases or making a referral decisions need to be made as to what would be most appropriate for the client, balanced against counsellor availability. Take the hypothetical scenario of a woman who has difficulty relating to men; it could be argued that it would be enormously useful if she worked with a male counsellor. Perhaps the very process of speaking to a person of the opposite sex could be therapeutic in itself. Then there are the more general issues of men and women working together (see Kanter, 1977), where the workplace counsellor might be involved in specific casework regarding discrimination and harassment.

Disability

Working with blind, physically or mentally disabled, hearing- or language-impaired clients presents the challenge of not labelling people and treating clients equally whilst not denying the reality of their situation. When working with disabled clients contracting might have a particular dimension, e.g. where you would work, whether or not you might need someone to sign or whether you need special aids for communication. Whilst a disabled person does not just bring their disability to the counselling session, just as with any difference it needs acknowledgement otherwise erroneous assumptions can be made.

Apart from any legal responsibility (Disability Discrimination Act 1995), setting the correct environment is crucial and certain adjustments will need to be considered when working with disabled people. For example, despite legislation not all transport and buildings are wheelchair accessible. Agreeing a suitable environment for a physically disabled person is more clear-cut than, say, working with a deaf client. Location for both is equally important, and in the latter case thinking about level of traffic noise would be important, for instance, as hearing aids amplify sounds that fall within their selected pitch range and can prove problematic. Light plays an important role in lip reading and so the counsellor needs to be in a position where their lips are well lit. These are simple and practical ways in which the setting can be made more accessible to the client. But what about the counsellor–client interaction?

Case example: 'Tuning in'

A client 'held court', thus avoiding the sensitive issues – not an unusual defence mechanism one might assume. However it took on a special meaning with a hearing-impaired client for whilst she was speaking she was not in danger of being embarrassed by not being able to hear what the counsellor was saying. The counsellor needs to be aware of a dynamic like this.

The counsellor with speech- or hearing-impaired clients might be tempted not to intervene for fear that they will interrupt, or alternatively fill the spaces with their own words. When the counsellor is speaking deaf clients sometimes pretend to hear what is being said and it is important to be aware of non-verbal clues as to whether the words have been heard. Listening, as has been said, is an art, but counsellors are human and in the face of stuttering or slow speech patience can be challenged. Adjusting interventions by making them short, being prepared to repeat them if necessary and generally being aware of the extra amount of concentration required for clients with these particular disabilities is essential.

For clients with disabilities, loss of independence and the issue of control can take on particular significance. Regaining control in other areas of their lives is important, easy to understand and can also be re-enacted in the counselling room within the counselling relationship. Once addressed clients often talk about how their lives have changed or how different and vulnerable they feel. Many have coped by suppressing their feelings of helplessness, anger and frustration.

Case example: loss

A competent woman, quite used to making her special needs known, was not consulted regarding a job change. The lack of consultation restimulated the loss of control she experienced in her life generally and the feelings of resentment at always having to make her needs known. Her frustration emerged and she sought the help of the workplace counsellor.

Working through issues of loss can be constructive in coming to terms not only with clients' situations but also with how they interact with others. In some cases it can be the main focus of the work.

With regard to finding the appropriate language, it has been my experience that people vary. Although some are particularly sensitive, most make it extremely easy. In terms of the counselling relationship I have found two aspects particularly interesting: first, that the individual's personality, if it has not been affected by brain damage, supersedes the disability; and second, the degree to which the client has come to terms with their disability affects the way they present themselves. Where they have reached acceptance they describe themselves as John or Mary, a person who just happens to have a disability, rather than labelling themselves 'disabled' – a subtle but important distinction.

Religion

Religious difference, we know, can be divisive and the workplace is no exception. The issue of religion may present because of discrimination but it is more likely to form an aspect within the overall casework, which could include other cultural issues. Sometimes cases present as 'work-related' problems, such as poor attendance or anxiety, and it is only after rapport has been established that the more personal issues emerge.

Here is an example where a life event triggered a crisis within a cross-religion relationship. Differences between partners can be minimised or even denied regarding value systems, only to emerge after they become a couple or are legally bound – or at a significant life event, as described below:

Case example: managing differences

Mr and Mrs Jones were from different ethnic and religious backgrounds and both families were against the marriage. All went well until the birth of their first child. Even though they had discussed how they would bring up their children it was not until the child, a son, was born that religious rituals became an issue. Previously they had clung together in the face of the rejection they felt, with any differences between them as a couple being projected onto the outside world, in this case their disapproving families. Now there were conflicting views between the two of them. It came as a shock to the wife when she realised that her husband had 'traditional' expectations of the mother of his child and wanted her to conform to the norm of his culture.

I would stress that these dynamics are common to many relationships. It is just that they are more easily identifiable where ethnic, religious or cultural differences exist. Whatever the cause other issues are usually involved, like the balance of power within the relationship and how they as a couple address and resolve their differences.

Let us look now at how religious difference would actually affect the counselling process. In Northern Ireland a counsellor's name can be sufficient to prevent the employee seeking help because their name indicates that they are not of the same faith. In a climate of mistrust security is a very real issue and takes on an enormous significance. But the following case is one where 'religious matching' of the counsellor would be of no advantage.

Case example: 'I need a transfer'

A Protestant and a Catholic had married in Northern Ireland. The wife was suffering from stress and her husband (the employee) presented asking for a transfer because of the threats they had received. In this instance they worked for a large organisation that was able to help on a practical level and arranged for a voluntary relocation. But in a small company this is not practicable and counselling would need to address how they as a couple can live with feelings of fear and a sense of isolation.

Case example: 'Angry and isolated'

Kevin came from a strict Calvinist background. He was also gay and HIV-positive. He was a very engaging young man to whom many had difficulty in saying 'no'. Estranged from his parents who rejected his sexuality, he was very challenging towards authority figures, his family and the church, but this was also acted out within the workplace. Within the counselling it became clear how angry he was. When he was diagnosed as having Aids the organisation was extremely supportive in terms of his workload but there was clearly a lot of unfinished business regarding his family, how he felt towards his church and his loss of faith. The counselling focus shifted to helping him try to resolve some of these conflicts before he died.

Different faiths often provide their own counselling services but clients may choose not to use them. Strongly defined religious groups may welcome 'a fresh perspective' whilst adhering to the basic principles of their faith, such as the role of women and girls' education. As a counsellor one needs to respect that there are calendar dates and dress codes that are fundamental to different religions. One needs as best one can to work with the client's religious frame of reference and respect their rights. This may require flexibility and can be challenging when their value system conflicts with one's own, but then this is a re-occurring theme throughout working with difference.

Other differences

I would like to acknowledge that there are many other subtle differences between colleagues that do not get as much public attention as those mentioned above: people who live alone, those who struggle to care for aged parents, working mothers – one could go on forever. Each difference brings its own issues and it is how one resolves those differences within the workplace that matters.

How does Diversity Impact on the Counselling Process?

The counselling culture

Issues of diversity and political correctness are often the subject of hot debate in the workplace, which can leave workplace counsellors rather bewildered and even a little frightened of knowing or asking more. This in turn can lead to avoidance or even denial of the impact of diversity on counselling practice and can affect the process either consciously or unconsciously.

As a starting point I think it is useful to bear in mind the socio-political circumstances in which counsellors live, train and work, and their impact on the counsellor's attitude. For instance, counsellors are not only influenced by their individual cultural upbringing but also by their training. As most theoretical schools devolve from Europe and North America it is argued (Lago and Thompson, 1996) that they are designed by and for people from a similar cultural background. Psychotherapy has been criticised for being predominantly white, Western, middle class and male in its assumptions and counsellors need to consider the legacy of theory itself, its belief systems, ethos and the philosophy of their own training culture. It is a bit like confronting one's own 'family system' – not always easy and likely to produce anxiety.

Perhaps culture is a collective unconscious programming of people. If so, then it has implications for how the counsellor's and client's cultures interact, how they behave and relate to others. As counselling is a two-way process prejudice can originate from the client or the counsellor. It seems to me that the difference lies in the counsellor's responsibility for being as aware and as available as possible for their client group. Acquiring knowledge of different races, cultures, religions, beliefs, rituals and value systems will help dispel myth and misinformation at a conscious level, but it begs the question of what remains at an unconscious level. We do not live or work in isolation, so do counsellors as a group reflect the range of difference in our society? We live in a multi-ethnic society, yet it is questionable whether counselling services reflect the proportion of ethnic minorities that they serve.

Why is it that participants on counselling courses are predominantly female, white and middle class? Is sufficient accommodation being made to encourage people from different social groups to be fully involved in training? What policies, for example, exist regarding age discrimination? And what about client uptake? On looking at statistics and geographical patterns, one counselling service manager concluded that apart from London where a large proportion of clients came from ethnic minority groups (and presenting problems were often about cultural misunderstandings or perceptions of discrimination), in other areas there was not a level of uptake commensurate with staff numbers. In discussions with others it would seem this is not an atypical pattern. This is particularly interesting in areas where there have been racial tensions and in major cities where many of the workforces come from Asian and Black communities. What conclusions can be drawn from these statistics? And what is the workplace counsellor's role in addressing this imbalance? How does a counselling service help the workplace to be more inclusive?

The therapeutic relationship

A workplace counsellor never knows with whom they will be working and what issues of diversity they will bring to the relationship. By recognising issues of diversity and how to manage them professionally the counselling process will become more effective. One of the first ways it impacts on the relationship is at the point of entry. Given the client's 'difference' it is debatable whether or not they will perceive a workplace counselling service as sufficiently approachable.

When working with differences it is all too easy to make assumptions and to look for patterns where they do not exist, to presume, for example, that the presenting problem is only to do with the client's particular 'difference'. The therapeutic relationship as described earlier in this book requires that the individual is not categorised or classified. In treating clients equally I think there is a delicate balance to be struck between the desire not to label people and the need not to deny the reality of the influence of their background or situation.

At the point of referral either party can make assumptions and a name might be sufficient to invoke a preconception of the other's cultural background. A supervisee told me of the reactions shown by some of her clients when they came for their first session and saw that she was black. 'You can see the surprise on their face?' 'How do you handle this?' I enquired. 'I just focus on why they have come to see me as a person and treat them with respect', she replied.

This is where one makes a professional judgement. Where the counsellor senses that race or difference of any kind – perhaps being blind – could be an issue then it is important to address this, as it could be a barrier to the counselling process.

Learning the Language of Difference

Have you ever been in a meeting where others are using technical terms and jargon as a form of shorthand and you do not know what they are talking about? I would suggest that clarification becomes essential for the meeting to be of any value to you. Similarly when two people of differing cultures meet, they will need to find a way of communicating and negotiating a common language. This is particularly important in the early stages of the counselling process. 'But I don't know what to say. I am scared of offending the client ... ' say counsellors. Often through fear of hurting people by using 'the wrong terminology' counsellors struggle to find the 'right words' and shy away from asking. They need to be free in their role and be genuine. At the contracting stage they could be direct and say something like: 'I am conscious that I am from a different culture and I would like us to be honest with one another, so, if there is anything I don't understand or if I use words that you find offensive can we agree to be direct about this?' Or if during the session they are struggling to understand nuances or terms with which they are not familiar then the counsellor should be direct with the client and discuss this with them. In my experience this kind of honesty is very much appreciated by the client.

Empathy is often described as being able to walk in the shoes of the client. Counsellors may not read Braille, but they can try and imagine what it must be like to be in a meeting where everyone else has the advantage of seeing the non-verbal interaction that passes between people. They may not 'sign' but they can wonder what it would be like not to hear the subtleties of voice tone. Whilst counsellors may not speak Urdu, Gujarati or Hindi they may have experienced the frustrations of being in a country where they are unable to make themselves understood. They may not be wheelchair users but they could try to imagine what it might be like to have difficulty entering buildings, being ignored because of height or constantly craning their necks at gatherings.

Whilst some counsellors do not believe that their work is affected by clients of different backgrounds or sexuality etc., others speak of feeling uneasy when the issue of working with diversity is raised, even though their work is in general of a high quality. Upon further exploration there seems to be a level of anxiety in workplace counsellors, verbalised by one counsellor in supervision who said: 'I feel I must get this right'. Where, I wonder, does this pressure come from? Why such caution? With regard to levels of anxiety one could argue that they reflect the dynamics within the system.

I cannot emphasise enough the significance of the workplace setting and the fact that the client–counsellor relationship does not take place in isolation. The organisational culture, its policy and complaints procedures regarding diversity may reinforce the levels of anxiety in the workplace counsellor. Working in environments where policy and practice are not always congruent can mean that both counsellor and client are the recipients of mixed messages. Counsellors in organisations are often perceived as being 'the best' at being understanding and open. This can reinforce their self-expectations and lead to pressure to 'get it right'. I would advise workplace counsellors to challenge these internal and external messages, take some risks and remember just how much they have to offer when they maintain their boundaries and do not get entangled in individual, organisational or political agendas. Speaking as an external supervisor, it seems to me that counsellors do not always value the work they do in such complex areas.

Supervision example: 'Am I racist?'

When discussing diversity in a supervision group a counsellor shared his anxieties, talking openly about his concern about being considered racist. He spoke of how he would treat differently a white and a black client, both presenting as being bullied. With the white client he would explore the situation, and discuss what he as a staff counsellor could offer by way of support should the client proceed with a complaint. But with the black client he recognised that he would immediately be thinking: 'This could end up as an official complaint and I must be very careful what I say because of our discrimination policies ... ' He admitted feeling very cautious.

How easy it would be to criticise, but I wonder how much open discussion exists regarding diversity issues. In a climate of political correctness and ever-changing legislation people, including counsellors, need to feel safe to explore their backgrounds and address their own potential racist or discriminatory views, which may have arisen not only out of lack of education but also by observation of the effects of grievance procedures which, when not handled well, can leave staff feeling inhibited.

It can be disheartening to observe lip service being paid to organisational statements regarding equality of opportunity. 'It sinks in at a surface level,' said one counsellor, 'but whether or not it changes people's attitudes is another matter.' It is therefore worth considering the organisation's motivation, methodology and effectiveness regarding diversity policies and procedures.

Another counsellor acted out of character when they 'became busy' and did more for a client from an ethnic minority than they usually did for their other clients, for example by writing letters on the client's behalf. As counselling is about helping clients to help themselves I questioned what this was all about. A defence mechanism manifesting itself in overcompensation, perhaps – but a defence against what?

With regard to race Marsella and Pedersen (1981) describe three potential reactions that the counsellor might exhibit:

1   *The illusion of colour blindness* – treating the client as just another white client. This denies many of the factors that are unique to black clients and suggests that therapists who say they are 'colour-blind' are not ready to work with black people. It also suggests that they may be resistant to confronting and dealing with these issues.
2   *Great White Father* – the expert who knows what is best for black people. They insist that they only wish to do good to the black person, who should put their trust in them.
3   *Assumption that all black people's problems start with being black* – although black people face discrimination, their problems do not all revolve round colour.

One could also imagine other situations of diversity where the three reactions mentioned above could equally apply – denial of the difference, seeing themselves as the experts and making assumptions that the individual's problem revolves around their particular difference.

Transference

When considering transference with regard to cross-cultural counselling I would emphasise the point I made earlier: that of considering one's own training background. Be aware of the need to be careful not to assume or interpret the importance of certain relationships. For example in some cultures brothers and uncles, or the tribe, may have more significance to my client than the mother–child relationship I learned about in my training. They will also have different rites of passage from those with which I am familiar.

Nevertheless transference, as described in Chapter 5, could be important in transcultural counselling. The client might, for example, unconsciously associate the counsellor with other people in authority and powerful feelings can be evoked. Initially the counsellor may be on the receiving end of some of the hostility and resentment that has accumulated, say, a black client's negative experience in a predominantly white school, and it is important not to be defensive when hearing clients' anger.

Where there is deeply ingrained prejudice borne out of transgenerational attitudes, counsellors are more likely to experience negative transference. Where they are unaware of the basis for such differences or where they hold different views of the world from their clients they are more likely to project negative feelings onto their clients. Kareem (2000) points out that working with minority ethnic clients in this way is not only ineffective but can create mistrust of therapy and its practitioners. He also says that:

> I believe that it is the responsibility of the therapist, from the very outset, to facilitate the expression of any negative transference which is based on historical context, and not leave the onus on the patient. The patient may be too needy or too afraid and thus may not recognise the existence of negative feelings or may not consider them to be an immediate issue – indeed, he may consider them to be something perhaps to be denied in attempting a 'good relationship' ... it is a fundamental clinical issue which must be acknowledged and brought out into the open. This may be a difficult task but it is one that must be undertaken in order to facilitate therapy.   (Kareem, 2000)

Whilst some clients may have a 'negative' transference towards a white counsellor others may have coped with their racial difference by copying white behaviour and may actively choose a white therapist, believing they are better than a black therapist.

In terms of countertransference the therapist could become overly sympathetic with diverse clients and suppress any negative feelings they might have, thereby not offering themselves as 'real' or as effective as they would be with other clients.

Gender and Culture Matching

How important is it for clients to be ethnically matched for a successful therapeutic outcome? Is transcultural counselling possible? What are the advantages of culture and gender matching?

Clearly there is an argument for matching helper with client. Perhaps the subtleties of a particular religious, ethnic or sexual grouping can only be truly understood by someone from a similar background. 'Gender and culture matching between the helper and the person in need are desirable because the person in need seeks to relate at as many levels as possible to the person who is helping them' (Murgatroyd, 1985).

A black supervisee told me how her visible difference helped the process, but not just with black clients:

> Clients open up a lot quicker because they assume I have experienced difference ... it doesn't have to be a black client but any one who is of a minority. It is just that by being different people can relate to me ... they think I will understand.

This poses the question: to what extent does the client's ability to identify with the therapist's ethnicity and background make it easier for them to work together? Because of their past experience of racism and prejudice black clients often find it difficult to trust a white psychotherapist and so find self-disclosure difficult. Sue and Sue (1990) note 'that there are black people who are very anti white and are angry with them', which affects the process.

Then there is the other view which says that 'matching done purely on the basis of race or colour can imprison both the counsellor and the client in their own racial and cultural identity' (Limentani, 1986). Although this might be the client's preference, ethnically matching clients does not in any way ensure therapeutic success. Clearly there are barriers to be overcome but overall I consider therapeutic attitude and style to be more important.

Eleftheriadou (1994) suggests that existential or phenomenological analysis can transcend culture and gender because it delves deep into the basic beliefs and values of the client, as defined by the client, and examines the client's fundamental ideas and assumptions about human existence. In talking to people from different cultures and minority groups some felt that it was not a case of seeing a white counsellor as better but that they wished to be counselled by someone who could offer a different perspective. As one client said: 'I know what someone from my own background would say.' Others feared that counsellors from their own religious background would put pressure on them to conform and others in smaller communities had concerns about confidentiality. Anonymity seemed to be an important factor in allaying their perceived fears.

Case example: sense of shame

I recall the case of Saima, an Asian client, who was encountering marital and financial difficulties. She had arrived in the UK some 15 years before, following an arranged marriage. There was a sense of shame attached to asking for help and yet, isolated from her own family, she did not know where to turn. It was difficult for her to ask for help but she felt that she would not have been able to discuss her problems within the Asian community, which she described as very close knit and where she thought criticising her husband would be frowned upon. She spoke of how helpful racial difference had been to the counselling process.

Whatever one's views regarding matching client to counsellor, in practice cultural incongruities are often unavoidable and in the workplace choice may be limited because of resources and logistics. This does not mean that a client's preferences should not be invited, particularly when working with diversity or gender, as illustrated below:

Case example: 'Can I see a woman counsellor?'

A young woman wanted a transfer to another part of the organisation where she would have less travelling time. However, she had recently failed a promotion board and it was difficult for personnel to find her a position.

She seemed hesitant about taking the appointment offered by the male counsellor. However, she kept the appointment. She was diffident and came across as lacking in confidence. The counsellor sensed her unease, but after several sessions it became clear as she talked more that she was extremely scared when travelling home on her own. It emerged that she had been sexually assaulted whilst working a late shift and had been too frightened to tell anybody for fear they would not believe her.

Clearly sensitive handling is required but the male–female component to the therapeutic relationship is a vital element in such a case, adding an additional challenge – in this instance for the male counsellor. Once her real concern emerged it was possible for them to consider finding her a female counsellor if she would prefer that.

A final thought about culture matching. In the chapter 'The Role of Counselling at Work' I discussed the different ways counselling services are provided in organisations. I believe there are parallels to be drawn when considering the advantages and disadvantages of a client working with someone within their own work culture (an in-house counsellor) as opposed to a client working with someone outside their own organisational culture (an EAP provider). I wonder what you think?

Counselling involves the whole person, and includes both the client's differences and their similarities. Often the problems that are brought to the workplace counsellor are multi-factorial and one should not allow diversity or obvious 'difference' to obscure the overall picture. When I first meet a client two questions have always stood me in good stead: 'Who is this person?' and 'What are they trying to tell me?' These questions are equally valid when working with diversity as they help to focus on understanding the person and to avoid stereotyping. But remember, to return to an earlier point, the counsellor can only do that after they have answered the question: 'Who am I?'

Summary

Absorbing the organisation's anxieties surrounding political agendas and fear of legal implications can inhibit the counsellor's natural style and the negative impact of political correctness can lead to unhelpful overcompensation. Having acknowledged how diversity presents itself in the workplace and considered the counsellor's role and the impact on the counselling process I hope this chapter will go some way to supporting workplace counsellors.

To be effective when working with diversity counsellors need to show consideration and commitment to their clients by:

- becoming aware of their own cultural, racial, ethnic and training background;
- recognising its impact on them and how they might view others;
- being aware of their prejudices and assumptions;
- not categorising the presenting problem as 'a diversity issue', thereby missing what may lay beneath the surface;
- watching out for stereotyping and allow for individuality within any group;
- considering other possibilities than the presenting picture or presenting problem;
- acknowledging, valuing and respecting differences;
- acquiring knowledge of others' cultures, religions and lifestyle to minimise misinterpretation;
- being even more explicit about their own philosophy and therapeutic approach in the contracting stage;
- demonstrating genuine interest in the client's culture, background, rules and rituals;
- daring to say when they do not understand, by being open and enquiring of the client;
- being prepared for transference issues to emerge, even if not directly worked with.

I firmly believe the issues involved in diversity are worth addressing. In this chapter I have covered some of the major 'differences' one might encounter – race, sexuality, disability and religion – but this in no way negates the importance of all areas of difference. The common themes and principles which equally apply to other areas of diversity should be clear.

Part IV

Intervention Strategies

INTRODUCTION TO PART IV

Having considered how to 'manage the process' of counselling I would like to revisit some of the issues raised at the beginning of the book to enable the counsellor to view the organisation as the client and, furthermore, to consider interventions that can be made other than individual counselling.

For the most part, the issues raised in Parts II and III relate solely to the counsellor and their relationship with their client. This section of the book, 'Intervention Strategies', returns to the arena of the workplace to consider ways in which the counsellor can move beyond the dyad to a broader organisational role. The chapter on 'Intervention' (Chapter 7) will take a counselling approach to organisational development and change management. I will return to the psychological processes that occur in organisations to illustrate the opportunities that exist to make counselling interventions. Whilst the majority of Chapter 8, 'Particular Approaches', will focus on group facilitation, initially it will offer a brief description of five aspects of current interest to workplace practitioners.

By concluding the book with a chapter on practitioner development (Chapter 9) I seek to make clear the value I place on the importance of effective selection and on-going training. This final chapter covers the processes of the developing counsellor as they mature and practice with the benefit of the client in mind.

7

INTERVENTION

Introduction

The development of any organisation usually takes a long-range perspective. One advantage in adopting a counselling approach, compared with 'quick fix' or prescriptive methods, is that decisions reached by the organisation as a whole are more likely to produce long-term benefits, as they will reflect individual and collective views which encourage ownership for change.

As in photography, there are times when the camera can zoom in and focus on one particular aspect of a scene and others when it can move back in order to have a wider view of the overall picture. I hope this chapter will leave you in a better position to feel able to do both. Initially I will focus on the 'organisation as the client', including the opportunities that exist for intervention using a systemic approach. Then I shall address change management, its effects on individuals and the organisation as a whole, before finally considering defence mechanisms at an organisational level.

Listening to the organisation

Addressing the real issues of improving work relationships requires hard work and a willingness to change systems. Most business transactions involve the use of intellect to absorb facts, figures and logistics in order to make connections. However, relying solely on an intellectual approach to addressing people issues can, in fact, get in the way of effective management, for example with regard to relocation, as illustrated in Chapter 1.

Interventions first and foremost require listening to the organisation. A counselling approach requires the working through of information and not just the assimilation of facts. A shift is required from relying on a purely

171

intellectual approach to one which pays attention to the attitudes and emotions which lie beneath the surface, some of which are already half-known, often based on familial experience and people's basic assumptions about handling relationships.

Often when organisations have problems they turn to training or the use of external consultants. In general staff welcome personnel development programmes aimed at increasing their awareness and skills. If, however, staff return to a work situation where their roles and structures have not been modified, it will defeat the purpose of the training as it makes it impossible for them to act upon any new insights gained. Often they are met with the 'now you are back in the real world' or 'give him a week and he'll be back to normal' syndrome.

That is why intervening at all levels in an organisation is essential if the health and performance of the organisation is to be maintained or improved. A counselling approach has the potential to play a vital role in this process as it can enable organisations to face and deal with their problems at several levels in a systematic way. A variety of interventions, often involving group work, help people acknowledge the realities of the workplace and also to communicate directly. This has the potential to develop climates of trust which enable people to change and achieve corporate goals.

Opportunities for Intervention

French and Bell (1973) and others suggest that organisational interventions range from changing individuals to changing the whole organisation. Table 7.1 outlines the methods and potential gains of intervention at various levels.

Before considering workplace counsellor interventions I would like to give a brief outline of alternative approaches within which counselling might have a role to play.

Organisational development

Organisational development (OD) is a term that describes a group of approaches, theories and techniques which, like systems theories, tries to change and improve organisational performance. Frequently organisations have departments dedicated to organisational development or they may buy in consultancy services. Organisational development is primarily concerned with adaptation, awareness of culture and process, problem solving and

Table 7.1 Methods of intervention and potential gains

Levels	Method	Potential gain
Individual	One-to-one counselling	■ Eases dyadic and triadic relationships
Work group	Group facilitation	■ Improves group communication
	Educative seminars, team building, debriefings	■ Offers preventative information (e.g. handling conflict, addictions, stress management)
		■ Optimises team effectiveness
Dyads and triads	Counselling, mediation	■ Lowers tension between people
Inter-group/corporate	Conflict resolution	■ Atmosphere of group co-operation
	Provision of statistics	■ Improves motivation and performance
	Input into strategic planning and innovation	■ Minimises absenteeism and potential litigation

technical and human resources – terms which are familiar to any counsellor. Taking a counselling perspective, the stages are the same as with individual work, except that the process embraces the whole organisation. This can be a daunting and an extremely exciting prospect. What both methods have in common is that they are catalysts for change.

Intervention requires staff counselling teams to think strategically and believe that they can make a real difference by working with all levels of the organisation. It requires the translation of counselling skills into facilitation and consultancy skills. The workplace counsellor can make a significant contribution to organisational development; however, they must decide their primary focus as they cannot be all things to all people.

Total Quality Management

Total Quality Management (TQM) is a way of managing the whole organisation, which attempts to ensure customer satisfaction at every stage. It involves a long-term effort to orientate employees towards a process of continuous improvement – often known as 'quality circles' (Juran, 1999).

The emphasis is on preventing errors rather than identifying and correcting errors. By the very nature of their work, workplace counsellors have a key role to play as they can ensure effective communication between employees and management on a continuous basis and can identify areas for improvement.

Consultancy and advisory services

Internal and/or external counselling providers offer a consultancy and advisory service that assists in forming effective policy and helps change the organisational culture.

Advantages and disadvantages exist in both forms of provision. External consultants, for example, may offer relative detachment in perspective and affiliation and in so doing misjudge the nature and needs of the organisation or impose inappropriate methodologies or solutions. On the other hand, internal consultants are constrained by their place in the politics of the organisation and may be limited in their awareness of context and wider opportunities. Perhaps the best likelihood of success is collaboration between internal and external specialists, working in close partnership with senior management (Department of Trade and Industry, 1997).

Taking the initiative and becoming involved at an early stage can be preventative rather than reactive work, helping organisations thrive rather than survive: for example where recession is anticipated, offering an input into any business recovery plans; or where staff are considered to be at risk counsellors can submit ideas to minimise damage.

Meaningful statistics, with clear interpretation, is one of the most powerful tools that counselling services can produce in order to promote organisational change. It is about making the invisible visible. The in-house staff counsellor is well placed to do this, particularly when they are attached to local offices or have a designated 'patch' for which they are responsible. By providing information about trends – e.g. some branches may generate more than their fair share of staff turnover, sickness absence or grievances – incalculable sums of money can be saved. Naturally client confidentiality must be preserved. EAPs' feedback to the organisation tends to be more quantitative and is less likely to identify trends gained from local 'informal' knowledge unless they are involved in specific projects.

Education and training

As well as offering to educate staff about counselling and its benefits there are particular specialist areas – bereavement, stress management, bullying, diversity, discrimination or mental health – where workplace counsellors have knowledge and experience which can benefit the organisation. In partnership with training departments they can help staff develop interpersonal skills, vital for effective communication and colleague collaboration. Organisations can gain considerably by developing counselling skills in their managers. This would be an intervention in itself, enhancing relationships and ultimately affecting the quality of output.

The Organisation as a Client

Viewing the organisation as the client, the counsellor/facilitator encounters many issues which are similar to individual client work. It is just the numbers involved, the permutations of alliances and the scale of the intervention that can be daunting.

Time is always an important factor in counselling but where the organisation is 'the' client it takes on another dimension. Diaries come out: managing to make a date to suit all often reflects the degree of ambivalence or commitment. The release of staff in whatever role, particularly when under-resourced, can make proposals non-starters. It would be easy, therefore, to do nothing in the hope that difficult situations will pass. However, limited interventions at an early stage, say of conflict, not only prevent other detrimental situations arising, they also clear ways forward for improved working relationships.

When staff pressure levels are high it is quite usual to encounter a variety of manifestations of anxiety such as scepticism, denial, cynicism and even despair. These attitudes can temper people's willingness to challenge the culture, to take risks and adopt initiatives. Naturally this makes effective intervention more difficult, but not impossible.

In order to gain commitment people need to be offered a clear view of the gains that can come from facing change, addressing unresolved issues and moving forwards. Without the good will and time commitment to see the process through, time, energy and money will be wasted. It is pointless just going through the motions; all parties need to be committed. The workplace counsellor will require good contracting skills and a willingness to be flexible.

As with individual counselling a sequence of sessions clearly designated and uninterrupted is required to deal with communication and relationships issues. At the initial stage it is important not to prejudge or challenge any organisational defence system in operation. From the first contact until the process is complete, gaining trust with each individual and with each group at each level and at each stage is vital. Counsellors acting as facilitators need to take a curious stance, enquiring about the organisation's beliefs and behaviours and asking questions such as: What is it like for them to be in such a situation? How are they dealing with it currently? What pleases them about what they have done so far?

Intervening in this way enables those involved to begin to think about their own ideas, behaviour and ideal outcomes. It is important to be alert to special alliances or hidden agendas, unwritten rules, who matters to whom and how much, and shared understanding about how people should behave. The organisation's current operating context also needs to be taken into account. Gradually a picture emerges of the organisation and its culture.

Counselling interventions

The following are some instances where change will be involved: company mergers and acquisitions, restructuring, changing from a training culture to a learning culture, introduction of a 360-degree appraisal system, change in dress codes, a traumatic incident requiring evacuation, disputes and relocation.

Take the following specific examples where an individual in an organisational setting is experiencing difficulty. Consider the ways you could intervene.

- A junior member of staff watches a senior member of staff become volatile and notices the smell of alcohol.
- The department is moving several miles away due to a recent merger. You have picked up concerns regarding parking spaces, transport and inadequate staff facilities.
- A manager is experiencing stress because he cannot meet targets with a reduced number of staff.
- Yesterday a member of staff was unable to travel to work due to anxiety about the threat of terrorism. There have been several evacuation practices since 11 September 2001.
- A recently appointed Chief Executive has been put in charge of a merged company and will need to cut staff.

In each of these situations there are a variety of approaches which can assist the organisation. The workplace counsellor may ask: Who is the client and in what way should one offer help? Is it the individual member of staff who has sought help or have they been referred? Is it the work-group who require some form of facilitation because of changes experienced? Or is it two sections that need to improve their working relationships?

The staff counsellor is dealing with a complex set of boundaries in each of the above examples. Accountability and confidentiality have to be explicitly negotiated with each role and with each boundary. Clearly in the above examples there are several opportunities for intervention. It is important to be clear about what changes these individuals would like to make and how they interact with the organisation's business, its policy and its culture. One way of classifying them in organisational terms is to concentrate on the primary focus for change. What do you think each focus might be in the above scenarios?

Sometimes the client may seem to be a victim of an impossible organisational situation, or it could be that situation has more to do with the individual's own psychopathology. It is much more likely to be a combination of both these factors – as illustrated in the case of Dennis in Chapter 1. Alternatively, perhaps it is the organisation itself.

Counsellor development

A developmental workshop for staff counsellors entitled 'Upstream or Downstream Intervention' – the metaphor of a river – emerged to consider ways of intervening in organisations. A river, as you know, is subject to tides, it has ebbs and flows and sometimes it gets blocked.

Participants were invited to consider where most of their intervention took place, just how much influence they felt they had and what were the implications for intervening 'upstream' or 'downstream'? Some were happy 'to paddle their own canoe' offering an individual counselling service, others preferred to sit 'on the side of the bank' observing, pondering what to do, whilst others with heavy caseloads felt 'deluged' and swamped by the river, hardly having time to come up for air.

They began to wonder whether there was any connection between their current 'torrent' of work and the fact that generally they did not intervene further up the organisational river. They also realised that by operating 'downstream' they were picking up 'flotsam and jetsam' and the odd floating 'undefused mine'. Participants began to think about the benefits to the organisation of what they described as 'paddling upstream', while realising the extra energy that would be required. By taking a more proactive stance perhaps they could be even more useful to the organisation thus minimising the potential for debris and wreckage? They started to consider what influence they had and what it would mean for them personally to work in a different way.

Why should workplace counsellors become involved 'upstream' when it can be such hard work? Well, often they have the 'ear of staff' who confide their fears and anxieties to them and, by being proactive and anticipating problems, early solutions can be sought. In turn this minimises unnecessarily heavy workloads. Furthermore, treating the organisation as a client provides a good service.

In order to operate at this level workplace counsellors need to develop sufficient confidence in their ability to influence, initiate, attend and make contributions to important meetings. They may choose to give formal presentations, use questionnaires, and write articles and follow-up reports.

Exercise

- What are the current trends in your organisation?
- What opportunities do you think exist to intervene in your organisation?

A Systemic Approach

A systemic approach says that a change in one part of the system affects other parts. Although it is desirable to involve all parties it is worth noting that setting in motion a small change can be a catalyst for overall change in the system, whether that be in a family or in an organisation. Initially it is important to work at the level which is presented but also to question what the potential is for change at other levels of the system and what the gain is for the organisation as a whole. In his novel *Anna Karenina*, Leo Tolstoy wrote: 'All happy families resemble one another and each unhappy family is unhappy in its own way'. This is equally true of organisations. The task is to unite with 'the family' or 'the organisation' and to work together to produce a 'therapist–family' or 'facilitator–organisation' system through which change can occur.

General systems theory provides a framework for considering the family as a system, rather than merely a set of individuals. It focuses on *the* organisation rather than on causality; it considers the family as a living system and looks at its capacity to adapt. This approach can be applied usefully in organisational settings. The workplace counsellor, when acting as an independent facilitator in an organisation, is like the family therapist who goes into a family without any definition of its pathology or knowledge of what dysfunctional patterns there might be. Let us compare two situations: one taken from clinical experience in a family, and the other in an organisation.

> **Example 1: a truant in the family**
>
> The Smiths were referred with truanting Billy. It would have been all too easy to focus on Billy as 'the problem' and not remember that it was all three people who had presented as clients. One view might be that the parents' relationship did not appear sound and put the focus on them as the problem, not Billy.
>
> However, during the assessment stage it became clear that there were many significant events, illnesses and deaths, involving parents and grandparents going back over time. Using a family therapy systemic approach the therapists worked with all members of the family, including both sets of grandparents and all the siblings of the presenting trio.

Clearly many complex forces were acting on the different members of the family. Working in this way events and history could be challenged. In this case taboos in terms of behaviour in what one was 'allowed' to say were acted out and changed. In this particular example the taboo was talking about the loss of a child and, moreover, anger was not seen as healthy. By allowing these issues to surface the family learned that they could manage to communicate more directly with one another and thus the rules of the family system changed.

> **Example 2: the organisational 'family'**
>
> A public-sector organisation was restructuring, which involved major national changes. In one region, 'Romanshire', staff relationships were particularly tense and these issues had not been addressed. During a meeting a senior member of staff 'Mr A' erupted, behaving in an abusive, irrational and unacceptable manner towards another senior member of staff, 'Mr B'. Mutual colleagues were left 'shell-shocked' and although the Regional Director, not present at the time of the incident, took the situation seriously he was not known for his people skills and underestimated the causes of the outburst and its implications.
>
> Complaints were made to Head Office regarding staff relationships and senior management's subsequent handling of the situation. The Head of Personnel considered several options:
>
> ■ a disciplinary interview for Mr A;
> ■ transfer Mr A to another section;
> ■ transfer Mr B to another section.

In organisations often a stiff warning followed by 'moving the presenting problem' is seen as a solution. It is rather like admonishing 'truanting Billy' in the earlier example and then sending him away to stay with relatives or go to another school.

> This is exactly what happened in 'Romanshire' except only one of the people in the conflict was transferred, the person seen as 'the offending member of staff'. The problem did not go away. Staff relationships were at an all-time low, two key members of staff were off sick 'due to stress' and the quality of work was declining despite long working hours. The Head of Personnel thought again. The organisation, under pressure from the threat of industrial tribunals, was keen to address the situation and do all they could to maintain good staff relationships during the restructuring. It was at this point I was given the brief 'to develop effective communication in Romanshire'.
>
> By the time I began working with the affected team relationships had improved considerably. However the speed with which emotions resurfaced indicated a delicate equilibrium, which was easily affected by outside influence. The fire might have gone out (outwardly people had settled down) but the embers were still burning and smouldering underneath. Management was perceived as having handled the situation badly and the general view was that it was 'all a bit late', 'someone should have been brought in straight away'. The main message was 'let sleeping dogs lie' but, of course, sleeping dogs have a habit of waking up when you least expect them to.

The short-term intervention

> An initial contract was made with the Head of Personnel but it was crucial to gain commitment at a local level so that the 'critical incident' could be addressed quickly. It was essential to involve the key players and the stakeholders, which in this case were personnel, unions and senior management, if any practical solutions or recommendations evolving from the intervention were to be taken seriously.
>
> Thereafter a phased approach, involving interventions at all levels of the organisation, was adopted. Initially I was perceived as yet somebody else in a long line of managers sent in 'to sort Romanshire out' rather like a social worker entering a disruptive neighbourhood family.
>
> Confidential individual sessions, facilitated group seminars, intergroup meetings and mediation sessions were held to allow for any residual issues to surface and to re-establish trust. Where individuals

were experiencing particular distress additional face-to-face or telephone consultations were offered.

The aim was to facilitate a more open style of interaction thereby minimising opportunities for further defensive behaviour or miscommunica-
tion. At times this was not easy and as I worked with their fears I
encountered ambivalence and clear resistance to taking forward the
agreed process. Given their prior experiences of 'not being heard' in
the organisation and the infamous outburst in a group setting, this was
not surprising.

Although the intervention needed to respect individuals' views, it was
essential that future recommendations ultimately reflected views
expressed openly and discussed collectively. It was time to confront the
process and our relationship. Whilst emphasising continued commitment to helping them achieve their goals, it was made quite clear that
the responsibility for the way forward – and the method – was up to
them. They were offered a range of options including facilitated team
meetings and a seminar on managing change. Apprehension eased
when fears of being coerced through a preconceived process did not
happen. From that point on individuals were co-operative and much
was achieved. Individuals began to confront differences and working
relationships recovered well. There now existed a potential energy for
creative change which, if nurtured, could benefit the region and organisation as a whole. But could this be sustained?

The long-term challenge

Without minimising the seriousness of the initial incident, for many it
had been superseded by other concerns, mainly the degree of instability caused by further organisational restructuring, accompanied by a
consistent theme of living with the effects of uncertainty. Even when staff
are highly committed to the organisation, working collectively is not
easy during periods of protracted change. Patterns emerged at all levels of insufficient recognition and support during the restructuring.
These reoccurring themes were seen by many as a reflection of a much
wider organisational culture: one which was under pressure, task
driven and insufficiently people orientated. It had become clear that the
original incident could not be viewed in isolation. The limited intervention in Romanshire could equally apply to other regions and at a
national level.

Public and media criticism of this organisation was another factor
which, when combined with the current levels of internal anxiety caused
by cumulative change, impacted on staff morale at all grades. This

181

combination affected motivation, stress levels and ultimately interpersonal styles of behaviour. What became clear was that the whole organisation was experiencing a lack of external and internal recognition leading to collective low self-esteem.

The organisation as a whole could learn a great deal from the 'presenting problem' in 'Romanshire' but would there be a sustained commitment to time being set aside for interpersonal development, a task which hitherto had not been valued in the same way as strategic planning? Such an approach would require leadership from Head Office, regional and local management, combined with a shared commitment by all members of staff regardless of grade.

Change Management

'Change management' are two words guaranteed to produce stifled yawns from most and the need for conclusive answers from others. Much is written about how 'to manage it' as though 'it' were something very tangible. Change management really challenges managers to think about how they manage people, as well as systems and equipment, through an organisational change.

Change is about endings, transitions and new beginnings. It's about being able to say 'goodbye' to something old in order to say 'hello' to something new. Inevitably there is an element of loss as well as gain. The process of change requires acknowledgement, an understanding of the processes involved for individuals within an organisation and it also requires time for the change to be fully integrated. Many who have been involved in mergers and acquisitions would liken them to the eighteenth-century writer Dr Johnson's view of marriage, as 'the triumph of hope over experience'.

Attitudes and communication

People are managing change every day of their lives as they face personal and work challenges in the context of a rapidly changing world. If people can do this why is it then that many organisations facing change find it so difficult? Perhaps one of the clues to the answer is that generally people do not talk about the amount of change they have coped with in the past and are coping with in the present (and how that affects their attitude towards any anticipated changes). It could be that organisations would benefit from pooling people's experience of change, thereby adding to their shared knowledge of individuals' strengths and ultimately the organisation's resources.

Perhaps a contributory factor to any potential blockage to sharing information is people's attitude towards change, some of which may have been developed earlier in their lives. Messages such as 'old habits die hard', 'better the devil you know' or 'a change is as good as a rest' and 'a new broom sweeps clean' may be reinforced by the organisation's own message about change. Add to this the organisational communication norm and perhaps we can begin to see where some of the blockages originate and what needs to be addressed in order to release energies and facilitate change – as opposed to denying it or resisting it in dysfunctional ways.

The challenge of change

Each person will react uniquely to changed circumstances. Some people will look forward to it, even seek it, and find the lack of it quite frustrating and demotivating, whilst others are drawn towards the status quo and security. For some the challenge is coping with 'change' whilst for others the challenge is coping with 'no change'. The former perceive it as a threat and resist it, whilst the latter perceive change as exciting.

Successful change involves a shift from the known to the unknown, from security to adventure, involving flexibility rather than rigidity and expression as opposed to repression. However, change is often experienced as an ordeal – something to be survived – and therefore resistance to change in some form is inevitable. As much energy can go into resisting change and repressing concerns as can go into facing change. The degree of resistance will affect how long the change(s) take. The challenge for an organisation is to minimise dysfunctional resistance and release creative energy.

> **Exercise**
> ■ Think of two changes you have made in your work and personal life during the past three years.
> ■ How have they affected you? What helped you? What hindered your progress through the changes?

One of the challenges of uncertainty is being able to live without being immobilised by its effects. Clearly the sense of isolation and social withdrawal that can occur in an organisation during a period of protracted uncertainty will affect staff's ability to communicate and their motivation towards their work. The use of counselling forums can be an extremely effective way to air tensions and release energy that would otherwise be redirected into dysfunctional personal or organisational behaviour. This is where the counsellor in the organisation can be 'an agent of change'.

The key factor is to release any blockages of energy which prevent knowledge and skills being fully utilised. Acknowledging difficulties and expressing emotions leads to hope and ideas for the future which can lead to smoother transitions. As with individuals it takes time for change in organisations to be fully internalised and incorporated. Where short cuts are taken there are hidden costs to be met.

Rosabeth Moss Kanter (1992) provides ten rules for stifling organisational change.

---

1 Regard new ideas from below with suspicion because they are from below.
2 Insist that people who need approval to act go through several levels to get signatures for action.
3 Ask departments or individuals to challenge and criticise each other's proposals. Pick the survivor.
4 Treat identification of problems as signs of failure.
5 Express criticism freely and withhold praise.
6 Control everything carefully.
7 Make decisions to reorganise or change policies in secret and spring these on people unexpectedly.
8 Make sure that requests for information are justified and make sure it is not given out to the manager freely.
9 Assign to lower-level managers, in the name of delegation and participation, responsibility for figuring out how to cut back, lay off, move people around, or otherwise implement threatening decisions. Get them to do it quickly.
10 Never forget that the higher-ups know everything there is to know.

Addressing change constructively requires senior management to recognise and understand the processes involved. Without an overt commitment from top management to introduce change management programmes they are less likely to succeed (Majoro, 1988). Policies incorporating strategies for facilitating change at a personal level create a climate where direct and open communication is possible. Where such a culture exists people feel safer to 'speak out' and meetings are not just 'time-serving' exercises.

Consultation has real meaning and recommendations are actually implemented. Perhaps policies could ensure that 'rituals' are included to help people acknowledge endings, speed the transition period and welcome new beginnings.

Individual reactions

It is important to recognise the individual within an organisation and the individual differences in response to announced changes. Adams et al. (1976) show the relationship between life transitions and self-esteem using a seven-stage model. The initial stage is one of immobilisation; followed by minimisation of the implications, then a 'downward curve' of depression and acceptance before climbing upwards through the final three stages of testing out new ways, searching for meaning and internalisation – phases which are familiar to those who experience a loss or bereavement.

In considering how to counsel those involved, factors to consider are whether the change is sought or imposed and what might be the individual's experience of change. Also consider the number of changes experienced prior to the current or envisaged change, the importance of this particular change, the significance of work in the individual's life and the current environmental support and opportunities available to them.

Example: a secure base

Shortly after the terrorist attack on the World Trade Center on 11 September 2001 an airline pilot sought the help of an EAP counsellor. He listed three incidents in his personal life during the preceding five years: the loss of a child, witnessing an automobile accident and protracted legal proceedings which had just been resolved in his favour. 'I am still feeling anxious and yet I don't know why,' said the client.

The counsellor was surprised that in his list of concerns he had not included the current pressures regarding his personal physical and psychological safety, given the nature of his work and job security. He did not mention them at all. The counsellor thought to himself, 'he keeps talking about his personal issues and yet this man is an airline pilot with a major airline and he doesn't even mention it. How long do I keep quiet?'

Often in a first session areas not mentioned or skated over can be, at an unconscious level, those that worry the client most. Whilst the counsellor did not want to minimise the client's personal life pressures, he wondered what it was like to be working in an organisation that was

---

185

> under threat from terrorist attack and where, by default, redundancies were already having an impact. Knowing that cut-backs had been already announced, the counsellor lightly enquired about the current work climate and how this affected him. 'I am fine, I am still in control.' The client had been managing multiple problems in his personal life, but what he had not mentioned was that his 'secure base', his work, the area of his life where he usually felt 'in control', was now clearly under threat. This seemed to tip the balance in terms of the client managing his anxiety levels, although he attributed the cause for his anxiety purely to his personal circumstances.

A secure base is crucial for human beings to learn, understand and develop their full potential.

> Familial security in the early stages is of a dependent type and forms a basis, from which the individual can work out gradually, forming new skills and interests in other fields. Where familial security is lacking the individual is handicapped by the lack of what might be called a secure base from which to work.   (Salter, 1940: 45)

The term 'secure base' in this instance is used to highlight the importance of the relationship between the individual and the organisation. Where instability exists it is likely not only to have a detrimental effect on the individual but also on the organisation's ability to develop and grow. It is important when working in organisations to recognise that managers too, at all levels, are undergoing change themselves and they too will have their own attitudes, preconceptions and feelings about the experience of past, current and anticipated changes. In order to help others in the organisation individuals need to put on their own life-jackets and recognise their personal experiences of change and their inner resources.

Stages of Individual and Organisational Change

The following models evolved out of a series of 'managing change' programmes carried out in three large organisations over a two-year period. They can be used in a variety of other situations. Table 7.2 offers an overview of organisational change, Table 7.3 looks at change interventions, and Table 7.4 focuses on skills.

Table 7.2 Overview of organisational change

Stages	Experience and perceptions	Emotions and behaviour experienced	Organisational structure/culture
Shock	Threat to existing structure, perceived as overwhelming 'This can't be!'	Panic, helplessness, high anxiety	Disorganisation; inability to plan, reason or understand the situation; often high level of activity and control
Defensive retreat	Attempt to maintain old structure Avoidance of reality, wishful thinking: 'Why?' 'Never mind, perhaps …' 'They should have …' 'Heard it all before'	Euphoria, relief, anger (fight/flight) joking, sarcasm, rationalisation, dreaming, blaming Absenteeism increases Sabotage of ideas and deadlines not met Increase in petty crimes	Defensive reorganisation; resistance to change; rigid positions taken, revival of 'old' ideas, practices and friends; lack of open communication, and an increase in indirect communication, subgroups form; an air of hostility and tension exists; alternatively uneasy bonhomie; blaming (employer, government) 'Us and Them'; withholding information

Table 7.2 *Continued*

Stages	Experience and perceptions	Emotions and behaviour experienced	Organisational structure/culture
Acknowledgement	Giving up existing structure and facing reality 'I should have …' 'If only …' 'Not worth it'	Depression, bitterness, guilt, self-doubt, despair, stress, low energy Lack of motivation to start or complete projects Poor decision making, time keeping and attendance Increase in sickness; decrease in ideas being put forward	Defensive breakdown: ■ Disorganisation; ■ Reorganisation in terms of altered reality
Adaptation and change	Establishing new structure, sense of worth. New reality testing, optimism, more energy 'Let's try …' 'Why don't we …'	Letting go; increase in satisfying abilities, experiences.	Reorganisation in terms of present resources and productivity improves; new projects are completed, new norms established; increase in creative energy, commitment and direct communication

Table 7.3 Organisational change interventions

Stages	Interventions
Policy making	■ Consultation at all levels ■ Consider human issues and number of changes involved ■ Identify key staff, training needs and budgets ■ Design communication channels, timing etc. ■ **Allow time to plan for future adjustments**
Announcement	■ Create good communicational environment ■ Set up a framework for discussion ■ Ensure accurate information available ■ Make clear the access and route to information ■ Clarify expectations of individuals ■ **Explain purpose, vision and gains of the change**
Shock	■ Be prepared to repeat announcements ■ Ensure congruency in messages ■ Minimise opportunities for distortions ■ Implement framework for discussions throughout the change process ■ **Exchange information as required**
Defensive retreat	■ Actively encourage discussion forums ■ Allow for ventilation of feelings ■ Encourage constructive criticism ■ Ensure support systems for key staff ■ Ensure education and training regarding the effects of change ■ Listen for ideas that can be incorporated ■ **Avoid secret decisions and excess control**
Acknowledgement	■ Make time to address all concerns ■ Do not minimise the effects of loss issues ■ Ensure practical programmes for stress management ■ Communicate through all levels ■ Share responsibility for implementation of policy – and any adjustments required ■ Invite ideas for realistic changes ■ **Allow for individual differences in staff**
Adaptation and change	■ Continue communication channels ■ Update all on progress and gains made ■ Allow for risk taking ■ Support new initiatives ■ **Encourage review of the change(s)**

Table 7.4 Preparation and skills for organisational change

Stages	Organisational skills
Policy making	■ Influencing skills ■ **Be open to new ideas and initiatives**
Announcement	■ Self-preparation – clarify own role ■ Awareness of individual reactions ■ Holding meetings for information flow ■ Breaking good/bad news ■ **Clarifying skills – minimise ambiguity**
Shock	■ Time management ■ Availability to staff ■ Active listening ■ Non-judgemental acknowledgement ■ Strategic planning – be aware of own stress level and put in place support systems ■ **Clear, unambiguous communication**
Defensive retreat	■ Skills as in previous stage ■ Facilitating open discussions ■ Listening for underlying concerns ■ Encouraging tensions to be aired ■ Distribution and exchange of information ■ Handling conflict issues ■ Care without colluding ■ Management of own stress levels ■ **Demonstrate respect for people**
Acknowledgement	■ Identification and acknowledgement of loss issues ■ Encouragement of expression of feelings ■ Exploration of individuals' attitudes to change ■ Recognition of number of changes ■ Assessment of potential risk factor ■ Balancing of individual and organisational needs, losses and gains ■ Demonstration of genuine interest ■ Practical help, e.g. time off ■ Recognition of strengths and efforts made ■ Knowledge of referral sources ■ Counselling skill – individual/group ■ **Acknowledge – don't trivialise**
Adaptation and change	■ Implementation of emerging ideas ■ Creative thinking and action planning ■ Encouragement of shift from insular to wider views ■ Support for risk taking and new initiatives ■ Review of achievements and praise ■ **Remember change takes time**

Exercise
- What are the effects on staff of the current changes in your organisation?
- How are they being expressed?
- In what way could counselling be used to assist the process?

Defence Mechanisms in Organisations

Any change brings a degree of uncertainty, which can be frightening even when it is something we actually desire. When embarking on a much dreamed-about holiday we may feel a degree of trepidation – something might go wrong and spoil the anticipated pleasure. In unwelcome situations where imposed threats exist, such as redundancy or relocation, people usually experience a loss of control and often believe it is unacceptable to express their feelings of uncertainty or anxiety.

Anxiety is personal and subjective. What evokes anxiety in one person, for example speaking at a meeting, might be a welcome challenge to another. However, in its acute form it can literally 'paralyse' individuals, groups of people and even organisations. Objective anxiety is that which is caused by an external or real threat, e.g. competing markets, mergers and currency fluctuations. Neurotic anxiety arises from within, possibly due to past experiences in the organisation.

If anxiety levels are not too high, adequate support mechanisms are in place and there are favourable environmental factors, then some realistic action is sufficient to deal with any 'perceived' threat. However, where stresses are excessive and insoluble the anxiety state may persist and become too much to bear. Equilibrium is now threatened and symptoms are liable to develop, manifesting themselves in illness. Individuals and or organisations are no longer able to function in a normal healthy way. In the short term with good support they (the individual or the organisation) can cope, but over long periods something usually gives.

It is not always easy at first to pinpoint the source of the anxiety as organisations are complex and anxiety can appear diffuse. When anxiety becomes overwhelming defence mechanisms come into play. Resorting to defensive behaviour means that organisations have less energy available to face reality such as changing markets, customer and employee concerns, cash flow and new business. If defences can be modified, abandoned, or

191

replaced with better adaptations then the health and performance of the organisation will improve.

Corporate-level anxiety

By now you should be able to recognise the defence mechanisms displayed by clients, as outlined in previous chapters, but how do they manifest themselves at group and organisational levels? An organisation threatened with survival because of outside factors such as recession may adopt a 'fight' or a 'flight' stance. For instance it may fight and project its anxiety onto an external source – competing companies or the government of the day. In this way the organisation rids itself of its anxiety and is given 'external' permission to treat people in certain ways, for example: 'We're going to blast the competition out of the water.' Or perhaps they will decide to shut up shop and get out of the market place, a form of external flight, saying: 'We've decided to sell/merge and unfortunately that means cutting jobs.' Corporate defence mechanisms come into play when internal organisational factors give rise to anxiety. Internally these anxieties may manifest themselves in the following patterns of organisational behaviour: fight, flight, dependency, wishful thinking, structured anxiety or alienation.

Fight–anger

Fight–anger cultures can develop internally with one division fighting against another. An 'us and them' blame culture develops with scapegoating of individuals or sections and the general blaming or bullying of others.

Flight–depression

Flight–depression cultures manifest themselves in withdrawal and apathy with people feeling isolated and noticeably not bothering to put forward ideas or challenge. Minimal interaction is observed in the workplace, where ideas are no longer put forward and there is a lack of creativity and effective corporate strategies.

Dependency

A dependent culture is recognised by a sense of powerlessness, with the underlying assumption that 'they', senior management, have all the power.

If the Chief Executive colludes in thinking she or he alone can put things right then the organisation is heading for trouble.

Wishful thinking

And then there is the 'after election' defence mechanism, one of wishful thinking where staff hope that some magical occurrence will transpire. All will be well once the new computer system is installed or when the new Chief Executive arrives.

Structured anxiety

Anxiety can manifest itself in the way the organisation is actually structured, as demonstrated in a famous study by Menzies (1959) of a nursing service in a London teaching hospital. She found that the organisation of the work itself became fragmented in the face of powerful emotions evoked by the work with patients, relatives and colleagues. Nurses looked after the patients 'indiscriminately' rather than allowing themselves to have any intimate or lengthy contact with an individual patient which might have exposed them to these powerful forces. Menzies (1991) suggests that among the needs that people have of institutions is their use as a defence against anxiety. If this is so, how do other organisations structure themselves to deal with pressurised situations? For example, to what extent does an organisation's structure relate to its staff who face hostility and abuse on a daily basis?

Alienation

Where powerful and primitive anxieties in an organisation exist, such as a deep sense of alienation or depersonalisation, one way of dealing with the situation is to externalise the source of the anxiety by using a 'palliative' approach – suggesting tangible solutions such as flexible hours, free tea and coffee or more holidays. Bain (1982) suggests this is an attempt to make life more bearable as opposed to addressing the root cause which is the organisation itself.

Working with bewildered organisations

I wish I could say this was easy work but in my experience it was not (although it was certainly challenging and often rewarding). Initially one needs to recognise and understand the particular defence mechanisms in operation and then there needs to be a recognition that despite the conscious desire for change there is an unconscious desire to avoid change and that sometimes an impasse will develop. Unravelling the deeper emotional features of 'resistance' and 'vested interest' is a familiar theme in organisational literature (Fineman, 1993).

It was Bion (1961) who brought our attention to the fact that groups work at two levels: the conscious level of the work-group and the unconscious level of the 'basic assumptions' group. It is the forces of the latter, originating from the unconscious world of the group, which is a powerful influence on how the group functions. After all, its purpose is to survive at all costs.

One of the key differences for workplace counsellors when working with groups is that one is potentially on the receiving end of projection and introjection. That is why co-working can be so helpful. It is only fair to alert you to the fact that when groups are faced with high levels of anxieties the facilitator can be the recipient of massive projections. I have experienced this and found it initially distressing and often perplexing, which is where my own supervision was so crucial. It seems to me that counsellors can become victims of organisational dynamics long before they realise that they exist. If they are to be effective in any professional sense it is important not to be sucked in or to collude with pressure or bad practice that compromise value systems. By maintaining boundaries and professional practice counsellors are not always going to be particularly popular and are in danger of becoming the 'scapegoat' of the organisation. Here lies the paradox because the pressure can be so great to 'toe the line' that in the end the client whom they wish to serve well, is let down because of 'mission impossible'.

Example: mission impossible

I was invited to run a seminar at a Counselling Service's conference. The branch had just undergone an internal efficiency review and they were seeking to improve their caseload and personal management. The organisation was known to have particularly high stress levels. Initially the brief was manageable, the time-slot realistic and the objective clear. Yet week by week the expectations increased, whilst the time-slot allocated to me dwindled and the outcome seemed less likely to succeed.

I arrived at the conference at a point when they were completing a day-and-a-half's exercise conducted by the organisation's 'Quality and Development Team'. I could see that it was nowhere near finished and

---

certainly not processed. What I witnessed was a pattern of communication where people were diminished, scapegoated or their views ignored. You could cut the air with a knife. Clearly there was much unfinished business to be addressed.

The conference went to lunch and I was most concerned about what could realistically be achieved in the afternoon session. On reflection perhaps I should have left there and then, but having spoken to many of the delegates over lunch it was agreed that we could use the situation creatively. Ever the optimist and 'seduced' by their trust in me, I began the session. I saw it as a perfect opportunity to illustrate creative change.

Choice point – how to proceed? The group had not succeeded in their previous task, their anxiety level was high and they certainly weren't listening to one another. I took the view that they would be unable to listen to me until they could 'offload' a little and so I quickly acknowledged the situation and offered people opportunities to talk before moving on to tackle 'the agreed task'. This went well but in the light of the previous events the pressure for them to experience some success meant that my brief to improve their personal management took on even more importance. Not only did they need practical help in managing their increasing caseloads, but now they also wished to deal with their own stress. It felt as though my session was to be 'the cure-all' for their overall situation. All of this was to be accomplished in a shortened afternoon! I, like them, was being asked to do more with less time available. Mission impossible.

Whatever I said did not seem to satisfy their need and I was left feeling devalued, deskilled and cross. When I could not ease their 'distress' and give them the miracle answer for which they yearned their disappointment and frustration was tangible. I was left feeling 'bad' and 'not good enough'. As hard as I tried, I felt I could not help them in the time allotted. The participants had also been left feeling 'bad' and 'not good enough' by the efficiency review and angry with the uncompleted previous exercise. So was I – a reflection of how the Branch was feeling, individually and collectively. It perfectly mirrored the dilemma the Branch was facing – a 'no win' situation. They felt damned if they did and damned if they didn't.

In this illustration the counselling service was unable to satisfy the unrealistic needs of the organisation and felt unable to state that clearly and say 'no'. Because they had just been reviewed they kept trying harder and harder. I got caught up in the dynamics but when I finally did say 'no' the Branch acted out the organisation's disappointment and vented their fury, albeit politely. I was a mirror image of their position within the organisation, but I was not quick enough to spot that I was getting caught up in the dynamics – if I had I could have been more helpful to the organisation by saying 'no' earlier on in the process. It was easier for them to place their dissatisfaction at the door of the external consultant and make them the 'bad object' – a strong projection which I had to contain until they were in a position for me to put it back to them. This can only be done when one has an ongoing remit with the organisation. In this illustration I believe it was important for the counselling service not to succumb to the pressure and become a casualty of the organisation's anxiety or fall prey to its collective projections. Using one's own self awareness' it can be helpful to say something like: 'I wonder if you and your team might at times feel unappreciated and undervalued, reflecting how your employees in the organisation might be feeling?' or 'Does it feel as though you can never say "no" to a request, that you take on more and more with unrealistic time schedules?' Naming what is happening in an organisation can be a huge relief but can only be done once one has 'caught hold' of the dynamics and has an opportunity to reflect it back to them. A one-off session where there are massive projections rarely gives you such an opportunity.

In this example there was so much talent, ability and energy waiting to be utilised by the counselling service team but its members were really struggling. They, like all the staff in the organisation, were under scrutiny and pressure with an increasing sickness absence record. It was vital that direct, honest and non-destructive communication be revitalised within the service if history was not to repeat itself.

Exercise

■ Think of examples of how defence mechanisms manifest themselves in your organisation.

In practice it helps to start at the level at which the client organisation presents, with counsellors asking themselves: Where is this organisation investing its energy? Is it in thinking, feeling or doing? For example, is it a task-orientated organisation obsessed with a compulsive search for more systems, more accuracy, more efficiency and more expertise? In such cases counsellors can end up as yet another 'system' that does not work. Is it an organisation which spends its energy issuing policy documents one after another? Or it is an organisation preoccupied with how it is feeling? It could, of course, be a 'depressed' organisation; one that has difficulty allowing itself to feel good about its achievements. It might just be an organisation that is undergoing the process of yet another change.

Summary

This chapter has considered the various processes that occur when viewing the organisation as 'the client'. Using a systemic approach, illustrated by case studies, it shows that many opportunities exist where a counselling approach can be incorporated into organisational interventions.

Just as with individual work, the first stage of systemic intervention with the organisation is assessment. Taking a psychodynamic perspective, there are other parallels with individual work including transference (see Chapter 5). The hidden forces of resistance often lie deep within the unconscious of the organisation's world and I have found that one ignores them at one's own peril.

Not every counsellor will feel comfortable or equipped to work in the ways described in this chapter but working with the whole organisation does offer counsellors opportunities to maximise their strengths and use of their time. It also shows the value of becoming involved with interventions other than counselling, such as education and training.

8
Particular Approaches

Introduction

This chapter will focus on six particular aspects of intervention: short-term therapy, mediation, telephone counselling, critical incident debriefing, co-working and group facilitation. I shall offer only a brief overview of the first five approaches, although ideally each could be a chapter in its own right. Interested readers are encouraged to seek further sources of information to gain a more thorough understanding of each approach. A more detailed account of group facilitation will follow, partly because of my own commitment to the value of groups, but mainly because workplace counsellors are increasingly finding themselves being asked to work in group settings.

Short-term Therapy

Over the past 17 years short-term therapies have been amongst the most rapidly expanding areas of growth within psychotherapy and counselling. As yet there is no exact definition as to what constitutes short-term therapy. Approaches use a variety of theoretical orientations, none of which automatically lead to a reduction in the number of sessions.

Today the number of organisations that would support long-term non-directive counselling is in rapid decline. With a growing need for psychotherapeutic services, combined with increased demands by government and insurers for accountability, there is a need for cost containment. Fuelled by downsizing and lack of funding there is an upsurge in client work, often accompanied by a reduction of resources. An attempt to find a solution to all of the pressures and constraints facing counselling services can lead to an almost desperate wish for a short-term 'quick fix' and the search for an approach or a technique which will answer the needs of all.

Perhaps these factors account for the renewed interest in short-term therapeutic methods and the rise in popularity of directive, problem-focused and brief therapies. The 'motorway route' can seem most attractive. It appears that it will get the workplace counsellor and the client to their destination more quickly even though the slower or 'scenic routes' might offer more interesting views and options. Being required to do more with less requires a re-examination of current working practices to ensure that all is being done to manage clients in a professional manner

Characteristics of short-term therapies

Butcher and Koss (1994) report that structured, time-limited intervention can be as effective as less structured, open-ended intervention. They outline common characteristics across approaches:

- limitation of therapeutic goals;
- directive management of the sessions by the therapist – therapist is active;
- centring the therapeutic content in the present;
- rapid early assessment;
- promptness of intervention;
- flexibility on the part of the therapist;
- ventilation or catharsis as an important element in the process;
- a quickly established interpersonal relationship to obtain therapeutic leverage;
- appropriate selection of clients, since not all clients can profit from a brief therapeutic contact;
- therapeutic management of limitations.

Time-limited Counselling

Rather than continue with the debate about definitions of short-term therapy it might be more helpful, within workplace counselling, to acquire the skills involved in working with clients on a time-limited basis, for instance clear contracting and focal techniques which help clients stay with central issues. This could then be seen as time-limited counselling (TLC) regardless of theoretical orientation. Counsellors will need to help clients focus on what issues are most prominent for them and be realistic about what can actually be achieved in the time given.

TLC offers a pre-arranged, non-negotiable number of sessions. When distress and tension impair clients' usual coping mechanisms, short-term contracts can provide support whilst the client mobilises his or her own coping capacities. As an approach it can be extremely helpful for those reacting to a crisis, e.g. bereavement, job loss, divorce or a particular work difficulty. Worden (1992) provides a practical approach to grief counselling which could be used alongside TLC.

A more general application of TLC is when staff return to work after a period of long-term sick absence. The workplace counsellor, in conjunction with line managers, can help employees, particularly those severely affected emotionally or coping with a mental illness, to adjust to the workplace again. A time-limited contract would not only seem appropriate but would also comply with the Disability Discrimination Act 1995. There are several advantages to using this approach. For some clients the conscious understanding that the work will be short-term can reduce their anxieties concerning potential dependency, thus enabling them to enter a therapeutic process. Others may feel more in control because they know exactly how long the counselling will last and this can assist them in focusing on their chosen goals. From the counsellor's point of view, where the motivation or ability for change is minimal then this becomes apparent quite quickly and this is helpful in managing caseloads and apportioning time constructively.

Nevertheless some clients will experience time-limited counselling as frustrating and disappointing. Having had access to the therapeutic process they become more aware of related connections to their presenting situation only to find the opportunities for working these through limited and resolution beyond their grasp. If time-limited counselling is an organisational method of working then the number of sessions allowed may be just the beginning of a referral process or the counsellor may need to renegotiate with their counselling manager or EAP manager to increase the number of sessions the organisation is prepared to offer.

Brief therapy

Brief therapy is a term used increasingly, around which there are misconceptions. Firstly there is the belief that there is one particular theoretical approach to brief therapy, secondly that 'brief' automatically means 'short' and thirdly that brief therapy and time-limited therapy are one and the same. Brief therapy, traditionally, refers to a limit in the focus (focal therapy) whereas time-limited refers to a limited time contract. Malan (1975) suggests that the three main differences in brief therapies are:

- that they have a limited aim which the patient is made to understand from the beginning;
- that the number of sessions is limited;
- that the techniques used are 'focal'.

'Focal' means that the counsellor is responsible for keeping in mind the aim and focus and bringing the focus back to the presenting problem. Long-term therapy is about intervention, treatment and reconstruction with no set period and number of sessions. Brief therapy, as described above, is similar in that it has no prefixed number of sessions but the end is determined by the extent to which the *focus* is satisfactorily addressed. (For further information see Dryden and Feltham, 1999.)

Solution-focused brief therapy

Solution-focused brief therapy (SFBT) is another approach that lends itself to time-limited counselling. Incorporating techniques based on the principles of systemic family therapy, the key characteristic of solution-focused therapy is the primary focus on the development of solutions rather than the exploration of problems (De Shazer, 1984). Contracting is much freer and less formalised, and there is less emphasis on history taking, exploration and understanding.

In a solution-focused interview there is minimal focus on problems and problem-free and solution talk is encouraged wherever possible. Techniques such as the use of the 'miracle question', 'problem-free talk' and 'exception finding' (George, 1990) are used to describe systematic goal setting and action planning, which are used frequently in cognitive and behavioural work.

Suitability of short-term therapies

Whether planned short-term interventions offer a more effective practice strategy than less structured, open-ended approaches to intervention in part depends on the nature of the problems and the objectives of intervention. Ideally the appropriate method will depend on the nature of the client's particular problem and the counsellor's assessment, but as discussed earlier there are external influences which can mean that in reality the counsellor has less choice than they would wish.

Short-term therapy should not be seen as an expedient counselling approach but used skilfully where and when it is appropriate. It is not suitable for all situations: for example, an adult survivor of sexual abuse may have a well-established and justifiable need to protect themself from intimate relationships. Sensitivity is required not to further 'abuse' the client's psychological space and it may take many sessions for such a client to feel safe enough to address their experiences. Treatment can be a long and complex process more suited to long-term therapy (Sanderson, 1991), as are clients suffering from alcohol or substance abuse.

This emphasises the importance of skilled assessment in the first session. If the case material is not suitable for TLC or SFBT then it is far better for the counsellor to be clear right at the outset about why they may not be able to take on the case. Setting clear boundaries is essential to counselling adult survivors of sexual abuse as they have a history of having boundaries violated. Obviously this requires sensitive handling and can be hard for the counsellor who would like to offer more but is unable to because of their contract with their employer. Perhaps saying something like: 'Given what you have told me today, you deserve more time to explore your situation than I am able to offer you ... what I can do, however, is to work together with you to find an appropriate form of counselling ...'.

Mediation

Mediation is a form of settling disputes without going to court and is increasingly seen as an alternative to costly litigation. Mediation can be offered internally in an organisation so long as it does not affect any subsequent legal action. Mediation agreements are binding in law. Seeking external mediation is another option, in the form of an independent organisation such as Advisory Conciliation and Arbitration Service (ACAS) or for public sector employees the Civil Service Ombudsman.

There has been considerable interest shown in recent years in mediation and its role in the workplace. Counsellors are well placed to mediate as long as they remain impartial. They may be asked to deal with grievances and harassment or help resolve conflicts between colleagues such as personality clashes and interpersonal rivalries. They can facilitate meetings between line management, personnel and employees to help resolve situations to the benefit of all concerned.

I would stress that mediation is not counselling, neither is it liaison work. Mediators do not make decision ; they are there to facilitate agreements and look to the future. If counsellors offer mediation it is essential that clear definitions and confidentiality boundaries are offered and understood. Those interested will need to feel comfortable working with more than one person and develop the necessary techniques. These deserve more elaboration than space permits in this book. Mediation is about compromise over conflict but it is not always possible to reach a positive outcome. Where this is the case then the task is about helping the parties acknowledge this and behave in a civilised manner.

Telephone Counselling

Along with the recent growth of the help-line industry there appears to be a shift towards telephone counselling as opposed to face-to-face work. It is particularly favoured by EAP programmes in the UK and yet American EAPs, many of whom have been in existence for far longer, have not found supporting evidence that telephone counselling is particularly effective. Telephone counselling deserves mentioning in the context of workplace counselling as sometimes practicalities mean that a face-to-face counselling session is not immediately possible. This may be because a counsellor is not available straight away in an urgent situation and could instead provide a 'holding' call. Telephone counselling could also be useful if the client has mobility difficulties or the client is geographically too distant from the counselling service.

Concerns and techniques

In terms of assessment and contracting telephone counselling involves similar processes to face-to-face work, but it has its limitations and requires the counsellor to make adaptations. Counselling over the telephone is different because both parties are denied visual information and need to rely mainly on voice contact and the information supplied by the client. This is particularly relevant to short-term counselling where the objective is to do a limited piece of casework, referring to a more appropriate service where necessary. The lack of face-to-face contact limits the assessment stage; therefore, it is less appropriate to use this method when only a limited number of sessions are available as it relies heavily on the client's self-diagnosis. Counsellors working in this way have often expressed concerns, such as whether they will be able to relate to a client over the telephone or knowing whether or not the client is crying.

The judgement of when to break a silence when using telephone counselling is more difficult because there is no visual information upon which to rely. If one is not sure whether or not it is a 'working silence' then taking a risk and saying something like: 'I'm wondering what is happening for you at the moment ... .' can ease the tension and clarify the situation. When working with a distressed client over the telephone it is useful to help the client verbalise other sources of help and to elicit whom they might speak to after they have finished talking with the person on the telephone.

When a counsellor is working with a client in this way it is still important to maintain time and appointment boundaries. For example when working over the telephone with a very distressed client, the counsellor could still alert the client to the fact that the time is approaching when they will need to bring the conversation to a close and subsequently signalling that perhaps it would be a good idea to talk in a day or two. One final point: note taking is less of a distraction when working over the telephone.

Points to consider when counselling over the telephone are:

No face-to-face contact	Some clients prefer speaking using the telephone. However, you may want to consider whether the client is using it as an avoidance strategy. Clients may feel more empowered in this way as they have a higher level of control. For example it is easier to just hang up than to walk out of the counselling room.
Cost	Clients may be concerned about the cost and the counsellor could offer to call the client back.
Voice	Tone of voice is very important, as is accurate listening to pick up messages client is trying to get across. Counsellor must convey a caring attitude to the client without the ability to smile or nod to convey empathy.
Issues	The counsellor can feel 'captive' to the telephone. Time management on the telephone requires skilled work.
Skills	Excluding the skills of visual observation and touch, all other counselling skills are relevant. Don't be afraid of silences. Use reflections and regular summaries to keep on track.

For further information on counselling by telephone see Rosenfield (1997).

New developments: E-listening

The day of cyber-counselling has arrived. Text-based counselling over the Internet is now a reality and the types of services vary widely – some simply enhance traditional delivery systems whilst others offer 'Therapy from your Couch'! The Samaritans have introduced E-listening in many of their centres and are finding that they are reaching a 'new' client group – often young men who indicate they do not want telephone contact. This group are presenting with similar presenting problems as telephone callers, including suicidal thoughts.

A large government department has recently introduced E-listening. Early indications seem to show that this will be well received as an out-of-hours contact and possibly will be more popular than the out-of-hours direct telephone help line, for those with Internet access. An online contract regarding confidentiality is established alerting the user to the limitations of confidentiality over the net (see Goss et al., 2001).

Critical Incident Stress Debriefing

Psychological debriefing

Psychological debriefing is a form of crisis intervention with groups of people who have been exposed to a stressful or tragic event. Its purpose is to decrease the likelihood of disturbing psychological reactions developing. Critical Incident Stress Debriefing (CISD) is based on the work of Mitchell (1983) and aims to reduce the incidence of Post-Traumatic Stress Disorder (PTSD) following a traumatic event. It has three main components: firstly, the initial debriefing for the ventilation of feelings; secondly, a detailed discussion of symptoms and the provision of reassurance; lastly an emphasis on the mobilisation of resources, providing information and forming future plans. In order to achieve its aims CISD has seven phases: introductory, fact phase, thought phase, feeling phase, symptom phase, teaching phase and the re-entry phase. Counsellors interested in debriefing work need to be properly trained and feel competent in handling group situations.

From an organisational perspective, having practical and psychological plans in place for emergencies is not just a case of behaving responsibly from 'a duty of care' point of view but is also sensible in business terms.

Debriefings are often associated with major tragedies, but sometimes traumatic events occur at work and early skilled intervention can prove invaluable – for example, witnessing accidents, being a survivor, reading through gruesome court or casework files, or even the suicide of a member of staff. It is not uncommon for a 'latent' period of months, and sometimes years, to lapse between the stressful event and the full symptomatic response.

Although debriefing work is widely carried out in this country most of the research has been done in the USA and Israel (Wilson and Raphael, 1993). In the light of current legislation, employers are increasingly realising the implications and benefits of preventative work in this area. However, the use of CISD in the workplace is being questioned, as reported in the *British Medical Journal* (Yamey, 2000).

Co-working

Two counsellors working together can be an extremely creative and effective way of intervening with dyads and in particular managing the dynamics of groups. When the relationship is based upon the mutual respect of each other's ability, each can trust the other to pick up on interactions otherwise missed, or see where there is a danger of becoming over-involved in the system. Together they are able to deal with the potential projections which form an important part of organisational work.

Co-workers who are able to discuss openly how their own organisation might be impacting on them and be reflected in what they see, think and feel, are in a good position to utilise this knowledge for the benefit of the client group. Where the counsellor is an employee of the organisation, prior knowledge of the dynamics involved can hinder objectivity, making the work more difficult, but not impossible. In such situations co-working with a colleague external to the organisation can be a very effective way to proceed. Again, external supervision helps support the counsellor and prevent them from being 'sucked in' to the organisational dynamics or being 'used' inappropriately. Co-working is a bit like a marriage or partnership, in that when it works well both workers feel supported and able to give of their best.

Group Facilitation

From counsellor to facilitator

Being a facilitator may look easy – but do not be fooled. It is rather like watching an experienced pianist effortlessly playing a Chopin sonata or a footballer making that critical strategic pass which leads to the ball going into the back of the net. Both examples, like group facilitation, require careful diagnosis, planning, knowledge and alternative strategies. The effective facilitator therefore needs to be willing to train in group-work skills and develop their own expertise through experience. A facilitator will also need to be aware of their own expectations and role in relation to the group.

Key factors to consider are: the group, the facilitator's role and the context in which they are working. When working with groups it is also important to maintain a sense of proportion and retain a good sense of humour. I like to compare group facilitation to social entertaining. Plan, prepare, expect the unexpected but above all relax and enjoy your guests. With a party nobody consciously plans a disaster; similarly most facilitators hope that their workshops, presentations or interventions will be helpful and enjoyable. Just as I consider the best dinner parties to be those where all guests make a contribution and enjoy being with one another, so I believe that a group will go well when each participant believes they have something to offer and is able to relax sufficiently to make that contribution. In order for this to happen part of the role of the facilitator is to pay attention to the following structural components:

■ **environmental** – room layout, seating, privacy, room allocation;
■ **organisational** – number of syndicates, allocation of members, use of plenary sessions, meal times, breaks and start/finish times;
■ **atmospheric** – the kind of atmosphere will predetermine the kind of development possible for a group;
■ **group rules** – how individuals wish to be treated, agreements, participation.

Whilst preparation and experience are key factors in group work, one cannot legislate for the unexpected. Effective facilitators plan for a group but do not arrive with 'the plan'. They are prepared to be flexible and have other resources at their disposal, so that if they detect a change in the group they can initiate an alternative plan as appropriate.

When beginning to work with a group I find it helpful to consider the following questions:

■ Who is asking me to work with this group and why?
■ What is the purpose of this group?
■ Do I have the necessary skills and knowledge required?
■ Who are the members of this group?
■ What is the composition of the group?

- What are members' needs likely to be?
- In what psychological state have individuals arrived?
- Are they voluntary or sent?
- To what extent have they been involved in the decision to have this event?
- What is the culture from which they come?
- What is the time framework within which we are working?
- What is realistic given the time?
- Given the task, how can I as the facilitator be most helpful?

Group participation

As has been said, all the planning in the world cannot legislate for the condition of the group at the point of commencement; therefore giving due respect and time to contracting with the group is important. Some form of 'psychological' contracting with the group helps group members learn co-operation and empathy instead of negative behaviour towards one another, such as passive aggression and manipulation. In this context the word 'contract' seeks to be an equal partnership between all members of the group, in which the facilitator has no greater or lesser responsibility for the group and its success than do the individual members. Like individual counselling facilitators need to consider their role and be explicit about what they offer the group and how they propose to work. Just as each person is an individual so is each group, and therefore each contract will be both different and unique.

Many people in organisations have never experienced true participative decision making as described above. When those with previous successful experiences are in the minority in a work-group contracting can be a difficult process. Often staff are used to strong leaders, who control rewards, establish the ground rules of a particular task and provide the necessary push to get the job done. They expect to be directed, motivated intellectually, and be impersonal and rational in their approach to problem solving. As a result there is a tendency to compete with other members for recognition and respond to authority rather than to members as peers. Such a climate is not conducive to establishing free and open communication, role flexibility and a truly non-evaluative atmosphere. To talk of the 'ideal' group is both risky and foolhardy; however, the successful working group has similar characteristics to those of thriving, functioning organisations as described in Chapter 1.

A successful working group should have the following attributes:

- A shared sense of purpose.
- Roles in the group are varied and there is acceptance of each participant's role or style.
- Communication channels are open and dissent is freely expressed.
- The group is not dominated or controlled by the personality characteristics of a few members.
- The whole group makes decisions and there is a flexible decision-making process.
- Innovation is encouraged and failure does not immobilise the group.
- The group has the skills and the necessary interest to diagnose any problems that minimise its effectiveness.
- Interpersonal problems do not become individual member problems but are seen as issues affecting the entire group.
- The group is responsive to its own changing needs and goals and is able to create new working patterns with minimum disruption.
- Balance of interdependency and flexibility.

As the workplace counsellor progresses to working with more than one person they will require an understanding of group dynamics and experience in facilitating skills in order to work with dyads and triads, as described in the previous chapter. 'Challenging' and 'scary' are often the words associated with group dynamics. These two words can take on an almost mystical quality, leaving some people overawed and others apprehensive about making the required shift from the dyad to a broader organisational role. Even those who have a good understanding of group dynamics can struggle in applying them in work situations. Perhaps this is because whilst groups have the power to be intensively therapeutic, at their worst they have the power to be destructive. Facilitators and group members alike will have personal histories and experiences of being in many types of groups. Part of the tension and challenge facing groups is that of being able to recognise the residual effects of prior experiences whilst using current opportunities constructively.

Stages of group life

It is useful to consider at which stage a particular 'group' is at any given time in its life before making any intervention. The following five-stage model offered here is an attempt to understand the conflicts and struggles that face groups as well as the satisfaction that can occur when human beings interact with one another. It is based on the work of Napier and Gershenfeld (1973) and I hope it will help you to make sense of some of the issues which arise when you work with groups.

1 The beginning

Issues to consider at this stage are the expectations and needs which individuals have prior to attending the event. These will be based on their personal experience of being in groups (including their previous life and training experiences). There is a need to survive in order to protect the 'self' and to feel secure in an unknown situation. At this point individual coping strategies and defence mechanisms are likely to become visible. It is a period of orientation where members will gather information, processing it as they 'wait and see'. Reminiscent of one's first day at a new school or starting a new job, there is a need to be accepted which means that individuals may carefully select what they disclose to one another. The facilitator at this point is often seen as 'all-powerful' and attitudes of passivity, dependency and idealisation may be displayed towards him or her. To sum up, this is a period of testing out where there is acquiescence to power where the group is concerned, with task issues at a public level.

2 Movement towards confrontation

Once the initial probing is over, a much more assertive environment develops as members seek more influence. Power issues begin to surface with definite stands being taken. Personality issues may surface; anger and overt blocking can emerge with issues often becoming polarised. The group becomes a testing ground for personal influence, status and prestige and some less assertive members may withdraw emotionally or even physically. As the group faces its own potentially destructive tendencies, confrontation is likely to take place in an effort to resolve these conflicts and tensions in order to get people working together again. This confrontation may manifest itself in resistance to the task in hand. The facilitator's authority may be challenged as they become the focus for the resistance and opposition which lies within the group. This is a period where tentativeness disappears, allowing underlying concerns to be made more public. This helps the group to become more 'real' than it was in the preceding stage.

3 Compromise and harmony

Once confrontation has taken place a period of goodwill ensues as members who are willing to compromise open up the lines of communication within the group. Competitiveness is played down and members are keen to avoid any signs of hostility. This period is often marked by a lot of joking and laughter. After recent events those who have taken opposite stands may come to realise that their needs are not being met. There is a genuine effort to build bridges and to look at issues, often to the point of over-discussing them whilst everyone has their say. The challenge now facing the group is how to resolve the discrepancy between what people are feeling and how people are behaving, i.e. whilst openness and honesty are encouraged on the one hand, there is subtle pressure on the other hand not to 'rock the boat' and spoil the harmony for which the group has fought so hard. It is the period which begins with a feeling of elation following the recent tensions and moves to a feeling of disillusionment as the group faces the fact that it still has a dilemma.

4 Reassessment

The group, having experienced relative structure at the beginning of its life followed by a period of less structure and control – neither of which seemed to satisfy its needs – faces the issue of 'Where do we go from here?' At this stage the group seeks new alternatives. The group faces the question of how honest it can be. At what level of intimacy and involvement does it need to work in order to achieve its goals? If the group is to survive shared responsibility, commitment and accountability will need to increase if trust and risk taking is to occur. The group at this point struggles to integrate both the emotional and the task components. In so doing it becomes more cohesive as norms and roles are developed. As the group takes more responsibility for its own management, the facilitator is seen in a less powerful position and is more likely to be used as a resource person with special knowledge and skills. This is a period marked by co-operation and reciprocity as expectations are reviewed, and where individuals reassess their positions.

5 Resolution and recycling

In any effective working relationship there are periods where tensions and conflicts occur and in this respect groups are no different. It is what the group does about them that is crucial, for if these tensions are denied, tension will increase and ultimately denial can lead to a decay of trust. Therefore, there will be times that a group needs to regress to earlier stages of behaviour, just as individuals do, but as the group matures it will resolve issues more quickly, using less energy and time to do so. This period is characterised by regression and progression. This stage is a reoccurring one and builds on the experience of the previous stage.

The challenge for the group is how quickly the period of regression can be overcome and the regressive cycle reduced.

The challenge for people working with groups is in grasping true understanding of what is happening to a particular group at a specific time in its life. The effective facilitator continually poses such questions, thus making their interventions appropriate, enabling and potent. In order to understand the dynamics of any given group it is necessary to know how to observe, analyse and evaluate in order to correctly diagnose the group process at any given time. Only then can the facilitator consider options and decide what type of intervention will be the most appropriate.

Termination of groups

When a group is not 'on-going' – and most are not, particularly training groups – it is important to recognise the termination phase. It is useful to be aware that individual members' responses to the approaching termination will vary. The basic underlying concern during this final stage is anxiety over leaving the group and applying the experiences and learning to the outside world. In some groups participants have formed very real bonds in order to further their development. Clearly reactions will vary and depend in part on the length of the group, its original task and its method. Clearly there would be a different emotional investment in a one-day workshop on workplace bullying or a half-day seminar on stress management, compared with a one-year change management programme. It is important to remember that individuals will cope with this closure and separation according to the degree of involvement they have experienced within the group, the duration of the group, its content and their own previous experience of endings.

Communication

A number of different types of group communication can be distinguished; they are called 'levels'. Each level stands in a hierarchical relationship with one another in terms of 'depth', with more superficial levels appearing easier to reach than the deeper levels. In general, deeper levels of communication seem to be the mark of longer-term, more trusting relationships whilst shallower levels appear to characterise shorter-term, less trusting relationships. The four levels are as follows:

Content   ■ Concerned with the subject matter at hand rather than its own emotional issues;

	■ working in a low emotional climate;
	■ dealing dispassionately with the facts.
Procedure	■ Setting and agreeing agendas;
	■ deciding on priorities and criteria;
	■ working in a relatively higher emotional climate.
Interaction	■ People are talking more and less likely to be actively listening;
	■ everyone talks at once;
	■ no one is talking because something is 'blocking' their ability or willingness to communicate;
	■ people are building alliances by selectively addressing certain members of the group;
	■ people are working in a more highly emotionally charged climate.
Feelings	■ The feelings of one or more members have become the salient issue;
	■ operating in a very high emotional climate;
	■ using facts and arguments to deal with the feelings discards these issues entirely to get on and deal with the feelings present.

Intervention skills

The first stage of intervention for the facilitator is to assess, from their observations of the group and by careful listening, the level at which the group is currently working, as illustrated in 'Mission Impossible' (Chapter 7). For example, if the group is dealing at a feelings level the facilitator needs to facilitate the feelings currently present. These may be overtly or covertly expressed. Were the facilitator to intervene at 'the procedure level', with an attempt to redefine the group's agenda or its priorities, this is likely to be ineffective. If the group is stuck on 'content' a reference to the 'agenda' may seek to move the group on by moving down one level. This may be a useful way to stop the flow and give group members the opportunity to refocus on their common objectives and ultimately the task of the group. Having diagnosed what is going on in the group, the next question is what to do about it.

The effective group facilitator has choices about the way in which they intervene by adopting an appropriate and consistent intervention style for each level. They may choose to intervene at a group level or at an interpersonal level, where the facilitator focuses on relationships within the group.

Alternatively, they may intervene with the individual behaviour of one member of the group only. The facilitator also has choices about the types of intervention they make. They may intervene on a conceptual level with planned or spontaneous theoretical input or the experiential, 'here and now' group experience. The facilitator could also intervene at a structural level, organising the range of activities the group is invited to perform.

When thinking about intervening, remember there is no one 'right way'. Facilitators may choose to do nothing but if they do so then this should be a conscious decision as 'no intervention' at all is still an intervention. Remember, silence can be extremely powerful. There is the world of difference between doing nothing because you believe that is the best thing to do and doing nothing because you do not know what to do. Facilitators need to bear in mind the possible consequence of their decision rather than abdicating responsibility.

Here are some suggestions. Consider the 'levels model', the type of intervention you might make (conceptual, experiential or structural), the intensity with which you intervene (low, medium or high intensity) (Cohen and Smith, 1976) and finally consider the stage of the group's life and what the issues might be for a particular group at a given time. In practice one uses a combination of all of the above. Whichever approach you take there will be implications but thinking through the needs of individuals and the group as a whole will assist you in being able to respond appropriately. Finally, as with individual work, the group practitioner needs to remember the value of being genuine in their role.

Group contexts

There does seem a lot to think about and to remember. This could be off-putting to the point that workplace counsellors say 'this is not for me' but they are often thrown in at the deep end regardless of their desires. They may be asked to work with groups of staff, offer an educational seminar or be called in to offer counselling for a section that has just received bad news. They may also become involved in conflict resolution as interventions designed to improve the effectiveness of inter-group relations inevitably involve a degree of disagreement. For example, where two departments or companies with different cultures merge, competition for resources is likely to occur and the counsellor needs to be confident in dealing with strong emotions, allowing them to surface in order to resolve conflicts. Here are some group scenarios and incidents you might encounter. Figure 8.1 considers the various ways in which a facilitator could intervene.

Perceiving	*Choice point*	Effective interventions
↓		
Being self aware		Responding
↓		
Listening and observing		At various levels
Making sense of what is happening		Using responding skills

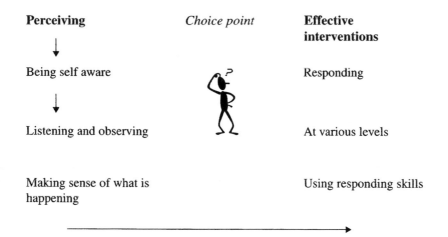

→

To decide how to intervene

Figure 8.1   Possible interventions

Example 1: conflict with the facilitator

Early to middle phase of group development, the group is task orientated, somewhat rigid and inclined to ignore emotional issues when they arise.

As a facilitator you have repeatedly called the group's attention to events the group has ignored 'as perhaps being too threatening' (traumatic event at work). One of the group members sits glaring at you as you finish another brief intervention. Finally s/he speaks directly to you in a loud, authoritative voice filled with anger and accusation.

Event preceding choice point

'I've been watching you and it seems to me that you are deliberately trying to stir everyone up, get us angry and share our feelings. I don't think our emotions have anything to do with why we are here and what we are discussing here. Every time we try to make a decision we get side-tracked and you seem to encourage it!'

The group falls silent, watching and waiting for your response.

Choice point
What would you do at this point and why?

Example 2: group norms

The group climate has evolved to the point where one or two group members begin to discuss highly personal issues. A group member who has typically been the most spontaneous and open has just finished sharing some intensely personal thoughts and feelings with other members.

Event preceding choice point

Following the member's personal statement, there is a long moment of silence at the end of which a very conservative and visibly upset member says: 'Wait a minute. I'm not sure I can go along with this. I thought we agreed not to talk about personal issues!'

Choice point

What would you do and why?

Example 3: the task versus the process

In this group there is a widening split between those group members who support 'task' issues and non-emotional involvement and those who endorse maintenance issues dealing directly with personal feelings. (This has sometimes been described as the conflict between the 'touchy-feelies' and the 'let's get on with the job' – task versus maintenance.)

The hostility between each subgroup has intensified and there is an inability to see the importance or relevance of the opposing subgroup's position. Following a particularly heated exchange, the group has fallen into a frustrated silence.

Event preceding the choice point

Two mutually antagonistic statements break the group's silence:

'I just can't understand why anyone would want to waste so much time on emotional issues, when we need to work on establishing an agenda and getting on with sorting the situation out!'

'I don't think an agenda has anything to do with what I want from this group, I can't understand your attitude at all.'

Various group members give support to each of these positions and express confusion about opposing stands. The group now lapses into an uneasy silence.

Choice point

What would you do at this point and why?

Example 4: emotions

This incident has occurred during the early to middle part of a group. There has been an emotional, painful disclosure of some intensity by a group member.

Typically other members have rushed in with supportive, comforting statements, which reduce the tension and block the individual from any further painful disclosure. As a result of this emotional 'sharing', the climate of the group may be described as an anxious closeness. Several, if not all, group members are involved.

Event preceding choice point

The group response to this event may be non-verbal, as when a group member gets up and goes over to sit beside or put their arm around the individual, or it may be verbal:

'I really appreciate your courage in telling us that…'

'Yes, I really have a great deal of respect for you, now.'

'I guess we have all had things that bothered us in the group and I appreciate your sharing your feelings with us.'

Choice point

What would you do at this point and why?

Example 5: token disclosure and collusion

This incident usually occurs during the early/middle phases of group life, often with intellectual, formal and non-expressive groups.

The group as a whole has made a few tentative thrusts at dealing with emotional issues. Two or three group members have revealed some personal concerns to the group, accompanied by displays of appropriate emotion. Following these emotional disclosures, the group climate seems to be one of quietness and tranquillity, with group members continuing to rework and reaffirm the importance of the personal disclosure. Inertia has developed, leading to group collusion to avoid future painful issues. It is becoming obvious that the group considers this to be a final, token gesture to the emotional aspects of group work.

Event preceding the choice point

'I really feel close to John after our talk: I think I know, now, how he really feels about the situation.'

'I feel the same way. This group seems very solid and completely supportive.'

'You know what we ought to do? We should all get together and go somewhere and have a drink and have ourselves a little party.'

Other members continue the conversation along the same lines.

Choice point
The facilitator needs to think whether this type of mutual support and approval should be encouraged and reinforced as a reflection of appropriate behaviour on the part of the group.

If it is a sincere attempt to provide mutual support then it should be encouraged. However, when groups begin talking about how warm, close and open they are, they can block or avoid unresolved issues. This is a 'flight into health' and a reaction to the increasing conflict and tension emerging in the group. It could be seen as an attempt to establish a norm of 'maintaining the happy status quo'.

What would you do at this point and why?

Discussion points

What were the issues involved in the above incidents? Were they surface issues or underlying issues? What are the circumstances in each scenario?

Summary

In this chapter I have sought to include approaches which are of topical interest to workplace counsellors. With changing work cultures there are many opportunities to develop the role of counselling and incorporate a variety of approaches. Using a group perspective workplace counsellors have much to offer in a range of situations. Whichever particular approach counsellors favour they need to distinguish between the opportunities and the limitations of their preferred way of working within their organisational environment and their own ability level.

Although at times workplace counsellors may experience a sense of frustration I have witnessed many who have made creative contributions in this field. With their perception and their courage to intervene, using many of the particular approaches described in this chapter, they have made a real difference and helped organisations to develop and change their cultures.

9

PRACTITIONER DEVELOPMENT

Introduction

Given the hidden constraints and forces of the organisation and the counselling world one might be forgiven for wondering why anyone would wish
to apply for a job as a workplace counsellor. Yet most who do, and are successful in their application, say that it is one of the best jobs they have ever
had. In this final chapter I would like to focus on what somebody interested
in entering the world of workplace counselling needs to consider before
they embark on that journey.

The Initiate

Selection

Although some organisations select an external candidate, already qualified
in a particular counselling approach, others will seek to appoint from within
their own staff complement and may already be committed to a particular
theoretical model and form of training. In the latter case, often there is
little choice for the initiate and the theoretical legacy is in a sense foisted
upon the newly appointed member of staff. In workplace counselling one
should not assume that there is always a choice of which theoretical school
the enthusiastic 'would-be counsellor' may wish to study or which training
course they may attend. In terms of practice initially counsellors may just
'go with flow' of what has preceded them without daring to question.

Once recruited, workplace counsellors need to allow themselves to be
influenced by real interpersonal experiences to form their own working
model and decide how theory relates to practice. Contact with clients and
testing their skills in practice are powerful learning vehicles. Once in post

it is likely that counsellors will have periods of 'off the job' training inter-spersed with periods of 'on the job' work experience designed to facilitate integration between theory, skills training and work-based practice.

An effective selection process endeavours to understand the candidate's motives and to establish whether they seek the role with a clear under-standing of what counselling means and involves. I have met candidates within organisations who have sought the role for a variety of reasons: some practical, such as a desire for relocation or grade promotion; whilst in other instances it is a question of a 'side-ways transfer' and the role has been thrust upon them and received rather reluctantly. For others it was just an 'add-on' part of their job description.

In the latter instances it came as no surprise to me when further down the line trainees would say, 'I did not know what I was letting myself in for when I took on this job.' Having said that I also recall the job satisfaction that many in those situations gained as they found themselves able to learn, develop personally and professionally and be of real help to others to the extent that, even when they were in mobile grades (as in the Civil Service) they resisted any suggestion of changing their job as a staff counsellor.

Preparation for training

Counsellors' reasons for seeking to become involved in therapeutic work are seldom entirely altruistic. For some the best solution to their own problems is to take their mind off them by helping others, as illustrated by Arnold Bennett when he said: 'The best cure for worry, depression, melancholy, brooding, is to go deliberately forth and try to lift with one's sympathy the gloom of somebody else.' Well intentioned perhaps, but this is hardly the most appropriate approach to counselling. It has been my experience that most people who enter the helping professions have their own personal rea-sons, but at the point of entry they are not always aware of them. For exam-ple, they may be attempting to understand themselves through other people's experience or using the work as a way of feeling needed.

The preparation for embarking on counselling training involves the hon-est study of one's own motives in helping others. These processes are not always easy and at times they may be painful; however personal factors are crucial in counselling relationships. This process of self-examination is one that enables counsellors to prepare themselves for meeting their clients on an equal humanitarian basis.

From a selector's perspective I would suggest that a trainee counsellor might find it both illuminating and practically useful as they begin their training if they were to ask themselves questions such as:

- How easy do I find it to ask for help?
- Would I go to see a counsellor?
- Have I been to see a workplace counsellor?
- Who gave me support when I really needed it?
- Who are the people who have helped me most?
- Why do I wish to do this kind of work at this point in my life?

If we as counsellors are not prepared to ask these questions of ourselves, what right do we have to ask them of our clients or to expect clients to share with us personal and often extremely intimate details of their lives?

Training

It is fundamental that the design of workplace counselling training programmes incorporate the question of how counsellors operate in organisational systems. Staff teams need to be aware of how easy it can be to reinforce a potential split, where counselling is seen as a separate activity neither influenced by the organisational context nor having opportunities to influence it in return.

Currently the standard of training is variable but from my experience as a provider of Civil Service Welfare Officer Training for some 22 years, I think that in order to practise effectively and ethically workplace counsellors need to:

- understand the theoretical foundations of counselling;
- be clear about their role and responsibilities;
- acquire knowledge about organisational systems;
- develop a range of counselling skills;
- be able to apply these to casework within workplace settings;
- acquire knowledge about specific client concerns and appropriate helping strategies;
- have a working knowledge of group dynamics;
- make appropriate organisational interventions;
- develop suitable attitudes and awareness, which correspond with the provision of a professional service within an organisational context;
- be aware of their limitations and able to refer clients to appropriate agencies;

■ be committed to the benefits of an on-going professional development programme, including supervision.

The role of self-awareness

As counsellors begin their journey they are often unaware of inner or semi-conscious messages. If they are too keen to succeed in life, then perhaps inadvertently they will put pressure on their clients to 'do well', to 'be worthy clients' seeking the counsellor's approval. As has often been said: 'The road to hell is paved with good intentions.' The counsellor might also enquire: Am I the sort of person who wishes to 'do good'? Do I tend to pre-plan the outcome for my clients? In deciding omnipotently what needs to be done it is so easy to forget the rights of clients. Under the guise of helping counsellors might unhelpfully put pressure on clients to conform to subtle messages. Whose needs are being served, those of the client or those of the counsellor? Answering such questions honestly not only increases the effectiveness of the counsellor, but also relieves some of the stresses and strains that can come from trying too hard. I believe it was Cervantes who said: 'Make it thy business to know thyself, which is the most difficult lesson in the world.'

But how does one begin 'to know thyself?' Personal therapy is often recommended and for some counselling training it is a prerequisite. For the purposes of this book I would like to offer you the following well-known diagram, the Johari Window, named after its originators, Joe Luft (1966) and Harry Ingham (see Figure 9.1). It is used in a variety of training arenas as it presents a structured model for learning about oneself – whether in the role of a manager, member of staff or workplace counsellor.

The process of becoming self-aware and increasing your self-understanding involves increasing the quadrant 'free and open', with the other three quadrants becoming correspondingly smaller. It involves being willing to ask for and to receive, non-defensively, feedback from others. It challenges the counsellor to take risks, for instance looking at the 'hidden

	Known to self	Unknown to self
Known to others	**Free and open** You know and others know	**Blind self** You do not know but others do
Unknown to others	**Hidden self** You know but others do not	**Unconscious self** You do not know and others do not know

Figure 9.1 The Johari Window

self' and taking the opportunity to share with others what they know about themselves, or in the 'blind self' asking how others perceive them.

The counsellor as a person

A common theme across the theoretical spectrum is the notion of creating a relationship that is sincere and authentic. This involves counsellors being themselves as people and requires on-going development. By realising that inside every counsellor there is a client and that inside every client there is a potential counsellor helps us as therapists to be genuine. Thinking about ourselves in relation to our clients helps us to treat them with the respect that they deserve.

I consider counselling as an art form, which depends not only on a combination of theory and technique but also on the ability of counsellors to express their individual personality. The counsellor who is an expert in the former at the expense of the latter is like the musician who practises her scales diligently, one who knows each note of the music, and yet gives a soulless performance.

Whichever theory you read I think you will find the words 'genuine' and 'real' occurring frequently and this requires the counsellor to be someone who is:

Free within role	does not use their role either to protect themselves or as a substitute for effectiveness.
Spontaneous	but not impulsive; if they filter what they communicate then they do so for the client's sake, not their own.
Non-defensive	is aware of own strengths and deficits, can examine negative criticism and responses honestly.
Consistent	does not have one set of stated values (e.g. justice and equality) which differ from their real values (e.g. power or money).
Self-sharing	is capable of disclosing about him- or herself.
Confronting	is able to be honest with others as to what they perceive. (Egan, 1977)

The following exercises will assist you in thinking about your own values, assumptions and philosophy of counselling. For example, my reason for becoming a counsellor at a conscious level was that I felt passionately about human injustice and was hungry to learn about people. Now I know that one of those people was me.

Exercise: practitoner development – counsellor's motivation

- What are my reasons for wanting to become a counsellor?
- What do I expect from the counselling relationship?
- What will be my satisfactions and rewards in helping others?
- What is my own philosophy about human nature?
- What philosophy do I bring to this work?
- List some of the thoughts (inner dialogue) you have about this work.

Exercise: self-awareness

- Ask for feedback from colleagues and friends and fill in as much as possible of your own Johari Window.
- Identify two aspects of yourself that you have kept hidden. Imagine yourself disclosing them to another person. What thoughts cross your mind? How might you feel?

The Relationship between Theory and Practice

I would now like to return to the theme of integrated training and consider the 'legacy of theory'. As with most inheritances parts of theory will be welcomed whilst others may appear to be of little use to you at this particular time in your counselling career. Whether counsellors study theory first or come to it at a later stage in their training, sooner or later it is natural for counsellors in training to ask such questions as:

- What has all this theory got to do with me?
- Where do I fit in?
- How does this relate to what I actually do in my day-to-day work?
- In what ways does workplace counselling differ from other forms of counselling?

The inheritance

From the knowledge you already have you will appreciate that the major traditions of psychotherapy and counselling have a long and rich history. However, the legacy they leave is a multitude of approaches to counselling, no shortage of definitions and ample opportunity for confusion. Corsini and

Wedding (1989) refer to some 250 schools or approaches. However, as yet there is no theoretical model for workplace counselling. It seems that a good starting point is to realise that as in everyday life some legacies are quite complex, some arrive with clauses attached and other legacies come with a burden of responsibility – perhaps to carry on traditions or to continue working in a particular therapeutic way. Rarely, in my view, are legacies unconditional.

Counsellors need to discriminate in how they apply theory to practice. They can use theory constructively, and likewise they can misuse it by not recognising its limitations – either by sacrificing clients to theory and or by imposing a particular theory onto their colleagues.

Bowlby (1996) suggests that many do excellent work using their intuition and without very clear ideas on theory, or even in spite of the theories to which they nominally subscribe. Applying theories works well when the theories are applicable but can be a big handicap when they are not:

> Perhaps my saving graces have been that I am a good listener and not too dogmatic about theory. As a result several of my patients have succeeded in teaching me a great deal I did not know and have contributed greatly to my understanding ... clearly, the best therapy is done by a therapist who is both naturally intuitive and also guided by appropriate theory. (Bowlby, unpublished paper)

The highways and byways of counselling

It is essential to discover one's own theoretical map in order to engage fully with managing the counselling process. One way of considering such questions is to view the main theoretical schools as major trunk roads with highways and byways coming off them. At some point in a counsellor's training it will become important to decide which of these 'major routes' they wish to use on their travels and which signposts they will need to look for. Will they be attracted by the 'fast lane' on the motorway or would they prefer the slower 'scenic' country roads? In what way does their organisation influence their choice of travel? And finally, how will they prepare for their journey in order to ensure that they and their clients travel safely?

These decisions are particularly significant in the early stages of practitioner development as they enable the counsellor to have reference points: a sense of familiarity and orientation from which to develop. This could be compared with 'the concept of a secure base' as introduced by Salter (1940). Her concept of a 'secure base', derived from observation of typical interactions between child and parent, is a stable foundation from which the child feels safe enough to explore. We could view the developing counsellor as the 'exploring child' and the 'parent figure' as a 'theoretical school' to which the counsellor becomes 'attached'. Developing this a little further, the 'child' in workplace counselling might have two 'parent' figures, one being the theoretical school and the other the organisation who may or may not share similar values. How well do these 'authority figures' get along? Is the 'child', in terms of the developing counsellor, in danger of receiving mixed messages, with all that that implies?

Whichever school or theory workplace counsellors finally choose, whether it be a conscious or an unconscious choice, they need to have a definition, a framework or 'map' in which they personally believe and within which they feel able to work. With this in mind workplace counsellors are better placed to differentiate between what is within their personal and their organisational limits and what is not, thereby offering clarity to their clients. Eventually, when counsellors are more confident in their role, they will be able to choose appropriate alternative 'routes'. An eclectic approach would then be sought not as a means of escape when the 'route' to progress is blocked – for example when the counselling process appears to have come to a halt and counsellors feel 'stuck' – but because counsellors, through understanding, make a considered decision based on informed knowledge.

Personal illustration

My own training, as a marital and family therapist, was based upon psychoanalytic principles, but with further study I began to incorporate other disciplines into my repertoire and skills into my toolbox. In that sense one could say I am an eclectic practitioner and I realise this declaration is open to criticism from purists. I remember many years ago I described my work as 'eclectic' to my then supervisor, who challenged me by asking me to consider 'whether eclectic meant lack of commitment.' His question brought me up short. Was I betraying my psychodynamic roots, my family of therapeutic origin, by daring to acknowledge that there were other ways of working, other methods I respected and wished to try?

'Did I truly lack commitment?' I wondered. I believe not, but to this day I am grateful to him for his challenging words for they have stayed with me and have served to remind me of just how important it is to have a good foundation, and sound training – and know from which counselling culture one emerges. Only then, in my view, can one venture forth and take risks.

As with Winnicott's (1972) concept of the child who has had 'good enough mothering', counsellors who are secure in their knowledge, aware of their limitations and confident in their ability to overcome any unforeseen obstacles, are able to move forwards seeking new opportunities and testing their limits.

Although this book has not been about debating the merits of each theoretical approach I hope that at this point you have realised just how much you do know from your own experience – about your own organisation, your 'family of workplace origin' – and that you might wish to delve a little more deeply into counselling and organisational theories.

Where roads meet

If when comparing the boundaries of different therapeutic schools we take a narrow view, zooming in to focus too much on detail and superficiality, we are unable to see the whole picture and it is easy to gain a distorted impression. At first glance it is all too easy to concentrate on the divergent views of 'the legacy' and ignore what therapeutic theories have in common and of course vice versa.

As human beings we are neither identical nor are we different and I would like to stress the importance of valuing the uniqueness of each client, each counsellor, each therapeutic school and, of course, each organisation, without forgetting the aspects which we as human beings share: for example, the need to belong, the capacity to love, to hate and the need to experience joy and sorrow.

It is also important to recognise to what extent the counselling service is provided in harmony or indirect conflict with the values of the organisation. Are their goals shared? If not, where is the difference and potential conflict? Perhaps recognition of overlap and common ground will provide a way forward. But conflicts do exist, so what is it like for a workplace counsellor to be in direct conflict with the requirement of the organisation? The counsellor may believe that the aim of counselling is to promote growth and autonomy and seeks to encourage clients to take personal responsibility and assert themselves, but he or she may work in a setting where passive employees are required.

Boundaries

In a changing world where, for example, the horizons of medicine and technology seem limitless, I think it is important for any practitioner to evaluate their own motives, rationale and boundaries at any given point in time – in other words, workplace counsellors need to bear in mind who they are, in which discipline they work and what they hope to achieve.

If one seeks to work therapeutically in workplace settings or groups, whether they be small or large, in order to avoid misunderstanding counsellors need to take into account a number of basic principles which underlie the way in which everyday groups function. One of these principles is the management of boundaries. I have found it helpful to consider which boundaries are permeable, which are restrictive and which are blurred to the point of not being recognisable. Counsellors need to be clear as to what constitutes a boundary. There is the world of difference between knowing that a boundary exists, recognising when one is crossed and not even being aware that one exists at all. It is important to know one's own discipline, whatever that might be, and the system in which we work, in order to serve those who seek our help, so that when faced with complex situations, one's knowledge, both objective and subjective, will stand one in good stead.

Skynner (1976), writing about systems, order and hierarchy, suggests that lack of systematic formulation can lead to confusion and conflict among schools of psychological thought. Boundaries therefore are required to preserve the identity of the individual practitioner and the role of counselling at work. If they are impermeable then any meaningful exchange, for instance with other disciplines, both within and outside the organisation, is prevented. On the other hand, if there is a lack of clear boundaries then the workplace counsellor's role will not be perceived with clarity, thus hindering the referral process. In addition, where there is a lack of identity counsellors can be subjected to inadequately controlled emotional involvement, which is helpful to neither the individual client, the practitioner nor the organisation as a whole.

Managing boundaries is not something new to people. Perhaps we can all relate to the tensions that can exist as we attempt to balance the demands of work and home boundaries. For instance, how flexible can we be with a work boundary when childcare is involved, and what is it like to work in a culture that says 'I am the first one in the office and the last to leave'?

The Counsellor and the Outside World

How counsellors view the world of counselling will in turn influence what they can offer their clients and equally how they are perceived by their individual clients and their organisation as a whole. Workplace counsellors need to consider:

- how they relate to their particular organisation;
- how they are going to relate to others in the organisation in which they practice;
- how they relate to the outside world (other agencies, organisations etc.);
- how they will work with counsellors who may hold different views from their own;
- how they relate to other therapeutic schools.

Part of any management function is to determine client or customer needs, the nature of the service one wishes to offer and how best to deliver and control that service. Attempting to understand the various approaches to helping people in a variety of therapeutic settings in the workplace is all part of the responsibility of managing the counselling process professionally. It underlines the importance of accepting that there are differing perspectives and different ways in which people can be helped. Although it takes time to sift through the various theoretical approaches, on a practical level it is useful to know where there are overlaps and where other disciplines might offer something very different, for example a specific form of treatment which would benefit the clients.

By acknowledging differences in practice and considering any similarities or overlaps, Clarkson and Pokorny (1994) suggest that the counsellor is better placed to establish their own identity as a practitioner and develop trust in other agencies and professions. Furthermore, counsellors are able to consider informed referrals based on knowledge of different services and establish boundaries between the self and other professionals.

Example: working in general practice

In the 1970s I worked as a counsellor in a general practice in the early days of GP counselling. The GP in question really tested me in more ways than one before he would, as he put it, 'let me loose on his patients'. Although I was clear about how I had been trained and what my boundaries were, I was entering a different system. I quickly realised that he was quite protective of his patients and his selection of referrals reflected that attitude. We both needed to trust each other's abilities otherwise it was clearly not going to work. In this instance we resolved our differences and over time I realised how much we could learn from one another, and also from the psychiatrists, community psychiatric nurses and social workers with whom we were both involved. After all, we were all there to help the patients and their families and as mutual trust developed we learned to respect each other's contributions.

Such an experience highlights the need to be tolerant, have an understanding heart and a forgiving nature – we are all human beings, vulnerable to prejudice and to making mistakes. Moreover, when working with another profession it is necessary to clarify right at the outset the methodology and expectations one has of the other's role. By identifying specialist knowledge and potential overlaps, ambiguity is minimised and the pressure on each other's role is reduced.

In thinking about the relationship between counselling, psychotherapy, psychology and psychiatry it is helpful to remember that in Rogerian terms 'respect' is one of the core conditions for counselling, and I live in hope that those involved in the therapeutic world aspire to being congruent not only in the way they practise but also in the way in which they treat other professionals. The idealised image of an all-understanding, non-judgemental therapeutic world is perhaps naive. Power struggles and conflicts exist just as they do in any other system, whether it is a family, a work-group or large organisation.

Exercise

- List other professions with whom you have had contact in this field and describe the approach they use.
- Imagine you are about to make a referral. Describe to your client the differences between a psychiatrist, psychologist, psychotherapist and a counsellor.
- How would you describe what you as a workplace counsellor can offer to your client that is different from the approaches mentioned above?

The Developing Counsellor

Stages of development

As the developing counsellor makes sense of their world through reading, practice and experience they are likely to go through recognisable stages. The following five-stage model is based on the work of Reynolds (1965):

- acute consciousness of self;
- sink-or-swim adaptation;
- stages of understanding the situation;

- relative mastery;
- teaching.

In the early stages the trainee's focus of attention is much more likely to be on himself than on the client and he is likely to silently question himself asking, for example, what have I done or how will I cope? One staff counsellor illustrated the last question beautifully when she told me that although she knew about time boundaries the more she thought about ending sessions the more difficult it became for her. The result was that her initial interviews were taking hours and leaving both her and her clients exhausted.

In an attempt to get on with the business of counselling the trainee is usually enthusiastic and keen 'to have a go'. They may demonstrate frustration when trying out new skills, knowing intellectually what they are trying to achieve but finding it difficult to let go of skills and attitudes acquired in previous jobs. In that sense counsellors can be compared with musicians who know they must learn and practise scales in order to acquire the necessary technique before developing their own interpretation of a piece of music. At one level both musician and counsellor intellectually accept that discipline of practice is required in order to develop, but at another level the experience can seem frustrating and pointless. After all, when one is eager to play a whole sonata or to engage in a complete counselling session, who really wants to practise scales or skills? Yes, it does require discipline and patience because this stage can last a long time.

The learner tends to depend on the experience of others who are familiar with the task. Too much correction at this stage can be counterproductive and so a balance needs to be struck between over-correction and letting mistakes go too far. Sometimes counsellors 'flounder' and literally feel they are 'sinking', believing that they will never cope and expressing a desire 'to give up'. Support, supervision and encouragement are of course necessary throughout training but they are crucial at this point. Skilled teaching should increase the trainee's ability to function and develop confidence in an atmosphere which is relaxing yet stimulating. It is important that the trainee is encouraged to trust and use their own spontaneous responses.

Encouragingly, most survive the initial stage and 'swim' and the counsellor now gets on with their work. In order to be effective and make sense of their own world counsellors at this stage seek to have more control over their environment, in order to develop self-confidence. What characterises this particular stage is that counsellors know what ought to be done but are not always able to do it. For instance they may know the 'right' counselling terms, such as 'therapeutic alliance', 'contracting' and 'the skill of reflecting', but without fully grasping the understanding or the principles underlying the terminology and concepts. This may manifest itself in a surface knowledge of jargon. Whilst they know their situation, as yet they do not have the ability to control their own activity in it and effectively implement new knowledge and skills. At this point, as there is unevenness in the level of the counsellor's skills, there can be a temptation for them – or others – to be overly critical and this is not helpful. Frequent and consistent supervision is essential at this stage.

As theory and skills become integrated into the practitioner's repertoire conscious intelligence and conscious response begin to work together. Much of the work is automatic in terms of employing skills. The practitioner now uses their mental and emotional energy to solve new problems and can be objective about his or her achievements. To return to the musical comparison, they are now able to express their individuality more creatively, putting the emphasis on particular notes. They now know when to 'play pianissimo' and when to 'play forte' and do so with confidence. At last counsellors experience themselves as both productive and creative. There is a danger if they feel they are 'finished' as a learner and get stuck by not availing themselves of further opportunities to develop.

Teaching what one has mastered is part of a life cycle. This stage of 'generativity versus self-absorption', as described by Erikson (1965) in his work on psychosocial development, is where experienced practitioners impart knowledge and understanding of what they consider to be effective, helpful and worthwhile to future generations. It can be a very satisfying experience to watch protégés develop, but it requires the ability to stand in the wings, allowing them to benefit from your knowledge and experience in a non-possessive way. Helping the counsellor define what they most want to learn reflects the process whereby a counsellor enables the client to define what is that they need to talk about. Remembering that their individual and organisational clients are not yours but those of the student or the supervisee enables those teaching to focus on the counsellor's development – which includes the right to intervene if you feel they or their clients are at risk.

Personal Development

Unrealistic expectations are a common trap in the face of the 'human need' in an organisation. Accepting that one has limitations and being able to say that little word 'no' is vital in managing the personal boundaries of organisational counselling. This requires an on-going commitment to self-development in the form of training, supervision and personal therapy. Developing counsellors need to explore their own way of conceptualising their counselling work.

So much of workplace counsellors' work is done on a one-to-one basis that there is the potential for isolation and work overload. It is useful, therefore, to set up support networks such as peer support, supervision and to commit to on-going professional development.

The apprenticeship model

The apprenticeship model is where the supervisor is seen as 'the expert' passing on their knowledge and skills, as with carpenters, electricians, nurses and doctors. The relationship in that sense is clearly unequal. Learning is primarily by 'doing' under careful supervision and is the result of the teaching, by instruction or by acting as a role-model. Following an initial assessment a learning programme will be designed by the supervisor, who will subsequently carry out the evaluation of the trainee's progress.

The growth model

In this model the assumption is made that earlier ways of behaviour persist into adulthood and emotional hurdles will have to be overcome. Learning is the result of freedom to learn, unimpeded by emotional blocks to learning. The role of the supervisor is to facilitate the learner's learning as opposed to mutual learning, and therefore the relationship is not an equal one. With regard to evaluation there is great emphasis on process rather than outcome and on feelings rather than behaviour.

The role systems model

The relationship in the role systems model is relatively equal, although authority derived from expertise and from an organisational role is acknowledged. Learning depends on continuous feedback on role performance. Learning goals will be designed by the learner and in dialogue, and they will focus primarily on analysing situations to determine what roles are appropriate in which circumstances. Feedback is seen as an essential ingredient of open communication and will be concerned with role performance of the learner and, of course, clients.

In the absence of any one model for supervision the above are some approaches used in other professions and trades. In an ideal world matching the individual's method of learning to the management style of their line manager or supervisor would be most appropriate. In reality this isn't always the case and here the new counsellor needs practical help and support as well as training to fully develop their role.

Making the commitment

In developmental terms a structured personal development programme offers the opportunity to break out of old patterns, take risks and experiment with different ways of working. Learning can of course be left to chance, but it is probably best done as a deliberate, conscious process. However, there may be barriers to engaging with the process. Under pressure of increasing workloads, time constraints and a variety of roles, self-monitoring one's own performance can easily be left as one goes from one interview or meeting to another. In the face of performance anxiety, a more defensive stance can be taken.

Throughout the process it is useful to learn to keep a developmental diary or learning log so that you can keep a balanced view of achievements and progress on a daily basis.

Counselling Supervision

To practise effectively and ethically counsellors need to maintain a balance between theoretical understanding, self-awareness and skills development. In addition they require a wider knowledge of other organisations and professional factors. Whilst counsellors can gain much by the critical reading of theories, their study needs to be balanced by understanding the processes and problems that are faced in everyday practice. Regular counselling supervision provides counsellors with the opportunity to address these issues and to monitor their work.

Supervision is increasingly seen as an essential part of on-going development in many professions. Whilst there are no mandatory regulations covering counsellor supervision in the therapeutic world, it is often a prerequisite for affiliation to professional bodies and a requirement for certain training courses. Supervision is encouraged and is seen as part of a professional responsibility to clients.

Aims of supervision

Supervision is a process intended to help supervisees maintain ethical and professional standards of practice, to enhance creativity by providing a forum where client work and the organisational dynamics can be discussed honestly. It enables the counsellor to differentiate between themself and the client.

Counselling supervision not only provides supervisees with regular opportunities to discuss and monitor their counselling work for the good of the client, but is also essential for the well-being of the staff counsellor. Counselling supervision should also take into account the client population and the setting in which the supervisee practises, in this case the workplace. Supervision offers counsellors the opportunity to:

- develop therapeutic competence;
- ensure that the needs of their clients are being addressed;
- monitor the effectiveness of the therapeutic interventions;
- be supported in the role;
- plan and utilise personal and professional resources effectively.

I would like to emphasise that the responsibility for obtaining good and adequate supervision lies with the counsellor, on a professional basis, and the employer who has a duty of care to provide for the health and safety of all staff, including counsellors.

Features of counselling supervision

Counselling supervision is a formal and mutually agreed arrangement for counsellors to discuss their work on a regular basis with someone who is an experienced and competent counsellor and familiar with the process of counselling supervision (see BACP, 2001b). It is also known as consultative support, clinical supervision or non-managerial supervision. It is considered an essential part of good practice, different from training, personal development and line management accountability. Ideally the counselling supervision role should be independent of the line manager role. The supervisor may be an employee of the organisation or they may be an external supervisor paid by the organisation to provide supervision. In practice supervision may contain some elements of training, personal development or line management; however, counselling supervision is not primarily intended for these purposes.

The organisational context in which staff counsellors work is an extremely important dimension of workplace supervision and one which is often overlooked. Supervision should take into account the client population and the setting in which the supervisees practise.

There are parallels to be drawn between an effective therapeutic alliance and an effective supervisory relationship. Even so, at times supervision will be experienced by the supervisee as being beneficial whilst at other times it will be experienced as corrective. Ideally it will be experienced as a working relationship based on mutual respect and one that is ultimately for the benefit of the client. The role is to facilitate the learning and thinking environment and the task is to work together to ensure and develop the efficacy of the supervisee's practice. Supervision takes the form of a constructive, collaborative working relationship, which has supportive and challenging elements. For further reading see Inskipp and Proctor (1993).

Personal Therapy

Nowadays a psychotherapist is expected to have their own personal therapy and psychoanalysts are expected to undergo a full psychoanalysis. With counselling the boundaries are less clear. It is becoming increasingly common in counselling training that the trainee has personal therapy or counselling and it is a requirement of most professional bodies.

There can sometimes be a temptation to use supervision as therapy. Most supervisors are prepared to support a counsellor through a personal crisis but where supervision sessions are clearly insufficient I believe it is important to encourage counsellors to seek additional help and or therapy where necessary. Apart from the benefits of self-knowledge, therapy is really important in that it protects both client and counsellor from the other's pain or unresolved issues. Being on the receiving end of good therapeutic skills is a wonderful way of learning about the client–counsellor relationship. The process of finding a therapist who will be good to work with offers us an insight into how it might be for clients who are considering seeking help for themselves.

Burn-out

You might wonder why I mention this term at the beginning of your career. Well, like 'stress', people often do not recognise that they are suffering from it until they are experiencing it. Burn-out is the process that describes the progressive loss of initial idealism, energy and sense of purpose experienced by people in the human services field, such as nursing, teaching, the police and of course counsellors. It can result in emotional exhaustion, negative attitudes towards clients, negative self-evaluation as a helper and emotional distance from clients. Some ideas, based on the work of Edelwich and Brodsky (1980) who described the stages of 'burn-out', follow.

Enthusiasm

This is the initial period of high energy, high hopes and often unrealistic expectations, when one is not fully aware of all that the job entails. It appears all important and because it promises to be everything and offer so much one can experience a sense of not needing anything in one's life other than the job. Over-identification with clients and excessive expenditure of one's own energy (including voluntary overwork!) are major hazards at this point. However, what people lack in knowledge and technique at this stage they make up for in enthusiasm and a belief in what they are doing.

Stagnation

After the initial burst of enthusiasm feelings of frustration begin to creep in, as the great expectations are not confirmed. Now the job is no longer so thrilling as to be a substitute for everything in life. Although one is still doing the job there is a realisation that it might be nice to have leisure time, a little money to spend, a car, some friends, a lover, more time, a home etc. More emphasis is now placed on meeting one's own personal needs and issues such as working conditions, hours, pay and career development become increasingly important. As one addresses one's own needs comparisons are made with other vocations, with those in higher paid jobs, with clients and with the tantalising alternative of working with another company.

Frustration

As frustrations build up people who set out to give others what they need find that they are not getting what they themselves want. Frustration is the core of burn-out. It is experienced in a variety of ways: 'a moment of stark enlightenment', 'a sudden blow', 'over a period of time'. At this point one calls into question one's effectiveness in doing the job and the value of the job itself. Much of the frustration encountered in the helping professions is expressed as 'powerlessness' and 'the system not being responsive to clients' needs'. These expressions refer to the earlier stage of expectations both for oneself and for one's clients. Emotional, physical and behavioural problems can occur at this stage.

Apathy

Basically one can respond to frustration in three ways. One can use it as a source of destructive or constructive energy, or one can walk away from it and not express the frustration. This is sometimes described as 'the retreat into apathy', a typical and natural defence mechanism when chronic frustration is in conflict with the need for a job in order to survive. It is typically expressed as 'a job is a job is a job'. It manifests itself in one putting in the minimum required time, avoiding challenges (even clients) and mainly seeking to keep oneself safe in the position. Apathy is a stage of 'getting by' and 'going through the motions', described as empathy having turned into apathy.

Intervention

Intervention can occur at any of the four stages prior to 'burn-out'. One of the challenges for supervisors and colleagues is to help staff experience the four stages with greater awareness and thus be less subject to swings of emotion. It is very important that helpers take responsibility for noticing the signs that show our systems are overloaded, and that they ensure support to deal with symptoms of stress sooner rather than later.

The aim of intervention is to break the cycle. It may be self-initiated, it may occur in response to an immediate or perceived threat or it may result because of an inner drive for change. It requires facing up to the reality of one's situation, understanding it, living with it and then taking constructive action.

Intervention may take on a variety of forms. It might mean modifying one's expectations, restructuring one's day or one's relationship with clients, colleagues or support systems. It could mean returning to education to obtain better credentials, or to stimulate one's life outside the job. The important intervention is the one that produces effective and lasting change.

These stages are cyclic – one can go through them several times and in different jobs. They are also contagious and enthusiasm, stagnation, frustration, apathy and intervention can affect our clients, colleagues and our personal relationships. We can move from enthusiasm to realism, stagnation to movement, frustration to satisfaction or apathy to involvement. Accepting that these stages will occur in the helping professions, and acknowledging them when they happen to ourselves and to our colleagues, puts us in a position to see them as a dynamic part of the job and to set up systems to address burn-out.

Caring for Yourself

Given increasing uncertainty in the workplace, issues of counsellor identity and the nature of the work it seems important to say something about 'who cares for the carers?'

When working in a shop or office environment there are tea and lunch breaks, opportunities for normal social interaction. Counselling, on the other hand, can be isolating work, particularly in the workplace. Staff counsellors have told me that they rarely walk down a corridor, 'go to the loo' or have a cup of coffee without knowing somebody who is either a client, an ex-client, the line manager of a client or colleague of a client. In this sense they are never 'off duty'.

It can be difficult, but not impossible, to be 'ordinary', to take time out and just be oneself. For some the dilemma is not worth the effort and they go through the day without any contact with people other than clients. Most of the work is sedentary and it is all too easy to get sucked into the needy world of casework. I think it is very important to guard against isolation. At the risk of generalisation, counsellors, like many in the caring professions, are notoriously good at caring for others and notoriously bad at taking care of themselves. The work is creative and fulfilling but it requires a high degree of concentration and the ability to tolerate listening to the distress of others.

It is useful for a counsellor to re-establish the equilibrium in their workweek by designing a care programme for themselves. Simple ideas like getting fresh air, moving around to balance the hours of sitting that are involved, or having fun all help to keep a sense of perspective. Having a good 'belly-laugh' is itself therapeutic and sometimes counsellors need to be reminded that it is still OK to have a sense of humour. Peer support networks and planned-in breaks are helpful. Stress management applies as much to the counsellor as to the client.

It is important for counsellors undergoing training to feel good about themselves if they are to be able to create an atmosphere of trust in the counselling room and elicit confidence from others with whom they interact within the organisation.

Keeping a perspective

I feel at this point that I need to balance the sense of seriousness and responsibility that a counsellor undertakes with the joy and creativity that can be experienced in doing this work. Counselling is not all doom and gloom; there can be laughter and wonderful moments that stay with you through a lifetime. In that sense it is a reciprocal relationship.

Finally, there is the ability to offer hope. Yalom (1980), when describing curative factors in groups, considered it important to have *faith* in the *effectiveness of the process*. I take the view that this is a powerful healing factor in itself. Workplace counsellors, like private practitioners, need to believe that the process can work.

Summary

When embarking on counselling development it is useful to recognise that people learn from a variety of sources including life experience, emotions, intellect and one's environment. Values, beliefs, needs and other personal characteristics permeate everything the counsellor does. In considering what is involved in selection, learning, personal development and self-care I have sought to help those of you who wish to pursue this type of occupation to think about what preparations you might need to make in order to enter the world of workplace counselling

Savouring tasty meals or seeing flowers bloom are for most of us rather pleasant experiences but watering and watching, preparing the soil for planting or peeling vegetables for cooking can be arduous work often willingly assigned to others. Similarly, in order to become an effective counsellor delegation is not a possibility. Personal preparation and practitioner development may inadvertently be overlooked but it is not something that anyone else can do for you.

POSTSCRIPT

Pressures and Pleasures

In this book I have looked at a variety of pressures that a counsellor working in an organisation may experience. Workplace counsellors need to think seriously about how they will manage conflicts, moral dilemmas, mixed messages and shifting priorities. All of these issues need to be resolved whilst maintaining credibility! Not an easy task. To balance this seemingly long list of pressures it needs to be said how rewarding counselling can be.

It was Freud who said that 'therapy was about enabling people to love and to work' (Hillman, 1983). He is often remembered for the former rather than the latter. Anyone working with an individual who has been helped by the process will know just what that experience feels like. It is at times a privilege. The challenge of working in organisations can be equally so, particularly where the counsellor has been able to make a difference at an organisational level.

When I was commissioned to write this book the contract letter arrived on my desk the very week I was told I had stomach cancer. The delight at my life's work being valued sat alongside the threat of death. Would there be time to write down what I wanted to say? Would I be able to make a difference? Physical survival took precedence and so it was some 18 months before I picked up my pen and began to write. Nothing happened. The trauma of surgery and chemotherapy affected my ability to remember and to think clearly, and so this book has challenged me in ways that I never envisaged. Having lived with this life-threatening illness for three years I would like to think that I am making death creative. However, in terms of the creativity of writing, I have struggled.

I know this book is not perfect, I know I could have done better but I hope it is 'good enough' to respect the work that workplace counsellors do every day of their lives. This last sentence not only reveals much about me but also about someone in my position reviewing his or her life. Life scripts of 'be perfect' linger. I am sure any writer can relate to this, for when is a book ever 'finished' to the satisfaction of the author? How hard it is to put the pen down and let the reader make up his or her own mind.

Note added in proof: Loretta Franklin passed away on 20th December 2002.

Appendix 1: Employment Law

Individual Employment Law Issues

Employees in the UK are entitled in general to a collection of rights. They come under two groups – contractual and statutory. Contractual rights arise out of the agreement reached between the employer and the employee. A company is required to give its employees a written statement of the terms and conditions of their employment. Currently employees in the UK have a number of statutory rights, the most important of which (subject in some cases to qualifying conditions) are the following:

- protection from unfair dismissal;
- rights to redundancy payments;
- protection from racial, sexual and disability discrimination;
- protection of health and safety.

Where individuals are working in certain professions – medical, legal or therapeutic – or the Crown employs them – then they may be required to sign an undertaking to abide by relevant confidentiality agreements and particular additional restrictions (e.g. the Official Secrets Act).

Collective Employment Law Issues

The majority of employees have individual employment contracts, which are enhanced by legislation. In the public sector and in certain industries where there are collective agreements with recognised trade unions then these agreements are treated as part of the terms and conditions of employees.

Tribunals

An Employment Tribunal (ET) is the main body for resolving employment disputes. It is empowered to make decisions and make financial awards. It is made up of a legal assessor (solicitor or barrister) and two lay people: one from a panel selected in consultation with employers, organisations, and the other from a panel selected in consultation with trade unions. An Employment Appeal Tribunal (EAT) is an appeal body made up of judges and lay members who have special knowledge of employment law. They are appointed by the Lord Chancellor. Mediation is a form of settling disputes (as described in Chapter 8).

Current Legislation

The Employment Rights Act (ERA) came into force on 22 August 1996. This Act consolidated existing legislation relating to individual employment rights in England, Scotland and Wales. Together with the Employment Tribunals Act 1996 (previously known as the Industrial Tribunals Act) it consolidates existing provisions. Current coverage of employment legislation is outlined below:

Employment Rights Act 1996	Individual Employment Rights
Trade Union and Labour Relations Consolidation Act 1992	Trade Union Law
Employment Tribunals Act 1996	Operation of ETs and EATs (Employment Tribunals and Employment Appeals Tribunals)
Transfer of Undertakings (Protection of Employment) Regulations 1981 (TUPE)	Transfers of Businesses
Equal Pay Act 1970	Discrimination Rights
Sex Discrimination Act 1975	
Race Relations Act 1976	
Disability Discrimination Act 1995	
Data Protection Act 1998	
Human Rights Act 1998	
Health and Safety at Work etc. Act 1974	Employers' responsibilities for providing a safe system of work
Access to Medical Reports Act 1988 and Access to Health Records 1990	Individuals' rights of access to their medical records and reports

(Note that the above is based on information available as at 18 January 2002.)

Appendix 2: Useful Addresses

Professional Bodies

British Association of Behavioural and Cognitive Psychotherapies (BABCP)
PO Box 9, Accrington
Lancashire BB5 2GD
Tel: 01254 875277
e-mail: babcp@babcp.org.uk

British Association for Counselling and Psychotherapy (BACP)
1 Regents Place
Rugby CV21 2JB
Tel: 01788 550899
Fax: 01788 562189
e-mail: bacp@bacp.co.uk

The Association changed its name in September 2000 from British Association for Counselling (BAC).

British Psychological Society (BPS)
St Andrews House
48 Princess Road East
Leicester LE1 7DR
Tel: 0116 254 9568

British Association of Psychotherapists (BAP)
37 Mapesbury Road
London NW2 4HJ
Tel: 0208 452 9834

Chartered Institute of Personnel and Development (CIPD)
CIPD, House Camp Road
London SW19 4HJ
Tel: 0208 971 9000
Fax: 0208 263 3333

Institute of Group Analysis
1 Daleham Gardens
London NW3 5BY
Tel: 0207 431 2693
Fax: 0207 431 7246
e-mail: iga@igalondon.org.uk

Institute of Welfare
Newland House
137–9 Hagley Road
Birmingham B16 8UA
Tel: 0121 454 8883
Fax: 0121 454 7873
e-mail: info@instituteofwelfare.co.uk

Nafsiyat, The Inter-Cultural Therapy Centre
278 Seven Sisters Road
London N4 2HY
Tel: 020 7263 4130
Fax: 020 7561 1870
e-mail: nafsiyat-therapy@supanet.com

National Association of Citizens Advice Bureaux (CAB)
115–23 Myddelton House, Pentonville Road
London N1 9LZ
Tel: 0207 833 2181

Relate
Herbert Gray College
Little Church Street
Rugby CV21 3AP
Tel: 01788 573241
Fax: 01788 535007

Royal College of Psychiatrists (RCP)
17 Belgrave Square
London SW1X 8PG
Tel: 020 7235 2351
e-mail: rcpsych@rcpsych.ac.uk

Tavistock Clinic (TAVI)
120 Belsize Lane
London NW3 5BA
Tel: 020 7435 7111

United Kingdom Council for Psychotherapy (UKCP)
167–9 Great Portland Street
London W1 5PF
Tel: 020 7436 3002
Fax: 020 7436 3013

It is impossible to list all organisations involved in counselling. A good starting point is to contact UKCP who have a comprehensive list of accredited counselling and psychotherapy organisations covering the whole spectrum of approaches. The BACP has a division designated to Counselling at Work and CAB is a useful source for general information and specialist associations.

Employment Law

Advisory Conciliation and Arbitration Service (ACAS)
Brandon House
180 Borough High Street
London SE1 1LW
Tel: 020 72103613

Age Concern England
1267 London Road
London SW16 4ER
Tel: 0208765 7200

The Commission for Racial Equality
Elliot House
10–12 Allington Street
London SW1E 5EH
Tel: 020 7828 7022
e-mail: info@cre.gov.uk

Disability Rights Commission
222 Gray's Inn Road
London WC1 8HL
Tel: 0345 622 633
e-mail: enquiry@drc-gb.org

The Equality Commission for Northern Ireland
Andras House
60 Great Victoria Street
Belfast BT2 7BB
Tel: 02890 500600

The Equal Opportunities Commission
Arndale Centre
Manchester M4 3EQ
Tel: 0161 833 9244
e-mail: info@eoc.or.uk

European Commission
Jean Monnet House
8 Storey's Gate
London SW1P 3AT
Tel: 020 7 973 1992

Human Rights Information Centre Council of Europe
F-67075 Strasbourg Cedex
Tel: +33(0) 388 412024
e-mail: humanrights.info@coe.int

REFERENCES

Adams, J., Hayes, J. and Hopson, B. (1976) *Transition: Understanding and Managing Personal Change* (London: Martin Robertson).

Aldrich, H.E. (1979) *Organizations and Environments* (Englewood Cliffs, NJ: Prentice-Hall).

BAC (1995) *Counselling: Definition of Terms in Use with Expansion Rational* (British Association for Counselling Information Sheet).

BAC (1997) *Nature of Counselling Supervision* in *Code of Ethics and Practice for Supervisors of Counsellors* (British Association for Counselling).

BAC (1999) *Counselling, Confidentiality and the Law* (British Association for Counselling guide no. 1).

BACP (2000) *Guidelines for those Using Counselling Skills in their Work* (British Association for Counselling and Psychotherapy).

BACP (2001) *Statement of Fundamental Ethics for Counselling and Psychotherapy* (British Association for Counselling and Psychotherapy).

BACP (2001a) *Counselling and Record Keeping* (British Association for Counselling and Psychotherapy).

BACP (2001b) *Ethical Framework for Good Practice in Counselling and Psychotherapy* (British Association for Counselling and Psychotherapy).

BACP (2001c) *Counselling Definition Training and Careers in Counselling* (British Association for Counselling and Psychotherapy).

Bain, A. (1982) *The Baric Experiment*, Occasional Paper no. 4 (London: Tavistock).

Balbernie, R. (1999) *Inadmissible Evidence: An Example of Projective Identification*, vol. 4, no. 2, Severn NHS Trust (London: Sage Publications).

Beck, A.T. (1976) *Cognitive Therapy and Emotional Disorders* (New York: International Universities Press).

Bell, G.D. (1967) *Organisations and Human Behaviour* (Englewood Cliffs, NJ: Prentice-Hall).

Berne, E. (1975) *What Do You Say After You Say Hello?* (London: Corgi).

Biestek, F.P. (1970) *The Casework Relationship* (London: Unwin University Books).

Bion, W.R. (1961) *Experiences in Groups* (London: Tavistock).

Blackler, F. and Shimmin, S. (1984) *Applying Psychology in Organisations* (London: Methuen).

Bond, T. (1993) *Standards and Ethics for Counselling in Action* (London: Sage).

BootsHelp (1997) 'Counselling and Support', leaflet (The Books Company Ltd).

Bowlby, J. (1988) *A Secure Base: Clinical Applications of Attachment Theory* (London: Routledge).

Bowlby, J. (1996) 'The Role of the Psychotherapist's Personal Resources in the Treatment Situation' (unpublished paper presented by R. Bowly at Seminar at the Institute of Group Analysis, 1996).

Brown, D. and Pedder, J. (1993) *Introduction to Psychotherapy: An Outline of Psychodynamic Principles and Practice*, 2nd edn (London: Routledge).

Butcher, J. and Koss, M. (1994) 'Research on Brief and Crisis-Oriented Psychotherapies', in Garfield and Bergin (eds), *Handbook of Psychotherapy and Behavior Change*, 2nd edn (New York: Wiley).

Capel, L. and Gurnsey, J. (1987) *Managing Stress* (London: Constable).

Carroll, L. (1999) *Alice in Wonderland* (London: Walker Books; originally published in 1865).

Carroll, M. (1995) *Counselling Supervision: Theory, Skills and Practice* (London: Cassell).

Carroll, M. and Walton, M. (eds) (1997) 'Educating the Organization to Receive Counselling', in *Handbook of Counselling in Organizations* (London: Sage).

Chartered Institute for Personnel and Development (2001) *Age Discrimination at Work* (London: CIPD).

Clarkson, P. and Pokorny, M. (1994) *The Handbook of Psychotherapy* (London: Routledge).

Cohen, M. and Smith, R. (1976) *The Critical Incident in Growth Groups: Theory and Techniques* (La Jolla, CA: University Associates).

Corsini, R.J. and Wedding, D. (eds) (1989) *Current Psychotherapies*, 2nd edn (Ithaca, NY: Peacock).

D'Ardenne, P. and Mahtani, A. (1989) *Transcultural Counselling in Action* (London: Sage).

Davies, D. (ed.) (1996) *Pink Therapy* (Buckingham: Open University).

de Board, R. (1983) *Counselling People at Work* (London: Gower).

Department of Trade and Industry (1997) *Best Practice in Learning, Education and Communications*, Report for Managing Change (DTI and University of Warwick).

de Shazer, S. (1984) *Four Useful Interventions in Brief Family Therapy* (New York: W.W. Norton).

De Vries, E.R. (1991) *Organisations on the Couch* (Oxford: Jossey-Bass).

Dryden, W. and Feltham, C. (1995) *Counselling and Psychotherapy* (London: Sheldon Press).

Dryden, W. and Feltham, C. (1999) *Brief Counselling: A Practical Guide for Beginning Practitioners* (Buckingham: Open University Press).

Durkin, W.G. (1985) 'Evaluation of EAP Programming', in S. Klarreich, J.K. Francek and C.E. Moore (eds), *The Human Resources Management Handbook: Principles and Practice of Employee Assistance Programs* (New York, Eastbourne: Praeger).

Edelwich, J. and Brodsky, A. (1980) *Burn-out: Stages of Disillusionment in the Helping Professions* (New York: Human Sciences Press).

Egan, G. (1977) *The Skilled Helper: Models, Skills and Methods for Effective Helping* (Belmont, CA: Brooks/Cole).

Eleftheriadou, Z. (1994) *Transcultural Counselling* (London: Central Book Publishing).

Erikson, E.H. (1965) *Childhood and Society* (New York: Hogarth Press).

Fairbairn, W.R.D. (1952) *Psycho-analytic Studies of the Personality* (London: Tavistock).

Fernando, S.J.M. (1991) *Mental Health, Race and Culture* (Basingstoke: Macmillan – now Palgrave Macmillan).

Fincham, R. and Rhodes, P.S. (1992) *The Individual, Work and Organization* (Oxford: Oxford University Press).

Fineman, S. (1993) *Emotion in Organisations* (London: Sage).

Firth, J. (1985) 'Published Case Studies', *Journal of Occupational Psychology*, vol. 58, p. 139.

Firth-Cozens, J. (1999) 'The Psychological Problems of Doctors', in J. Firth-Cozens and R. Payne (eds), *Stress in Health Professionals: Psychological and Organizational Causes and Interventions* (Chichester: J. Wiley & Son), pp. 79–91.

Foulkes, S.H. (1975) *Group Analytic Psychotherapy: Methods and Principles* (London: Karnac).

French, W.L. and Bell, C.H. (1973) *Organization Development: Behavioral Science Interventions for Organization Improvement* (Englewood Cliffs, NJ: Prentice-Hall).

French, J. and Raven, B. (1967) 'The Basis of Social Power', in D. Cartwright and A. Zander (eds), *Group Dynamics Research and Theory* (New York: Harper & Row).

Freud, S. (1962) *Five Lectures on Psychoanalysis* (first published 1910; London: Pelican).

Freud, S. (1923) *The Ego and the Id*, in J. Strachey (ed.), *Standard Edition of the Complete Psychological Works of Sigmund Freud*, vol. 19 (London: Hogarth Press, 1953–73), pp. 1–66.

George, E., Iveson, C. and Ratner, H. (1990) *Problem to Solution: Brief Therapy with Individuals and Families* (London: BT Press).

Goss, S., Anthony, K., Jamieson, A. and Palmer, S. (2001) *Guidelines for Online Counselling and Psychotherapy* (Rugby: British Association for Counselling and Psychotherapy).

Hall, B. and Moodley, R. (2001) 'Using an African World View in Therapy with Black Clients', *Counselling and Psychotherapy Journal*, vol. 12, no. 3.

Handy, C. (1976) *Understanding Organizations* (Harmondsworth: Penguin).

Handy, C. (1993) *Beyond Certainty: The Changing Worlds of Organization* (Cambridge, MA: Harvard Business School).

Harrison, R. (1972). 'Understanding Your Organisation's Character', *Harvard Business Review*, May–June.

Hawkins, P. and Shoet, R. (1989) *Supervision in the Helping Professions* (Buckingham: Open University Press).

Helman, C. (1985) *Culture, Health and Illness* (Bristol: Wright).

Highley, J.C. and Cooper, C.L. (1995) *An Assessment and Evaluation of Employee Assistance and Workplace Counselling Programmes in British Organisations*, unpublished report for the Health and Safety Executive.

Hillman, J. (1983) *Interviews* (New York: Harper & Row).

Hoel, H. and Cooper, C. (2000) *Destructive Conflict and Bullying at Work* (British Occupational Health Research Foundation).

Inskipp, F. and Proctor, B. (1993) *Making the Most of Supervision* (Twickenham: Cascade Publications).

Iveson, G.E. and Ratner, C.A. (1990) *Co-operative Therapy* (London: Brief Therapy Press).

Jaques, E. (1961) 'An Objective Approach to Pay Differentials', *The Manager*, vol. 29, no. 1, pp. 27–57.

Jung, C.G. (1969) *Man and his Symbols* (New York: Doubleday).

Juran, J. (1999) *Quality Handbook* (New York: McGraw-Hill).

Kagan, N. (1980) 'Influencing Human Interaction – Eighteen Years with IPR', in A. Hess (ed.), *Psychotherapy Supervision: Theory, Research, and Practice* (New York: John Wiley).

Kanter, R.M. (1977) *Men and Women of the Corporation* (New York: Basic Books).

Kanter, R.M. (1992) *The Change Masters: Corporate Entrepreneurs at Work* (London: Routledge).

Kareem, J. (1978) 'Conflicting Concepts of Mental Health in a Multi-Cultural Society', *Psychiatrica Clinica*, 11, pp. 90–95.

Kareem, J. (2000) 'The Nafsiyat Intercultural Therapy Centre: Ideas and Experience in Intercultural Therapy', in J. Kareem and R. Littlewood (eds), *Intercultural Therapy* (London: Blackwell).

Kareem, J. and Littlewood, R. (eds) (2000) *Intercultural Therapy* (London: Blackwell).

Kelnar, J. (1975–6) *Lectures on Character Structure* (unpublished) under the auspices of London Marriage Guidance Council.

Kennedy, E. (1977) *On Becoming a Counsellor* (Dublin: Gill and Macmillan).

Kets de Vries, M. (1991) *Organisations on the Couch* (Oxford: Jossey-Bass).

Kfir, N. and Slevin, M. (1991) *Challenging Cancer – From Chaos to Control* (London: Routledge).

Klein, Mavis (1980) *Lives People Live* (New York: John Wiley).

Klein, Melanie (1952) 'Notes on Some Schizoid Mechanisms', in P. Heimann, S. Isaacs and J. Riviere (eds), *Developments in Psychoanalysis* (London: Hogarth Press).

Klein, Melanie (1963) 'On Identification', in *Our Adult World and other Essays* (London: Heinemann).

Koss, M.P. and Butcher, J.N. (1986) 'Research on Brief Psychotherapy', in A.E. Bergin and S.L. Garfield (eds), *Handbook of Psychotherapy and Behavior Change*, 3rd edn (New York: Wiley).

Lago, C. and Thompson, J. (1996) *Race, Culture and Counselling* (Buckingham: Open University Press).

Laplanche, J. and Pontalis, J.B. (1988) *The Language of Psychoanalysis* (London: Karnac).

Lazarus, A. and Fay, A. (1975) *I Can if I Want To* (New York: William Morrow).

Lemma, A. (1996) *Introduction to Psychopathology* (London: Sage).

Limentani, A. (1986) 'Affects and Psychoanalytical Situation', in G. Kohon (ed.), *The British School of Psychoanalysis: The Independent Tradition* (London: Free Association Press).

Littlewood, R. (1989) 'Glossary', in *Report of the Royal College of Psychiatrist Special (Ethnic Issues) Committee* (London: Royal College of Psychiatrists).

Lowen, A. (1976) *Bioenergetics* (London: Coventure).

Luft, J. (1966) *Of Human Interaction* (Mountain View, CA: Mayfield).

Majoro, S. (1988) *The Creative Gap: Managing Ideas for Profit* (London: Longman).

Malan, D.H. (1975) *A Study of Brief Psychotherapy* (London: Plenum).

Marsella, A. and Pedersen, P. (1981) *Cross-Cultural Counselling in Psychotherapy* (New York: Academic Press).

Masson, J.M. (1989) *Against Therapy* (London: Collins).

McClellan, K. (1989) 'Cost Benefit Analysis of the Ohio EAP', *Employee Assistance Quarterly*, vol. 5(2), pp. 67–85.

McLeod, J. (2001) *Counselling in the Workplace, The Facts: A Systematic Study of the Research Evidence* (Rugby: British Association for Counselling and Psychotherapy).

Mearns, D. (2000) 'How much Supervision Should you Have?' (Rugby: British Association for Counselling and Psychotherapy: Information Sheet 3).

Menzies, I.E.P. (1959) *The Functioning of Social Systems as a Defence against Anxiety* (London: Tavistock).

Menzies, I.E.P. (1991) 'Changing Organisations and Individuals', in F.R. Kets de Vries (ed.), *Organisations on the Couch* (Oxford: Jossey-Bass).

Miller, A. (1990) *The Untouched Key* (London: Virago).

Miller, E.J. and Rice, A.K. (1967) *Systems of Organisation* (London: Tavistock).

Mitchell J.T. (1983) 'When Disaster Strikes: The Critical Incident Stress Debriefing Process', *Journal of Emergency Medical Services*, vol. 8(1), pp. 36–9.

Moorhouse, S. (2002) 'Quantitative Research in Intercultural Therapy: Some Methodological Considerations', in J. Kareem and R. Littlewood (eds), *Intercultural Therapy* (Oxford: Blackwell Science).

Murgatroyd, S. (1985) *Counselling and Helping* (London: British Psychological Society and Routledge).

Napier, R.W. and Gershenfeld, M.K. (1973) *Groups: Theory and Experience* (Boston, MA: Houghton Mifflin).

Nelson-Jones, R. (1993) *Practical Counselling and Helping Skills* (London: Cassell).

Noonan, E. (1992) *Making of a Counsellor* (London: Tavistock & Routledge).

Ogden, T. (1982) *Projective Identification Psychotherapeutic Technique* (London: Aronson).

Parkes, C.M., Stevenson-Hinde, J. and Marris, P. (1972) *Bereavement: Study of Grief in Adult Life* (London: Tavistock).

Parkes, C.M., Stevenson-Hinde, J. and Marris, P. (1991) *Attachment Across the Life Cycle* (London: Routledge).

Parkin, W. (1993) 'The Public and the Private: Gender, Sexuality and Emotion', in S. Fineman (ed.), *Emotions in Organisations* (London: Sage), pp. 167–89.

Perls, F.S. (1969) *Gestalt Therapy Verbatim* (Moab: Real People Press).

Peters, T.J. and Waterman, R.H. (1982) *In Search of Excellence* (New York: Harper and Row).

Pincus, L. and Dare, C. (1978) *Secrets in the Family* (London: Faber and Faber).

Proctor, B. (1978) *Counselling Shop* (London: Burnett Books-Deutsch).

Proctor, B. (1997) 'Supervision for Counsellors in Organisations', in M. Carroll and M. Walton (eds), *Handbook of Counselling in Organizations* (London: Sage), pp. 342–58.

Reynolds, B. (1965) *Learning and Teaching in the Practice of Social Work* (New York: Russell and Russell).

Rice, A.K. (1958) *Productivity and Social Organisation* (London: Tavistock).

Rogers, C.R. (1951) *Client Centred Therapy* (Boston, MA: Houghton Mifflin).

Rogers, C.R. (1961) *On Becoming a Person* (London: Constable), pp. 61–2.

Rosenfield, M. (1997) *Counselling by Telephone* (London: Sage).

Rowan, J. (1983) *The Reality Game* (London: Routledge & Kegan Paul).

Salter, Mary D. (1940) *An Evaluation of Adjustment Based upon the Concept of Security*, Child Development Series (Toronto: University of Toronto Press).

Salzberger-Wittenberg, I. (1970) *Psycho-Analytic Insight and Relationships* (London: Routledge & Kegan Paul).

Sanderson, C. (1991) *Counselling Adult Survivors of Child Sexual Abuse* (London: Jessica Kingsley Publications).

Schein, E.H. (1980) *Organisational Psychology*, 3rd edn (Englewood Cliffs, NJ: Prentice-Hall).

Siebert, A. (2000) 'How Non-diagnostic Listening Led to a Rapid "Recovery" from Paranoid Schizophrenia: What is Wrong with Psychiatry?', *Journal of Humanistic Psychology*, vol. 40, no. 1, pp. 34–58.

Skynner, A.C.R. (1976) *One Flesh: Separate Persons* (London: Constable).

Skynner, A.C.R. and Cleese, J. (1983) *Families and How to Survive Them* (London: Mandarin).

Storr, A. (1979) *The Art of Psychotherapy* (London: Secker & Warburg).

Stroebe, W. and Stroebe, M.S. (1978) *Bereavement and Health* (New York: Cambridge University Press).

Sue, D.W. and Sue, D. (1990) *Counselling the Culturally Different: Theory and Practice*, 2nd edn (New York: Wiley).

Sutherland, V. and Cooper, C. (2000) *Strategic Stress: An Organisational Approach* (Basingstoke: Palgrave).

Tolstoy, L. (1986) *Anna Karenina*, trans. Rosemary Edmonds (1954; Harmondsworth: Penguin).

Trist, E.L. and Bamforth, K.W. (1951) 'Some Social and Psychological Consequences of the Longwall Method of Coal-getting', *Human Relations*, vol. 1, pp. 3–38.

Warr, P. (1987) *Psychology at Work* (Harmondsworth: Penguin).

Weiner, M.F. (1993) 'Role of the Leader in Group Psychotherapy', in H. Kaplan and B.J. Sadock (eds), *Comprehensive Group Psychotherapy* (Baltimore, MD: Williams and Wilkins).

Wilson, J.P. and Raphael, B. (1993) *International Handbook of Traumatic Stress Syndrome* (New York: Plenum).

Winnicott, D.W. (1972) *The Maturational Process and the Facilitating Environment* (London: Hogarth Press).

Worden, J.W. (1992) *Grief Counselling and Grief Therapy: A Handbook for the Mental Health Practitioner* (London: Routledge).

Yalom, I.D. (1980) *Existential Psychotherapy* (New York: Basic Books).

Yamey, G. (2000) 'Psychologists question "debriefing" for traumatised employees', *British Medical Journal*, vol. 320, p. 140.

INDEX

absence: as stress indicator 25
Adams, J. 185
addiction 202
Advisory Conciliation and Arbitration
  Service (ACAS) 202
age: discrimination 144
Aldrich, H. E. 13
alienation 193
anger: corporate anxiety 192
authority: problems dealing with 30
anxiety: corporate-level 192–3; and defence
  mechanisms 191; structured 193

Bain, A. 193
Balbernie, R.: 'Inadmissible Evidence'
  130
Bamforth, K. W. 7
Beck, A. T. 109
behavioural approach: transference 117,
  118
Bell, C. H. 172
Bell, G. D. 3
bereavement: cultural differences 152;
  time-limited counselling 200
Biestek, F. P. 62
bioenergetics approach 118
Bion, W. R. 129, 194
Blackler, F. 5
Bond, T. 93
Bowlby, J. 82; transference 113; using
  intuition 225
brief therapy 200–1; solution-focused
  201
British Association for Counselling and
  Psychotherapy (BACP): confidentiality
  39; power relations 139; on record
  keeping 71; supervision of counsellors
  235; task of counselling 28

Brodsky, A. 237
Brown, D. 121
Buddhism 152
bullying: challenging organisations 24;
  conditions 15; survival culture 12,
  13–15; vulnerable groups 14
burn-out: of counsellors 236–9
Butcher, J. 199

Carroll, M. 70
change management: attitudes and
  communication 182–3; coping with
  innovation 7–8; reactions to 185–6;
  stages of experiencing 187–91, stifling
  184; and stress 23; tensions and
  energies of 183–4
Children's Act (1989): and confidentiality
  37
Clarkson, P. 137, 229
Cleese, John: *Families and How to Survive
  Them* (with Skynner) 111–12
Client Centered Therapy (Rogers) 117
client-centred counselling: transference
  117, 118
clients 31–3; cancelled appointments 93;
  common needs of 57; diagnosis and
  assessment 72–3; disclosure and defence
  90–3; domiciliary visits 67–8; ending
  the relationship 97–100; first contact
  with 68–9, 77–9; groups 76;
  interaction with counsellor 60–2;
  motivations of 57–9; planning and tasks
  94–5; resistance 59–60; seeking help
  55–7; *see also* employees; individuals;
  transference and countertransference
cognitive behaviour therapies: goals 94;
  transference 118
Cohen, M. 214

communication: with difference and diversity 160–3; facilitates tasks 7; in groups 209, 210–11, 212–14
confidentiality 174, 177; changing concepts of 37; contracts for 41–2; disclosure 39–40; and evaluation 70; interaction in therapy 61; and the law 37–9; reports 89
conflict and confrontation: challenging projection 133–4; group confrontation 210; professional role of counsellors 33–6; and roles 20
consultancy and advisory services 174
continuing professional development (CPD) xiv
contracts: with clients 73–6; and confidentiality 41–2; as counsellors 73
Cooper, C. 24, 70
corporate abuse 16–17
corporate anger 192
corporate defense mechanisms 192
corporate level anxiety 192–3
Corsini, R. J. 224–5
counsellors: attitudes and motivation 52–5; burn-out 236–9; characteristics of 55; contribution to process 78; co-working 206; development of 177–8; emotional involvement 105–8; equilibrium and perspective 239–40; experience and development 230–2; as group facilitators 206–8, 213–14; interaction with clients 60–2; matching for gender and culture 164–6; and the outside world 228–30; as people 223–4; personal development 232–4; personal therapy 236; professional role 33–6; recruitment and selection 219–20; roles of 46–7; as scapegoat 194–6; self-awareness 222–3, 224; self-disclosure 134–7; setting limits 108–10; supervision 234–6; training 87–8, 220–2; see also transference and countertransference
crisis counselling: time-limited counselling 200, 205–6
Critical Incident Stress Debriefing (CISD) 205–6
culture: cross-cultural differences 151–3; matching counsellors and clients 164–6;

of organisations 10–13; questioning 12; survival 12–18; thriving 18

D'Ardenne, P. 153
Dare, C. 73
DASIE model 65
Data Protection Act (1988) 71, 87
Davies, D. 154
De Board, R. 30
De Shazer, S. 201
De Vries, E. R. 11
debriefing 205–6
decision-making: of clients 61; clients' needs 57; groups 209
defence mechanisms 91–3; bewildered organisations 193–6; of counsellors 223; dependency 192–3; fight or flight 192; of organisations 191–2; projection 127–34; reactions to change 187, 189, 190; wishful thinking 193
depression 192
disability 151, 155–6
Disability Discrimination Act (1995) 37, 155, 200; disclosure 40
Disability Rights Commission 151
discrimination 142; and confidentiality 37; counsellors' responsibilities 150–1; disability 155–6; historical context 143–5; legislation against 143–4; prejudice 149–50; and religion 156–8; sexuality 153–5
diversity: context of 146–9; counsellors' own backgrounds 158–60; cultural differences 151–3; issues of 142–3; language of difference 160–3; managing 144–5; matching counsellors and clients 164–6; in therapeutic relationship 160; transference 163–4; see also discrimination; ethnicity and race; harassment
Dryden, W. 201
Durkin, W. G. 70

E-listening 205
Edelwich, J. 237
education and training: of counsellors 220–2, 225; as organisational experience 5; for organisational

staff 174–5; personal development for counsellors 232–4
Egan, G. 64–5, 223
Eleftheriadou, Z. 147, 151, 165
emotions: within organisations 4–5
empathy 55; balancing 106–7; working with diversity 161
Employee Assistance Programmes (EAPs) xiv, 2, 166, 174; counsellors' reports 36; external provision of counselling 29; telephone counselling 203
employees: flexible employment 19; and identity 6; legal aspects 241–2; organisational problems 175–6; see also clients; individuals
Employment Rights Act (1996) 242
employment tribunals 24–5, 241–2; counsellors as witnesses 35
Employment Tribunals Act (1996) 242
Erikson, Erik H. 232
ethics: confidentiality 37–42; diversity 150–1; roles of counsellors 33–6
ethnicity and race: bullying 14; challenging discrimination 24–5; counsellors' own 158–60; definition and cultural context 146–9; three potential reactions to 163
European Union 151

Fairbairn, W. R. D. 89–90
families: cultural norms 149; organisations as 179–80; religious conflicts 157
Fay, A. 96
Feltham, C. 201
Fernando, S. J. M. 146
Fincham, R. 44
Fineman, S. 4, 6, 194; culture of organisations 10
Firth, J. 30
Foulkes, S. H. 108
French, J.: types of power 44
French, W. L. 172
Freud, Sigmund: analyst as mirror 135; countertransference 119; super ego 4; transference 111

George, E. 201
Gershenfeld, M. K. 210

Gestalt approach 118
goals: of groups 209; process-based contract 75–6; setting with clients 93–4; short-term therapies 199–202; visualization 96–7
groups: attributes of success 208–9; emotions and intervention 214–18; facilitating 206–8, 213–14; stages of 209–12; structural components 207; termination of 212

Handy, Charles: freedom for employees 18; stress and strain 19–20
harassment 142; legal obligations 150–1
Harrison, R.: types cultures 11
Hawkins, P. 107
Hawthorne Experiment 29
Helman, C. 147
helping process see intervention; therapy
Highley, J. C. 70
homosexuality 153–5, 158
humanistic existential approach 64; therapists' self-disclosure 135; transference 117

identity: and work 6
individuals: versus community 152; influence of organisations 5; life stages 30; and organisational culture 11; within organisations 18–19; personhood of counsellors 223–4; reactions to change 185–6, 187–91
industrial tribunals see employment tribunals
Ingham, Harry 222
insecurity 29
internet: E-listening 205
intervention: bewildered organizations 193–6; in burn-out 238–9; change management 182–91; defence mechanisms 191–3; listening to the organisation 171–2; organisational opportunities 172–3; organisations as clients 175–8; systems approach 178–82
interviews: types of 30–1
Investors in People (IIP) xiv
Islamic cultures 152

Jacques, Elliott 18–19
Jewish culture 152
job development 30
Johari Window 223–4
Jung, Carl G. xiii, 131
Juran, J. 173

Kagan, N. 69
Kanter, Rosabeth Moss 154;
  organisational change 184
Kareem, J. 140, 151; on transference 164
Karpman triangle 146
Kelnar, J. 111, 114
Kennedy, E. 107
Klein, Mavis 146
Klein, Melanie: projective identification
  128
knowledge: objective and subjective 53–4
Koss, M. 199

Lago, C. 159
Lawrence (Stephen) enquiry 143
Lazarus, A. 96
legal aspects: confidentiality 37–9;
  contracts for counsellors 42; diversity
  issues 150–1; individual and collective
  241; record keeping 70–1; tribunals
  241–2; witnessing at tribunals 35
life skills 65
Limentani, A. 165
listening 61; art of 62–4; and disabled
  clients 155; later reflection 85; to the
  organisation 171–2; theory *versus*
  practice 225; and transference 126–7
Littlewood, R. 147
Lowen, A. 137
Luft, Joe 222

McClellan, K. 70
McLeod, J. 28
Mahtani, A. 153
Majoro, S. 184
Malan, D. H. 200–1
management: as clients 32; source of
  stress 21
Marsella, A. 163
Masson, Jeffrey M. 140
mediation 202–3, 242
Medical Report Act (1998) 89

Menzies, I. E. P. 193
Miller, Alice 139
Miller, E. J. 7
Mind survey on stress 23
Montagu, Sir Nicholas 149
Moorhouse, S. 147
motivation: of clients 57–9; and survival
  culture 13
Murgatroyd, S. 164

Napier, R. W. 210
Nelson-Jones, R.: DASIE model 65;
  interviews 31
non-judgemental attitudes 55, 61
Noonan, E. 67

objectivity: as therapeutic issue 105–8
Ogden, T. 129, 130
organisations: bewildered 193–6; as
  clients 175–6; corporate abuse 16–17;
  cultures of xv, 10–13, 24–5; defining
  3–4; development 172–3; economic
  uncertainty 17–18; emotions in 4–5;
  as family system 32; influence on
  individuals 5; internal problems 30;
  long- and short-term systems approach
  178–82; perceptions of counsellor
  228–9; reactions to change 187–91;
  and systems 6–10
organisational change 184

Parkes, C. M. 82
Parkin, W. 5
Pedder, J. 121
Pedersen, P. 163
person-centred approach 94
personal development: of counsellors
  232–4
personal life: and stress 23
personality development: psychodynamic
  theory of 61
Peters, T. J. 11
Pincus, L. 73
Pokorny, M. 137, 229
politics: systems of 9–10; types of
  power 44
Post-Traumatic Stress Disorder (PTSD)
  205

power relations 230; counsellors' role 42–5; culture of 11; political systems 9–10; in therapy 138–40; types of 44
Prevention of Terrorism Act (1989) 37
Proctor, B. 117
projection: analyst as mirror 135; and bewildered organisations 194; challenging 133–4; containment 129–30; examples 126–7; identification 128–9; returning client's experiences 130–2; 'stuckness' 132–3
psychodynamic approach 64, 118; analysis for therapists 236; in counselling xiii; family relations 82; personality development 61
publicity: for counselling services 45–6

Raphael, B. 206
Raven, B.: types of power 44
reality therapy: transference 116
reflection: group reassessment 211
relationships 33; in groups 209–12; organisational development and 172–3; organisational 'family' 179–80; personal 29
religion: and discrimination 156–8
respect 55, 230
retirement: and work identity 6
Reynolds, Bertha 230–1
Rhodes, P. S. 44
Rice, A. K. 7
risk: domiciliary visits 68; in relationships 107
Rogers, Carl R.: Client Centered Therapy 117; resistance 59–60; risk in relationships 107; unconditional positive regard 55
roles: ambiguity 19, 20; of counsellor 33–6; culture of 11; modern ambiguity 19; stress and strain 19–20
Rosenfield, M. 205
Rowan, J.: and countertransference 126; on self-disclosure 135; transference 117

safety 23
Salter, Mary D. 186; secure base 225–6
Salzberger-Wittenberg, I. 125–6
Samaritans: E-listening 205
Sanderson, C. 202

Schein, E. H.: on organisations 3–4
self-determination 61
self-esteem: low 56
sexism see discrimination; harassment
sexuality: abuse 202; counsellor–client relations 139; diversity and discrimination 153–5, 158; harassment 14; matching counsellors and clients 164–6
Shimmin, S. 5
Shoet, R. 107
Siebert, A. 58
Skynner, Robin 228; Families and How to Survive Them (with Cleese) 111–12
Smith, R. 214
Storr, Anthony: on self-disclosure 135
stress: causes of 23–4; counsellor burn-out 236–9; debriefing 205–6; management of 25; and strain 19–20; understanding 21–2
Sue, D. W. and Sue, D. 165
suicide: and confidentiality 40
supervision: of counsellors 234–6
Sutherland, V. 24
systems theory 178–82; open 8–9; within organisations 6–10, socio-technical 7–8

tasks: culture of 11; planning and 94–7
teamwork: organisational development and 172–3; see also groups
telephone counselling 203–5
terrorism 185
therapy: brief 200–1; for counsellors 236; counsellors' self-disclosure 134–7; debriefing 205–6; developing the relationship 89–90; different approaches 64–5; disclosure and defence 90–3; end of process 97–100; ending sessions 82–5; evaluation 70; expectations 81–2; first session of 77–80; frequency and duration 76–7; goals 93–4; interaction of 60–2; Karpman triangle 146; listening 62–4; monitoring progress 69–70; notes and recordings 85–8; planning and actions 94–7; power relations 138–40; reflection 85; reports 88–9; a 'secure base' 225–6; short-term 198–202; subjectivity and objectivity 105–8;

therapy – *continued*
  telephone counselling 203–5; theory
  versus practice 224–8; therapeutic
  alliance 51–2, 114; time-limited
  199–200; and touch 137–8; *see also*
  groups; intervention; transference and
  countertransference
Thompson, J. 159
time-limited counselling (TLC) 199–200
Total Quality Management (TQM) 173–4
touch 137–8; cultural differences 152
transference and countertransference:
  being aware of 110; 'classical'
  countertransference 118–20; in
  counselling relationship 112; cultural
  diversity and 163–4; definition and
  concept of 110–12; and listening
  process 126–7; message in
  countertransference 120–1; other
  approaches to 116–18; positive and
  negative 113–14, 125; process of
  transference 114–16; self-monitoring
  125–6; working with
  countertransference 121–5
traumatic events 205–6
Trist, E. L. 7

uncertainty: economic conditions 17–18;
  source of stress 23

visualization 96–7

waiting lists 59
Walton, M. 70
Warr, P. 25
Waterman, R. H. 11
Wedding, D. 225
Weiner, M. F. 76
Wilson, J. P. 206
Winnicott, D. W. 227
wishful thinking 193
women: bullying 14
Worden, J. W. 200
workplace: conditions for stress 23;
  dynamics of 116; workload 20;
  see also employees
workplace counselling 27–9; cancelled
  appointments 93; client contracts
  73–6; contracts and legal status 42;
  development of xiii–xv, 2;
  discrimination issues 145–6, 150–1;
  external and internal 166; first
  contact 68–9; influence and power
  of counsellors 42–5; initial
  referrals 80–1; internal and external
  provision 29, 34; by other
  professionals xvi; publicising
  services 45–6; range of problems
  29–30; record keeping 70–1; setting
  for 66–8; theory *versus* practice
  224–8; *see also* clients; counsellors;
  organisations; therapy

Yalom, I. D. 240